# D-DAY
## THE AIR BATTLE

# D-DAY
## THE AIR BATTLE

KEN DELVE

The Crowood Press

First published in 1994 by
Arms & Armour Press

Revised edition published in 2004 by
The Crowood Press Ltd
Ramsbury, Marlborough
Wiltshire SN8 2HR

**www.crowood.com**

**British Library Cataloguing-in-Publication Data**
A catalogue record for this book is available from the British Library.

ISBN 1 86126 704 5

*Photo previous page:* A-20s of 416th BG en route to Le Havre.
(US National Archives)

Typeface used: Bembo.

Typeset and designed by
D & N Publishing
Lowesden Business Park, Hungerford, Berkshire.

Printed and bound in Great Britain by CPI Bath.

# Contents

# Introduction

OPPOSITE: *A small part of the thousands of ships in the invasion convoy.*

ABOVE: *The invasion under way as photographed by a Mustang of 2 Squadron in the early evening of 6 June.*

In the early hours of 6 June 1944, the long-awaited return to Europe became a reality as Allied forces stormed ashore in Normandy. Although the German military machine managed to prolong the war for almost another year, there was no doubt that the 'writing was on the wall' for the Nazi empire. There was much hard fighting still to do, but after the initial forty-eight hours it was all but impossible for the bridge-head to be eliminated. This successful lodgement was the culmination of months, arguably even years, of planning and preparation. One overall fact is evident from the records of both sides: Allied air power was the key to the success of Operation *Overlord*. One assessment stated that:

> The success of *Overlord* depends on three major conditions:

7

1. Air superiority to ensure that the initial assault and build-up is not prejudiced by enemy air action.
2. Surprise is essential for the assault to succeed; without it we would not get ashore.
3. Winning the 'build-up race' by preventing or retarding the build-up of enemy land forces.

This, of course, relates to the immediate pre- and post-invasion period and does not encompass the full range of tasks given to air power during the preparation phases. How far back one extends the preparation phase is a matter of some debate; Montgomery, for example, saw victory in the Battle of the Atlantic as an essential element for the success of the invasion of Europe when he said 'winning the Battle of the Atlantic was essential to ensure the passage of the vast volume of personnel and stores from America and Canada to the battle front.' It could equally be argued that the effects of the strategic bombing offensive by RAF Bomber Command and the US 8th Army Air Force had a direct effect on German war potential, and therefore the ability of the German regime to sustain the war effort in the West, one direct example being the need to employ the construction organization on rebuilding projects in the Reich, rather than on military projects such as the Atlantic Wall.

One vital operation was the air assault on the invasion area in the months prior to June, although an even greater effort had to be expended on surrounding areas as part of the overall deception plan, thus fulfilling item two of the conditions mentioned above. The effective sealing off of the invasion area allowed the Allied forces to build up their strength whilst the defenders were reduced to moving reinforcements by night and, because of poor communications routes, committing them piecemeal to the battle, thus fulfilling the third requirement. None of this 'air power won the day' attitude is intended to detract from the courage, resilience and capabilities of the Allied land forces; to many a soldier on the

*A-20* La France Libre *was the first such aircraft in 9th Air Force to complete 100 operations. The whole point of D-Day was encapsulated in the aircraft name.* (US National Archives)

beach, any comment that air power had made life easy would have met a blunt rebuttal!

The air battle for D-Day was by no means the story of a single day: in this short account the author hopes to highlight the significant aspects of this crucial campaign.

## Acknowledgements

As usual, my gratitude to the Air Historical Branch for their unstinting help, especially to Mr Graham Day; also to the Office of Air Force History (USAF) for generous help with the USAAF elements of this story. Photographs are from a variety of sources. Most plans and target photographs are Crown Copyright via the Air Historical Branch.

# 1 The Long Build-Up

In early summer 1940 the German war machine was in the ascendancy after lightning campaigns in Poland and France; the combined power of German tactical air operations and brilliant use of armoured forces simply overwhelmed the opposition. When the last of the armada of 'little ships' had returned and the 'miracle of Dunkirk' was over, the most immediate concern of the British was the defence of their island. Surely the Germans would come – how could they be stopped? So much military material had been left behind in France, and the morale of the army was poor after its ill-fated campaign on the Continent.

*Re-loading the guns on a Hurricane during the Battle of France 1940: this was the RAF's first experience of intensive operations and a steep learning curve for all involved.*

*Spitfires of 616 Squadron landing at Rochford during the Battle of Britain; even whilst Britain was fighting for its survival, outline plans were being made for the return to Europe.*

However, to Prime Minister Winston Churchill, one of the major considerations was how to get back into Europe; he was already thinking in terms of the invasion of the Continent and the eventual defeat of Nazi Germany. To many, this was mere wishful thinking, but it was this dogmatic determination that, despite his frequent interference with military strategy, made Churchill a fine war leader. It was, of course, to be many months before any realistic consideration could be given to this concept; the hard-fought and close-run Battle of Britain had first to be won, and the threat of a German invasion of the British Isles defeated. In the meantime the only offensive weapon with which the British could strike back was RAF Bomber Command, and this force waged almost nightly battles over Germany and occupied Europe.

The desire to show that Britain had not abandoned its intention to free occupied Europe was further expressed by active support and encouragement of the various Resistance movements and, in a more overt military fashion, through

the creation of Commando forces whose job it was to carry out raids against German-occupied Europe. All of this was small scale and took some time to build, but it set the tone of an overall policy that wanted to put as much pressure as possible on the Nazi regime.

The German invasion of Russia in summer 1941 brought a new ally into the field, an ally whose potential was great but whose immediate future appeared bleak. German armies advanced towards Moscow making spectacular captures of Russian men and material on the way. However, of even greater significance was the entry into the war of the United States in December 1941. The World was now truly at war, with the Axis powers (Germany, Italy, Japan and their allies) facing the Allied nations (Britain, the USA, Russia and their allies).

Although it was in the Far East/Pacific theatre that American interests were most directly threatened, the Allied leaders agreed a 'Germany First' policy, whereby the majority of assets would be focused on the defeat of that nation. This was a crucial strategic decision, and meant that the might of American industrial and military muscle would be focused on the European theatre: it was no longer a question of *if* the Allies would return to the Continent, but rather *when* they would return. The Russian leader, Josef Stalin, made strong pleas for the creation of a second front in Europe at the earliest opportunity, so that the Germans would be forced to divert forces away from the Eastern front to deal with the new threat. Whilst the Western Allied leaders understood the need for such a strategy, they simply did not have the resources with which to carry it out with any guarantee of success; the convoys of war material being sent to Russia were in themselves proving to be a serious drain on Allied resources, the very same resources that would be needed to pursue the desired long-term aim of a return to Europe. This failure, as Stalin saw it, to open a second front in 1942 or even 1943, became a cause of much bitterness in the post-war period.

As the Germans had found in 1940, a major amphibious operation required a huge amount of planning and a number of pre-conditions in order to stand any chance of success. What was true for them in summer 1940 when the British defences were weak was far more relevant for the Allies when they contemplated an attack on the European continent. During 1942 and 1943 a number of lessons were learned that would have crucial effects on the eventual assault.

## The Strategic Bombing Offensive

On the first day of the war, RAF Bomber Command launched a daylight attack against German shipping, the only target type that the bombers were permitted to attack. These were the opening moves in a bomber offensive that was to last almost six years, and which led to the development of the most powerful strike force ever assembled. But these early daylight missions were a disaster, and the much-vaunted bomber weapon appeared impotent. The vulnerability of the bombers in daylight attacks led to the decision to abandon such operations, except in certain circumstances. The bomber force thus became, by default, a night bomber force trying to find pinpoint targets in Germany, targets such as oil installations and armament works, the destruction of which, the economic warfare experts predicted, would have a devastating effect on the German war effort.

In the first two years of the war Bomber Command achieved very little in military terms, although the effect on morale at home and in the occupied countries must not be overlooked. This was the only means of striking back at the heartland of the enemy, especially at a time when news from the various theatres of war was invariably bad. Bomber Command was also, however, building for the future, gaining experience that, when combined with more capable aircraft and equipment, and better tactics, would

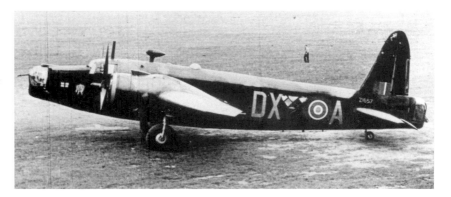

*Wellingtons bore the brunt of Bomber Command's offensive against Germany from 1940 to 1943; DX-A is a 57 Squadron aircraft at Methwold in 1942.*

*Air Marshal Harris as commander of Bomber Command was called on to commit his heavy bombers to the* Overlord *campaign.*

lead eventually to the forging of an effective weapon. The elements began to come together in 1942, almost co-incident with the arrival of a new, dynamic commander: Air Marshal Arthur Harris. To counter a mounting tide of criticism as to the lack of effectiveness of the bombers, Harris mounted a 1,000 bomber raid to demonstrate the offensive power of his bomber weapon at the strategic level. The chosen target was Cologne, and on the night of 30/31 May 1942 a force of 1,046 bombers attacked the target, causing huge amounts of damage to the industrial and residential areas of the city, with a low loss rate amongst the attackers.

Even if this raid, and two follow-up attacks of a similar magnitude on other German cities, did not convince all of Bomber Command's detractors, it at least gave Harris a breathing space in which to reform and strengthen the Command. Harris was a firm believer in the value of the bomber offensive, and he considered it better to destroy the tank, gun or warship in its factory than on the battlefield. He also considered that experience had shown that the so-called war-winning 'panacea' targets favoured by some experts, a typical target system being oil installations, were not only hard to hit but also appeared to be not as critical as was suggested. This negative view was subsequently challenged – and changed. With his new and more potent four-engined bombers such as the Halifax and Lancaster entering service in reasonable quantity, Harris was able to build an offensive force capable of carrying a large bomb tonnage into the heart of Germany.

As the threat from Bomber Command increased, the Germans were forced to dedicate an ever-increasing level of resources in a defence network of fighters, searchlights and guns. Indeed, it has been estimated that over one million men were involved in the defence of the Reich, along with thousands of guns and aircraft, all of which could have been used elsewhere if the bomber threat had not existed. The detractors of Bomber Command argued that the mass of resources used by the Command could equally have been used elsewhere.

In August 1942 the US 8th Army Air Force launched its first attacks, and what came to be termed the Combined Bomber Offensive was under way. The American bomber chiefs also believed, like the RAF, that the best prospects of success lay in attacking pinpoint industrial targets, such as oil installations, in daylight. But initial bombing results were equally poor, and the losses amongst the bombers, mainly to enemy fighters, reached alarming proportions. Once again the need for air superiority as a pre-requisite for a successful daylight bombing campaign had become apparent. However, unlike the RAF response of retreating to the cover of night – perfectly reasonable, given the capabilities available in 1939 – the American response was to face

ABOVE: *Armourers prepare another load of bombs for a Bomber Command Lancaster.*

*B-24s en route to Germany.* (US National Archives)

*Hurricane BD867 was lost during the Dieppe operation; the lessons of Operation* Jubilee *were invaluable.*

the challenge and attempt to achieve the necessary level of air superiority. It was also in this year that the first real moves were made in planning a return to Europe.

An RAF special planning staff had been set up under Air Chief Marshal Edmonds in May 1942, to examine all air aspects of the invasion planning (this organization was later reorganized, and integrated into Supreme Headquarters Allied Expeditionary Forces, or SHAEF). In the two years leading up to D-Day, many planning organizations had inputs into the *Overlord* plan, and many contrary concepts were put forward; and at times there was a distinct danger of 'too many cooks spoiling the broth'. At times there was also a dangerous level of political in-fighting amongst the top military leaders.

### Operations *Jubilee* and *Torch*

In Operation *Jubilee* – often termed a 'reconnaissance in force' by some historians, and a 'bloody disaster' by others – a Canadian force, supported by British Commandos, attacked the French harbour town of Dieppe on 19 August 1942. They were supported by the largest array of RAF aircraft yet employed on a single operation, with some sixty-eight squadrons flying over 3,000 missions in a period of just sixteen hours. Many squadrons, such as 616 Squadron

with its Spitfire VIs, were called upon to mount three operations in quick succession, as Allied commanders endeavoured to employ air power in an attempt to salvage something out of the gathering disaster. The air battles over and around Dieppe were the largest yet experienced, claims and losses being roughly equal on both sides. It certainly reinforced the now accepted principle that air superiority was an essential pre-requisite for the support of a major amphibious landing, both to protect friendly forces from air attack and to use aerial firepower to make up, to some extent, for the lack of heavy weapons on the ground. Unfortunately, little progress had been made in developing air support tactics, although this situation would soon be rectified by some outstanding work in the Desert War.

The whole Dieppe operation had indeed been a disaster for the Canadian forces involved: losses were high, and many brave men were condemned to years of captivity. However, Operation *Jubilee* had taught the Allies a number of valuable lessons and useful experience had been gained, which together would be put to good use by the *Overlord* planners. For the remainder of 1942 it fell to the bomber forces to continue the offensive against Germany in Europe. The scale of these operations could certainly have justified the title of a second front, albeit not in the way that the Russians desired.

By mid-1942 it was seen as increasingly important to find a way of satisfying Stalin's demands for a second front – whilst not engaging in any project too hazardous, or with only limited prospects of success. The defences of Western Europe were far too strong for the available Allied forces to have any hope of making a successful landing in France; furthermore, the campaign in North Africa had been progressing reasonably well; therefore the decision was taken to mount an amphibious assault in North Africa that would clear Axis forces from that theatre of operations and provide a springboard for possible moves into Italy or southern France. It would also provide additional information on conducting a major amphibious landing. The level of opposition was unknown; some Allied commanders hoped to simply walk ashore and be greeted as liberators by the French garrison, others believed that fierce resistance was possible. A comprehensive air support campaign was devised, although because of the limited number of land bases, much of the tactical air power involved was carrier-based.

When Allied forces landed in Tunisia on 8 November 1942 in Operation *Torch*, they were in many respects testing out amphibious operation concepts that had already benefited from the Dieppe experience – even though in North Africa the assault troops did not face the same type of defensive system as would later be the case in Normandy. It was also the first operational experience for many of the American tactical aircraft, and as such paved the way for the doctrine adopted by the late UK-based 9th Air Force.

## 1943: The *Overlord* Air Campaign Commences

When Churchill and Roosevelt met at Casablanca for the 'Symbol' conference in mid-January 1943, they laid down the basic Allied strategy for the overall 'Germany First' policy. The immediate strategic aim for 1943 was to knock Italy out of the war, whilst at the same time continuing to concentrate men and material in the UK for the invasion of Western Europe. Needless to say, Stalin was not happy, even though it was argued that a campaign in Italy would provide a second front in Europe. It was further argued that the increasing offensive power being employed by the heavy bombers of RAF Bomber Command and the US 8th Air Force in itself comprised a second front that absorbed a great deal of the German military capability that could otherwise be employed against Russia.

As a result of the Casablanca decisions, a new directive was issued to the strategic bombing forces for their pursuance of the Combined Bomber Offensive:

> Your primary objective will be the progressive destruction and dislocation of the German military, industrial and economic system, and the undermining of the morale of the German people to a point where their capacity for armed resistance is fatally weakened.

This directive, issued on 21 January, listed five target systems for attack, none of which was new: submarine construction yards, aircraft industry, transportation, oil industry, and 'others in the war industry'.

This is a convenient point at which to review one aspect of the D-Day air campaign that has usually been ignored: the Battle of the Atlantic.

### The Battle of the Atlantic

The shipping lanes leading to Britain were essential to the nation's continued survival. For the prospects of a return to the Continent, those routes from North America became particularly vital from early 1942 onwards, with the transfer of men and materials from America. By 1942 an increasing number of improved U-boats were entering service, and Allied shipping losses approached critical proportions – total losses that year amounted to 1,664 ships, representing almost 8 million tons capacity, not to mention thousands of lives. This was largely due to the German 'wolf packs' concentrating in the Greenland Gap where there was no Allied air cover. The critical situation in the Battle of the Atlantic was high on the agenda of the Casablanca Conference.

The outcome was a directive to the British air commanders, and in particular Bomber and Coastal Commands, that greater efforts would have to be made. Bomber Command attacked the U-boats in their home bases in France, usually with little result as the installations were too well hardened for conventional bombing to have much chance of success, and against U-boat construction and training centres; Coastal Command, aided by the advent of improved longer-range aircraft, increased the scale of its anti-submarine patrols.

By mid-1943 the increase in air protection, more escorts, and a change of tactics meant that the situation had changed, and in the face of increasing losses the German naval commanders withdrew the majority of submarines from the North Atlantic. Between June and August 1943 only fifty-eight Allied ships were lost to U-boats, whereas the latter suffered seventy-nine losses. Air attacks on submarines in transit across the Bay of Biscay to and from their bases proved very worrisome for the Germans, who responded by increasing the patrols by Junkers Ju 88s – which in turn were countered by Mosquito and Beaufighter patrols. Air cover was further improved in August with long-range patrol aircraft operating from bases in the Azores. The Allies had therefore gained the initiative, and technological improvements such as ASV (air-to-surface vessel) radar, Leigh Light aircraft and improved weapons also made day and night attacks equally successful.

With the U-boats now taking a very low toll of the constant stream of Allied convoys that were passing into the ports of western Britain, the build-up of men and equipment gathered pace. By the spring of 1944 the Battle of the Atlantic was virtually over, and the Allies never again lost the advantage. Nevertheless a significant air effort had to be maintained in order to ensure the continued suppression of the German submarines.

*Depth-charge attack on a U-boat – 120 Squadron, 23 April 1943. Air power played a significant part in winning the Battle of the Atlantic.*

*2nd TAF pilots spent months prior to the invasion training for operations from limited facilities – a tent and a table sufficed for planning and operations.*

## Composite Groups

A great deal of consideration was given as to how the Allied air units would be organized during the period immediately before and after the invasion. On 8 December 1942, Air Marshal Leigh-Mallory, AOC Fighter Command had written to the Under-Secretary of State at the Air Ministry concerning the re-organization of units:

> It is essential, if units are to move overseas and operate effectively on the Continent, that they should be placed on a mobile basis well in advance of their move, and that trials should be carried out to determine how mobility may best be achieved. I wish to carry out trials as early in 1943 as weather permits of a minimum number of representative units. It is foreseen that the general trend of movement of air forces to the Continent will take the following general line: Servicing Commandos will proceed early, followed as quickly as possible by the Mobile Air Reporting Organisation. The Aerodrome Defence squadrons must then go over so as to protect landing grounds that are being made ready by the Aerodrome Construction Groups. Station HQ and a mobile Sector HQ will be the next units to move. The next move is for fighter squadrons to move permanently to the Continent, followed by reconnaissance squadrons.

Exercise *Spartan*, which took place in early March 1943, was the first major exercise designed to test the new composite group and airfield organization. The exercise employed a limited composite mobile group, designated 'Z' Group, and was one of the largest training exercises to involve air-ground elements. Despite poor weather for part of the period, this was an invaluable 'first look' at how the new concepts could be applied. There was no appreciable American involvement, and the composite group doctrine was very much a British/Canadian one. The American tactical air forces were already organized in a composite manner, incorporating bomber and fighter types within the same overall command structure.

17

Extensive reports were written following the conclusion of *Spartan*, including one by Lt Col R. Stockley, commander of the 'British side' during the exercise:

> Calls for close support from forward tentacles were rare. The vast majority of requests for support were formulated as a result of air reconnaissance. The time lag between time of origin of a request and the time over target was often as much as two to three hours. On occasions, calls for support were answered in seventy minutes or less, and I saw no reason why in the future this figure should not be the normal one – and often improved upon.

These comments were important, and revealed two aspects: firstly, that not all the lessons of the North African campaign had been absorbed; and secondly, the importance of improving forward air control. His closing comment was also instructive: 'I feel that *Spartan* showed even more clearly that the provision of light inter-communication aircraft, such as are used by air observation posts, for commanders and liaison officers, are not a luxury but a necessity.' Much debate also centred on how staffs should be integrated, and how requests for air support should be forwarded. It is to the credit of RAF and army personnel, and in large measure to the work of Army Co-operation Command, that issues such as this were resolved and did not degenerate into inter-service wrangling.

On 17 April 1943 the RAF's inspector general, Ludlow-Hewitt, circulated a memo concerning the reorganization of air support for the army:

> In general, the organization of the composite groups now operating in the Western Desert Air Force is sound and should be adopted as a pattern for continental operations. The AOC composite groups works at army level and, while responsible for directing day-to-day air operations, he should not directly concern himself with the direct control, co-ordination, plotting and timing of attacks.

*Forward control posts in the front lines with ground forces were an essential element of the army support (close air support) mission.*

> This should be done by an intermediate headquarters. The operational units of the composite groups should be organized into functional wings.

This accorded with the philosophy expounded by Leigh-Mallory as AOC Fighter Command, whose 'Big Wing' concept, when he was AOC No. 12 Group, had caused such debate during the Battle of Britain. Ludlow-Hewitt was also proposing the disbandment of Army Co-operation Command, on the grounds that:

> Conceptions of army/air co-operation have recently undergone radical changes, and the indirect form of co-operation with specialized aircraft has become subordinated to the overriding requirement of direct air support, which may now involve potentially the entire strength of at least so much of the air force as

can be effectively employed in the battle area. Air support will no longer therefore depend upon the limited resources of a detachment or air component or some such ancillary formation of the army, but will have squarely behind it the whole strength of Fighter Command.

This doctrine of subordination of the entire air resource, tactical and strategic, to the needs of the ground forces was to cause much wrangling, the bomber chiefs in particular seeing it as a misuse of their forces.

The disbandment of Army Co-operation Command took effect on 1 June 1943 as part of a general reorganization of tactical air assets. The references to the Desert Air Force experience are highly relevant, as air power played a major role in the success of land operations in the North African theatre, and was also required to be highly mobile and flexible. Of equal import was the fact that in due course a number of its commanders took up senior appointments within the Allied Expeditionary Air Force, although this itself was to create a certain amount of friction.

Whenever air power is discussed it tends to focus, for obvious reasons, on the aircraft and their combat capabilities, to the exclusion of what is a most essential element: keeping aircraft serviceable and armed. A great deal of attention was paid to this aspect as part of the mobility exercises. The aircraft servicing organization was reorganized to cover three areas: the advanced landing grounds, the airfields and the base area. According to Air Publication (AP) 3397:

It was appreciated that under active service conditions there would be occasions when to ensure quick 'turn-round' it would be necessary to use advanced landing grounds forward of the airfield areas. To perform the servicing task on these landing strips, servicing commandos were established under the control of Group Headquarters. These personnel were taught to operate with a minimum of equipment and to improvise as much as

possible, besides being instructed in self-defence. Their essential duty was to perform refuelling, rearming, between-flight and daily inspections, and repairs of a minor nature.

The success of these servicing commandos is one of the unsung aspects of the RAF's air effort and they played a vital role, especially during the initial weeks of the air move into Europe. The second tier, the airfield, was the basic operational level, with each airfield designed to have three flying squadrons. Technical personnel were divorced from the squadrons, not always a popular arrangement, and centralized at the airfield, leaving only one sergeant tradesman with each squadron for 'technical continuity purposes'. To maintain the concept of mobility the technical squadron was not meant to undertake repair work scheduled to last longer than forty-eight hours; such tasks were allocated to the Repair and Salvage Unit (RSU). The establishment for the RSU was one for every two airfields and they had a mobile and a static element to handle aircraft outside or inside of the airfield boundary, respectively. They were not intended to undertake work scheduled to last longer than seven days. The final element of the chain was the base area, with a remit to handle 'all servicing work beyond the capacity of the airfield'.

Exercise *Spartan* showed that the basic organization was workable, but the divorcing of groundcrew from their squadrons proved to have an effect on the overall *esprit de corps* of the squadron, and it was decided that 'as far as possible the echelons be established to support specific squadrons, their number being correlated to that of the squadron. It was the policy of the Command for the echelon to accompany the squadron whenever possible.'

In mid-May, Leigh-Mallory informed General Sir Bernard Paget, GOC 21st Army Group, that: 'AOC No. 83 Group will be affiliated to 2nd Army and move his advance headquarters to Oxford. The Group's squadrons will deploy to ALGs in Sussex.' No. 83 Group had formed

*This official photograph is entitled thus: 'At a Tactical Air Force station in Britain, June 7th, 1944. Masses of fighter aircraft collected at a group support unit of the AEAF, and hundreds of RAF vehicles assembled at a forward repair unit on the same airfield. Mechanics in the foreground are getting a fighter ready for future operations.'*

at Redhill on 1 April out of a cadre provided by those units of Exercise *Spartan*'s 'Z' Group that had been kept in being for this purpose. Leigh-Mallory also stated that a second composite group was being formed using squadrons from No. 11 Group, and would in due course be assigned to the 1st Canadian Army. Two weeks later, 29 May, he wrote again to say that the plan had changed, and that No. 83 Group would go to the Canadians, whilst the second formation, No. 84 Group, due to form in July, would belong to 2nd British Army. This change was a result of pressure from the Canadian government, but it was subsequently reversed again nearer D-Day

when the final details of the amphibious assault plan were agreed.

## Into Europe: from the South

The surrender of German and Italian forces in North Africa on 12 May 1943 brought the Tunisian campaign to an end, and enabled the Allies to move forward to the next strategic step, a return to the European mainland. Although British and American commanders had worked together during the Tunisian campaign, there had been a tremendous amount of friction, and it was only the appointment of certain key 'co-operative' players such as Eisenhower, Tedder and Coningham that brought any measure of successful integration; it is significant that these were also to be amongst the principal commanders for Operation *Overlord*. It would, of course, be foolish to suggest that all friction vanished; it certainly did not, and the Allies were to be plagued with nationalistic and inter-service rivalries for the remainder of the war. However, the campaigns in North Africa and Italy, and the operational experience they gave to the commanders, were to prove invaluable in the management of the far greater scale and complexity of *Overlord*.

The joint Allied air command of MAAF (Mediterranean Allied Air Force) was reorganized and strengthened during the summer of 1943, and in June commenced anti-air operations in preparation for the invasion of Sicily. The requirement to gain air superiority before mounting a major amphibious operation was well understood and was now applied with vigour; meanwhile, the anti-shipping squadrons sank any enemy vessel that moved, and the strategic bombers hit enemy lines of communication.

The assault forces landed on the beaches of Sicily on 10 July under the cover of a huge air umbrella. Not all aspects of the initial phase went well – the airborne operation was a disaster, and almost 50 per cent of the gliders carrying 1st Airborne Division ended up in the sea. As bridgeheads were secured, so landing strips were constructed to enable tactical aircraft to keep up with the advance, supported by men of the RAF Servicing Commando. Sicily was taken by 15 August, but substantial elements of the German forces had escaped across the Straits of Messina into Italy, despite intense air bombardment. The first ground troops landed in Italy on 3 September, only a few days before the Italian capitulation. Allied air strategy concentrated on Operation *Strangle*, an interdiction campaign aimed at cutting all lines of communication into southern Italy. The

*During Allied operations in Italy, Operation* Strangle *was implemented to cut enemy lines of communication and prevent the Germans moving reinforcements to the battle area. In this photo, 12th Air Force B-26s hit a rail target. It was the success of this campaign that prompted Allied planners to adopt a Transportation Plan for the Normandy campaign.* (US National Archives)

success of this tactic, although disputed by some, was seen as playing an important role in the initial Allied advances. This anti-communication strategy became a central feature of the pre-invasion bombing campaign for D-Day.

At this point we can leave the Italian campaign with the final comment that German defence lines were established, and in a series of fighting withdrawals the defenders slowly retreated northwards. By this time many of the

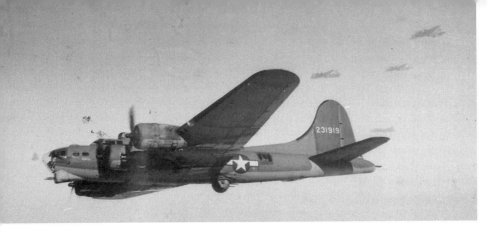

*Flying Fortress* Mon Tête Rouge III *of 452nd BG. The pre-invasion bombing strategy relied on the British and American 'heavies'.* (US National Archives)

*P-51* Fools Paradise IV *of the 380th FS/363rd FG; the creation of the 9th Air Force as the American Tactical Air Force for* Overlord *provided a major enhancement of Allied air power. Groundcrew watch a four-ship of Mustangs returning from yet another mission.* (National Archives)

BELOW: *2nd TAF Mitchells taxi out; the 2nd Tactical Air Force was a core element of AEAF and initially comprised No. 2 Group and No. 83 Group.*

senior commanders had been moved back to the UK to join the staffs for *Overlord*, taking with them the ideas, concepts and principles of the campaigns in the south. Without doubt the single important lesson learned was the indivisibility of the air/land battle; this may seem an obvious statement, but in the early years of the war, airman and soldier had little understanding of the requirements or capabilities of the other, and until such an understanding was reached, co-operative operations were impossible. The Desert/North Africa campaign had been a fertile breeding ground for new ideas and doctrines, and the presence of such air leaders as Coningham provided the catalyst. In essence, the doctrine was that the air force kept the enemy air away from the ground forces and provided firepower when and where needed, and the army secured the airbases so that the air force could operate as near the front as possible; co-ordination was carried out by a joint tactical HQ. It did not always work quite as planned, but by the end of the North African campaign the basic routine was well established.

## *Overlord* Planning

Amongst the many topics for discussion at the 'Trident' Conference held in Washington in May 1943 was the date for the landings in north-west Europe. In view of other calls upon Allied resources, the need to ensure that the air campaign had sufficient time to achieve its objectives, and also the time-scale for the build-up of adequate force levels, it was decided that spring 1944 was the optimum date. It was essential, therefore, that all operations be geared to this effect, and all planning effort be suitably oriented.

Throughout 1943 Allied air strength continued to grow; more bomber and fighter groups joined the rapidly expanding US 8th Air Force, and this organization was soon putting formidable effort into the Combined Bomber Offensive. However, the major factor in the expansion of air power was the decision to create a new American tactical air force in the UK, specifically for operations in conjunction with *Overlord*, the longer-term plan being that this organization would move to the Continent as the land forces advanced. Rather than form a new air force from scratch, it was decided to reform the 9th Air Force, which had operated in North Africa, in Britain.

Other changes were being made to the air power organization: No. 2 Group moved from RAF Bomber Command on 1 June to join the newly formed 2nd Tactical Air Force (TAF). At this stage, 2nd TAF was part of RAF Fighter Command and comprised only two operational groups – No. 2 and No. 83. For other units there was re-equipment or even a change of role, as the majority of the RAF's home-based power was reorganized in preparation for the invasion. By August 1943, the Chief of Staff to the Supreme Allied Commander (COSSAC) planning staffs had a tentative invasion plan drawn up, and this was duly circulated to the various departments for comment. An inter-service study of the invasion coast, using information from air reconnaissance (as well as covert material from the Resistance movements), had confirmed two suitable beach areas within the areas of interest; this latter requirement was based upon the need for fighter cover of the assault, and so was limited by fighter range to the area between Flushing and Cherbourg. The two areas were the Pas de Calais (Gravelines to the Somme river) and Baie de la Seine, Normandy (Orne river to the Cotentin peninsula).

The COSSAC plan had its origins in 1942, devised by a team headed by Lieutenant General P. Morgan as Chief of Staff to the Supreme Allied Commander Designate. What this team did was to analyse air power and air–sea–land lessons of other theatres and previous operations in order to apply such lessons to the problem now faced, the entry back into Europe. Without this corpus of information and experience from Dieppe, North Africa and Sicily, the planning for *Overlord* would have been far more difficult and far less reliable in its strategy.

The next major consideration was 'where should the landings take place'. An enormous effort was to be expended convincing the Germans to expect the invasion in the wrong place; thus as soon as the decision had been taken in favour of Normandy, it became vital to make the Germans look to the Pas de Calais. The major aspect of this, as far as the air campaign was concerned, was to be the policy of attacking two targets outside the designated invasion area for every one attacked within it. The overall plan, codenamed *Bigot*, was incredibly complex and not confined to north-west Europe alone; but anything that could make the Germans concentrate resources in the wrong area was worth a try.

## Airfields

With the 'Germany First' decision the Americans had agreed to allocate the bulk of their combat air power to the European theatre; this, combined with the continued growth of the RAF's own strength, meant an enormous requirement for airfields – preferably as close as possible to the enemy. The latter consideration was particularly important for the short-range fighters and fighter-bombers, and a massive construction programme had been instituted in late 1941/early 1942. The allocation of units to airfields, and the jigsaw puzzle of trying to ensure that the right units were in the right places, was one of the most important juggling acts that the air commanders had to make, especially as the US 8th, and later 9th, Army Air Forces needed geographic clutches of airfields for their respective combat wings. However, there is one aspect of the airfield programme that is particularly relevant to the D-Day campaign: the construction of a series of advanced landing grounds (ALGs).

In the autumn of 1942, work started on a series of ALGs in southern England, temporary airfields that would accommodate British

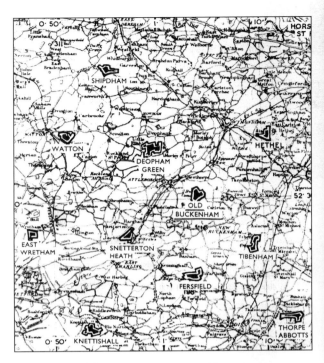

*The massive airfield construction programme left some parts of England dotted with airfields; this area of East Anglia was home to part of the American Army Air Forces.*

and American tactical squadrons for a limited time in the pre-invasion period. With the massive weight of air power being assembled for the invasion, the question of where to base units became increasingly acute, and whilst the construction programme for permanent airfields was accelerated, an even more acute need was for airfields for use by short-range tactical aircraft; a network of ALGs was therefore constructed in southern England, primarily in Kent, Hampshire and Sussex. A large number of possible sites was surveyed, and once a selection had been made, plans were drawn up for the construction of twenty-three ALGs for use by the RAF's 2nd TAF.

The initial work involved the clearing of woodland and the draining of marshland, after which an RAF Airfield Construction Service (ACS) team of three officers and 200 airmen would be given an average of three months to complete the construction of the site. In

ABOVE: *Temporary airfields made great use of metal tracking for runways and, as here, dispersal points.*

*Steel mesh being laid down to create yet another new airfield for use by tactical aircraft.*

general terms each airfield was constructed to the same pattern, although local conditions did require some variation, with two metal-track runways, 2.5 miles (4km) of perimeter track, plus an additional SMT track. A typical ALG construction involved:

- Levelling of site: 10,000 tons of earth to be shifted.
- Laying of runways: two runways each 1,600 × 50yd (1,463 × 46m), metal track.
- Aircraft standings: 80in (2.03m) metal track.
- Perimeter track and MT road: 2.5 miles (4km) perimeter plus 2.5 miles MT road in metal track or hardcore with tarspray cover.
- Hangars: eight blister type.
- Petrol installation: sufficient for 18,000 gallons (82,000ltr).

Other than the blister hangars, very few buildings would be provided, so tents or requisitioned buildings would be the norm. Each airfield was to be capable of supporting up to fifty day-operational aircraft. Most of the work was carried out by the RAF's Airfield Construction Service, although Royal Engineers, American Engineer Aviation Battalions and civilian contractors all contributed. Target date for completion was March 1943, and eleven of the sites were allocated for USAAF use, the remainder being for the RAF. For a variety of reasons the programme was soon behind schedule. The first airfield to open was Chailey, 3 miles (5km) east of Burgess Hill, in April 1943, but like many of these airfields there was no initial attempt to move in operational units. Most of the new airfields had been completed by the end of 1943, and some

TOP: *Laying the tarmac perimeter track at Shipham in May 1943; note the Liberators in the background.*

ABOVE: *Wire-mesh surfaces being laid by the 833rd Engineer Aviation Battalion (EAB).* (US National Archives)

had been used by squadrons on evaluation exercises.

## Advanced Landing Grounds

| Opened | Location | Closed |
|---|---|---|
| 1 Apr 1943 | Chailey | 20 Jan 1945 |
| 30 May 1943 | Selsey | 19 Aug 1944 |
| 1 Jun 1943 | Bognor | 26 Sep 1944 |
| 2 Jun 1943 | Appledram | 6 Nov 1944 |
| 15 Jun 1943 | Swingfield | 28 Apr 1945 |
| 25 Jun 1943 | Lydd | 13 Dec 1944 |
| 1 Jul 1943 | Kingsnorth | 20 Jul 1944 |
| 2 Jul 1943 | New Romney | 1 Nov 1944 |
| 2 Jul 1943 | Newchurch | 13 Dec 1945 |
| 28 Jul 1943 | Woodchurch | 18 Sep 1944 |
| 6 Aug 1943 | Lashenden | 29 Jun 1945 |
| 6 Aug 1943 | Staplehurst | 18 Jan 1945 |
| 11 Aug 1943 | Ashford | 15 Sep 1944 |
| 20 Aug 1943 | Headcorn | 9 Jul 1944 |
| 15 Sep 1943 | Funtingdon | 13 Dec 1944 |
| ? Sep 1943 | Brenzett | ? Dec 1944 |
| ? Mar 1944 | Lymington | 25 Jun 1944 |
| 3 Mar 1944 | Bisterne | 23 Jun 1944 |
| 1 Apr 1944 | Deansland | 12 Jan 1945 |
| 1 Apr 1944 | Coolham | 1 Aug 1944 |
| 4 Apr 1944 | Wington | 6 Jul 1944 |
| 10 Apr 1944 | Needs Oar Point | ? Nov 1944 |
| 13 Apr 1944 | High Halden | 15 Sep 1944 |

The ALGs were only part of the overall requirement, and in October 1943 a draft airfield disposition plan was issued, which in essence was an allocation of airfields for specific phases of *Overlord*:

*Phase I*: Period up to April 1944, with American groups arriving in the UK and requiring winter quarters, plus concentrating on training and gaining operational experience.
*Phase II*: April 1944 to D+8, units move to battle stations, take part in the invasion, and British units commence move to the Continent.
*Phase III*: D+8 onwards, British units continue to move to the Continent, followed by American units.

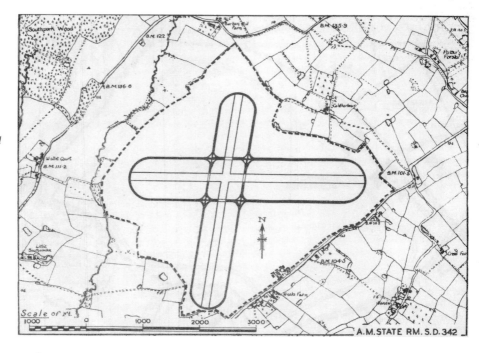

Plan of the ALG at Headcorn, which opened in August 1943. The creation of a series of temporary airfields in southern England was needed for the mass of tactical air power being assembled.

The construction, maintenance and defence of airfields remained a key issue for planners and commanders; this programme was one of the most successful elements of the overall campaign. The sheer scale of effort (and cost) in building the air bases from which Allied air power would dominate the European battlefield was astounding when you add up the millions of feet of timber in Nissen huts, the miles of asphalt and concrete on runways and taxiways, and the countless hours spent in preparing airfield sites to take three runways of over a mile long – and a host of other construction details. Sixty years later, large parts of the UK landscape retain traces of this time when southern and eastern England became a giant 'aircraft carrier'.

## Combined Bombing Offensive 1943

Whilst tactical air power developed its strength and doctrines, the major offensive effort remained that of the heavy bomber forces, although an increasing number of medium-bomber attacks, fighter-bomber operations and fighter sweeps were being made over north-west France, Holland and Belgium. The increased threat to the German war economy brought an increasing level of resources into the air-defence network – fighters, radars, guns and searchlights. This in turn caused bomber losses, by day and night, to rise, and made the question of air superiority of primary importance, a subject debated at the Washington Conference in May 1943, and reflected in a directive (*Pointblank*) issued on 3 June 1943, which stated that:

> …the offensive has caused an increase in day- and night-fighter defence, and therefore we must check the rise in fighter strength; the priority is to attack the German fighter forces and the industries upon which they depend:
>
> 1. The destruction of German airframe, engine and component factories, and the ball-bearing industry on which the strength of the German fighter force depends.
> 2. The general disorganization of those industrial areas associated with the above.
> 3. The destruction of those aircraft repair depots and storage parks within range, and on which the enemy fighter force is largely dependent.
> 4. The destruction of enemy fighters in the air and on the ground.

The success of the *Pointblank* bombing offensive was considered to be an essential part of the overall pre-invasion air strategy. The twin prongs of this offensive were to be the daylight raids by the US 8th Air Force, and the night raids, mainly against industrial targets in cities, by RAF Bomber Command. Not only would the German air force be destroyed in the factories and on the ground, but when the fighters rose to meet the bomber streams they would face increasing numbers of Allied

*Bombs dropping from a formation of B-17s. From June 1943 Operation* Pointblank *focused bombing effort against the German fighter organization.*
(US National Archives)

*Bombing up a Lancaster of 83 Squadron.*

fighters. Throughout this period numerous communiqués stated the general war aim:

> Since 1942 it had been the ultimate intention of the Western Powers to re-enter the Continent from the UK, concentrating the maximum of resources in the most convenient theatre so as to force unconditional surrender upon Germany.

Although the British war effort was still badly stretched, the entry into the war of the USA meant that eventual victory was now rather more certain and so future planning could take on a more positive approach.

**Allied Expeditionary Air Force**
The overall air chain of command was confirmed on 15 November 1943 with the creation of the Allied Expeditionary Air Force (AEAF), with HQ at Stanmore Park under Air Marshal Sir Trafford Leigh-Mallory (whose appointment as Air Commander-in-Chief, Allied Air Forces had been announced in August), with 'responsibility for providing air support for the invasion and consolidation of Allied forces in NW Europe'. On the same day Fighter Command was 'disbanded' and the home defence elements reverted to the pre-war title of Air Defence of Great Britain (ADGB). With the creation of the

AEAF, various air elements were transferred to the new air organization, including 2nd TAF, 9th Air Force, and elements of ADGB. In due course other commands and units would be subordinated to AEAF for the *Overlord* campaign.

Perhaps sensing that the chain of command needed emphasizing, Leigh-Mallory issued a memo two days after his appointment: 'My directive states that I will have under my operational command RAF TAF, 9th US Air Force, ADGB and such other units as may be assigned to AEAF at a later date.' Politics were indeed never far beneath the surface, as evidenced by a memo (14 October) from General Arnold (Commander USAAF) to ACM Portal (British Chief of Air Staff):

> *Overlord* hangs directly on the success of our combined aerial offensive, and I am sure that our failure to decisively cripple both sources of German air power and the GAF itself is causing you and me concern. I am afraid that we are not sufficiently alert to changes in the overall course of the air war. In particular I refer to the fact that we are not employing our forces in adequate numbers against the GAF in being, as well as his facilities and sources. On my part I am pressing Eaker to get a much higher proportion of his forces off the ground, and put them where they will hurt the enemy.

*Formation of Spitfires from 41 Squadron; Fighter Command's squadrons undertook offensive sweeps from 1941 onwards, taking the war back to the enemy.*

BELOW: *Trafford Leigh-Mallory was appointed as Air Commander-in-Chief of the Allied Expeditionary Air Force in August 1943.*

One of his main points was the lack of fighter support for the daylight bombers:

> As presently employed it would appear that your thousands of fighters are not making use of their full capabilities. Our transition from the defensive to the offensive should surely carry with it the application of your large fighter force offensively. Is it not true that we have a staggering air superiority over the Germans and we are not using it.

Arnold also made the point that the P-47's basic design had a shorter range than that of the Spitfire, but when fitted with long-range tanks it was working well as an escort. The implication was that the American daylight offensive could be far more effective (and less costly) if the RAF's fighters were used as escorts and employed in an offensive way to destroy the Luftwaffe's remaining combat power. The RAF comment was that attempts were being made to improve the range of the Spitfire, but that an external tank only gave an extra 50 miles (80km) – and besides, 'our fighter force has been designed to obtain air superiority over northern France, for which it is eminently suitable.' It could have been added that on short-range penetrations and offensive fighter sweeps, the Luftwaffe seldom made an appearance.

On 23 November Leigh-Mallory issued Command Order No. 1, part of which read:'... as Air Commander-in-Chief of the Allied Expeditionary Air Forces and the ADGB I am privileged to lead a joint force of which much is expected in the coming months. I know that all ranks will justify my confidence in the future as they have done in the past.' On 6 December he issued a directive to the tactical air forces:

> The objective of Operation *Overlord* is to secure a lodgement area on the Continent from which further offensive operations can be developed. The lodgement area must contain sufficient port facilities to maintain a force of twenty-six to thirty divisions, and enable that force to be augmented by follow-on shipments. Target date is 1 May 1944, and there are two phases:
>
> Phase I: Effecting a landing in the Caen sector, early capture and development of airfield sites in Caen area, and capture of the port of Cherbourg.
>
> Phase II: Enlargement of the area captured in Phase I so as to secure the whole of the Cherbourg, Loire and Brittany group of ports.

He also outlined the expected air strength for the target date (*see* box below).

With over 10,000 aircraft, the air forces arrayed for the invasion of Europe would be the

---

### Expected Air Strength

|  | Type | Established Aircraft per Squadron | Squadrons | Allocated to AEAF |
|---|---|---|---|---|
| 8th AF | Day heavy bomber | 12 | 162 | – |
|  | Day fighter | 25 | 45 | – |
|  | Photo-recce | 12 | 4 | – |
| 9th AF | Medium bomber | 16 | 32 | 32 |
|  | Light bomber | 16 | 12 | 12 |
|  | Day fighter | 25 | 54 | 54 |
|  | Night fighter | 12 | 3 | 3 |
|  | Fighter-recce | 18 | 4 | 4 |
|  | Photo-recce | 12 | 4 | 4 |
|  | Troop carrier | 13 | 52 | 52 |
| British | Day fighter | 18 | 59 | 42 |
|  | Fighter-bomber | 18 | 18 | 16 |
|  | Fighter-recce | 18 | 8 | 5 |
|  | Night fighter | 18 | 22 | – |
|  | Light bomber | 20 | 6 | – |
|  | TAF | 18 | 12 | 12 |
|  | Photo-recce | 18 | 8 | 4 |
|  | Heavy bomber | 20 | 82 | – |
|  | Troop carrier | 20 | 9 | 9 |

*Airborne lift*

| | |
|---|---|
| IXth TCC | 624 C-47, Gliders – 2,000 CG-4A, 400 Horsa, 40 Hamilcar |
| No 38 Gp | 330 aircraft*, 900 Horsa, 40 Hamilcar |

*80 Albemarle, 80 Stirling, 20 Halifax, 150 Dakota

*A-20s cruise over an airfield pock-marked by craters.* (US National Archives)

most powerful ever assembled. Whilst the number of aircraft was impressive, the list of targets prepared by the planning staffs was equally impressive. Added to this was the fact that it was a diverse group in terms of aircraft, experience and capabilities; it also suffered from variations in doctrines and dogmatic stances amongst certain of its commanders. All of these aspects would cause problems as the campaign unfolded.

On 12 December, Leigh-Mallory chaired a conference on the employment of tactical bombers: '…study of tactical bomber operations carried out in the past few months showed that attacks carried out on airfields appeared to have done the enemy little harm, and had not provoked any appreciable defensive reaction.' It was agreed that there was 'little to be gained from attacking his airfields at this stage', and instead set two new priorities:

1. Attacks on suitable industrial objectives with sufficient weight to reduce still further

the enemy's already strained economic and industrial resources, in particular those in the Paris and Lille–Lens–Béthune areas.
2. Attacks to provoke the enemy fighter defences to react in force, thus offering us the opportunity to destroy them.

The second target category was simply an extension of the *Circus* operations that the RAF had been mounting since 1941, but without any appreciable reaction from the German fighter force. It was hoped that with the increased number of tactical bombers, operating with strong fighter escort and co-ordinated with fighter sweeps, the Germans would have no option but to react in order to prevent the destruction of vital targets. For the Allied planners one of the perennial problems was deciding which targets fitted this 'critical' requirement. The December meeting proposed that weekly target lists be drawn up for each of the tactical air forces; the first list (21 December) comprised:

*IXth Bomber Command*
Chocques – glycol production.
Meulan-les-Mupeaux – Bf 109 components and single-engine fighter factory.
Albert – aero engines and components.

*2nd TAF*
Bully-les-Mines – methyl-alcohol production.
Ghent/Terneuzen – oil storage.
Lille/Fives – engine and railway workshops.

*No. 2 Group*
Woippy – aero-engine works.
Limoges – BMW aero-engine assembly plant.
Hengelo – electrical equipment.

*No. 38 Group*
Beaumont-le-Roger – fighter airfield.

December brought another round of command appointments, General Eisenhower taking up the post of Supreme Commander, Allied Expeditionary Force, with Tedder as his deputy. At the same time, General Bernard Montgomery was confirmed as Commander of 21st Army Group and, more significantly, as overall commander of Allied land forces for the initial phase of the invasion. The last of the senior posts, that of Allied Naval Commander, Expeditionary Force had been granted to Admiral Ramsay in October.

It was inevitable that the appointments would result in changes to the outline plans already in preparation; in particular, Montgomery objected to certain elements of the COSSAC plan concerning the strength and frontage of the initial assault phase (too small) and the scale of the airborne operation. The original plan called for an airborne operation by less than one division, whereas in his view:

> ...it was evident that airborne forces could play an extremely important role in the assault, and it seemed unfortunate that such a small lift should

*A Bomber Command 'before and after' view of an aircraft factory at Toulouse, the attack taking place on the night of 1/2 May 1944.*

BELOW: *Another German fighter falls prey to an Allied fighter, in this case a Spitfire, on 17 May 1944.*

be at our disposal when there would be three or four airborne divisions available for operations on D-Day.

Nevertheless, the general elements of the COS-SAC plan were adhered to; after all, the plan had undergone numerous changes since its first draft, and was based upon operational experience. The planning staffs worked long and hard, taking great care to maintain inter-service and inter-allied co-operation.

As 1943 drew to a close the Allies appraised the position and the effect of the air campaign to date. The majority of effort had been that expended by the strategic bomber forces, especially the campaign designed to gain air superiority through the destruction of German Air Force fighter capability, and by bombers and maritime aircraft against the U-boat threat. Both of these elements were assessed as progressing well, albeit the GAF was proving more resilient than some forecasts had predicted. The various fighter sweeps and fighter-escorted daylight raids by medium bombers had not produced the air battles through which it had been hoped to destroy the remaining *Luftwaffe* fighter strength. Nevertheless, the planners were confident that the campaign was more or less on schedule, and that with ever-increasing offensive

power the Allied air forces would be able, given suitable weather conditions and accurate intelligence, to complete all that was asked of it. The prospects for the invasion in 1944 looked good, although it was realized that there was still much to be done.

# 2  The Air Battle Builds to a Climax

The outline overall Air Plan called for four phases of air operation in support of *Overlord*:

1. Preliminary: January–February 1944, but also a continuation of the air offensives of late 1943.
2. Preparatory: March–May 1944, main weight of attacks on invasion targets.
3. Assault: D minus Two to D plus One.
4. Follow-up: D +2 onwards.

On 21 January, Leigh-Mallory was promoted to Air Chief Marshal – but this did nothing to reduce the wrangling amongst the Allied commanders. There is, unfortunately, insufficient space in this account to detail the many debates (arguments), or to analyse what one author has called the 'war between the generals'; what I have attempted to do is to highlight those debates and conflicts that had some direct bearing on the air campaign. One source of friction was the relationship between Leigh-Mallory and the Deputy Supreme Commander, Tedder; as an airman, and with his experiences in the Middle East campaigns, Tedder was deeply interested in all aspects of the air campaign and plans for the employment of both tactical and strategic air assets. Leigh-Mallory

*Tedder and Coningham – the two air leaders established an excellent rapport during the Desert campaign, and both joined the Allied Expeditionary Force, Tedder as Deputy Supreme Commander, and Coningham as Commander of 2nd TAF.*

was determined to brook no 'interference', and expressed his dislike of the command arrangement; however, in February, Tedder was given greater control of air planning in an attempt to clarify the overall chain of command. Leigh-Mallory also found it difficult to work with Coningham, perhaps because of the latter's connections with Tedder, the two of them having worked together in the North African campaigns.

The situation remained less than ideal, and was further complicated by the desire of British and American bomber chiefs to remain independent to pursue their own strategies; although Harris in a post-war communiqué stated:

> It was obvious to me that the heavy bomber offered the only conceivable means of breaching the Atlantic Wall, destroying the enemy's interior lines of communication, and thus enabling the army to break out of its beachhead when it gathered sufficient strength.

This post-war comment was materially different to statements he made at the time, in which he often railed against any diversion of his bomber effort from its true strategic target – German cities and their industries. For example, in January 1944 he wrote:

> It is clear that the best, and indeed the only effective support that Bomber Command can give to *Overlord* is the intensification of attacks on suitable industrial centres in Germany as and when the opportunity offers. If we attempt to substitute this for precision attacks on gun emplacements, beach defences, communications and dumps in occupied territory we shall commit the irremediable error of diverting our best weapon from the military function for which it has been equipped and trained, to tasks which it cannot effectively carry out.

Whilst this was his firmly held conviction, he nevertheless employed his force to great effect

*With one engine feathered, a 15th Air Force B-17 returns from a target in northern Italy. The integration of the heavy bombers based in Italy (15th AF) and the UK (8th AF) into the United States Strategic Air Force was an important policy decision.* (US National Archives)

on a range of pre-invasion targets as dictated by AEAF.

In general terms Eisenhower had a relaxed command style whereby he preferred his subordinate commanders to work out their difficulties, a policy that has elicited adverse comment. The overall chain of command continued to cause friction during the remainder of the preparatory phases; at one stage, control and planning of all 2nd TAF and 9th Air Force operations was devolved to Coningham, this arrangement to remain in effect for a limited period running from just before to just after the assault phase. As all strategic bomber ops came under Tedder, this meant that Leigh-Mallory was almost 'minister without portfolio', a situation summarized quite well as:

> …The control of the Air Commander-in-Chief over the operations of the strategic bombing forces was so reduced as a result of the differences of aims, ideals and doctrines between the various air authorities, with differences due perhaps to national pride and ambitions and to the clash of strong personalities, that even before D-Day he was only able to set out the objects of the attack and co-ordinate their timing.　　　　　　　　(RAF Narrative)

The daily air commanders' conference did little to ease the situation, although it must be stressed that amidst all the wrangling none of those involved lost sight of the overall aim and intent of the air campaign.

A further change in January was the creation of the United States Strategic Air Force (USSTAF) under Lieutenant General Carl A. Spaatz. This organization brought the operational control of US 8th and 15th Air Forces under one commander, such that he could direct the strategic bomber effort from England (VIIIth Bomber Command) and Italy

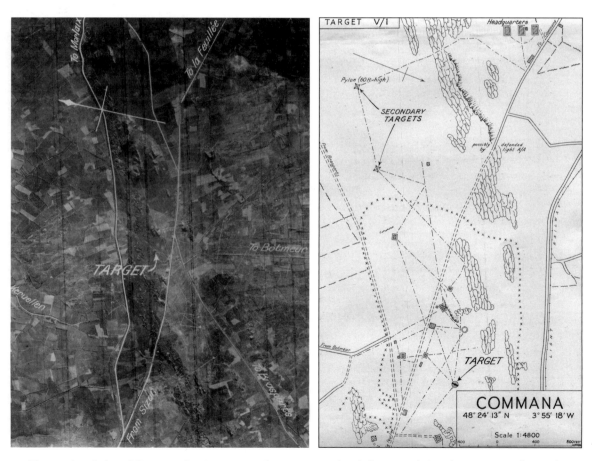

*Photograph and plan of Commana showing a variety of targets associated with this site, including the primary aerial array, the secondary Benito towers and the Headquarters area. Note the photograph has been rotated 180 degrees when compared to the map.*

37

(15th Air Force) to the same overall strategic aim of supporting *Overlord*. This was of greater value when the original plan of a simultaneous landing in the north (*Overlord*) and south (*Anvil*) of France was still viable. In due course, however, the latter operation had to be delayed – shortage of landing craft being a major consideration. The main co-operative effort of USSTAF then became the anti-oil campaign. Although the command problems were severe they should not be overstated. In view of the size and complexity of the Allied organization it is amazing how smoothly the general relationships went, much of this due to the willing co-operation at the middle and lower operational levels.

The AEAF Bombing Committee was formed on 10 January 1944 to consider:

1. Suitability of targets for bombing.
2. Relationship of bombing commitments to the scale of effort estimated to be available.
3. Allocation of priorities to the various commitments.
4. Apportionment of the available bomber effort.

As mentioned above, the scale of Allied air power available for *Overlord* was incredible – but so too were the tasks it would be called on to perform. The Bombing Committee had a host of inputs to consider, many of which were contradictory, and they also had to take into account feedback from operational experience as well as evaluations conducted by various trials organizations. It was all very well for a committee to allocate a particular scale of effort against a target, but if the effectiveness of the weapons delivered was inappropriate, then the entire process would be flawed. It was also important to consider the capabilities of the enemy to repair any damage, as this would dictate when a target should be attacked, or if a re-attack would need to be programmed. Throughout this account the reader will come across references to effectiveness of attack; for

example, in respect of heavy bombers being employed against coastal gun batteries. Unfortunately, until all air assets were put under the operational control of Eisenhower (in spring 1944), much of the committee's work was treated as advisory by the bomber chiefs.

A major conference was held on 21 January, the first one at which Eisenhower was present, and many objections were raised to elements of the *Overlord* plan. However, it was agreed to confirm the invasion date for 1 May, thus satisfying the ground commander's desire for the longest possible campaigning season.

Throughout the first few months of 1944 the specialist committees sat to decide the best way of dealing with the particular set of problems with which each of them had been tasked; most of the major target categories had such a committee, and typical of these was the Airfield Committee. Plans were then presented to the AEAF command organization, and at one such meeting (26 January) the outline anti-airfield plan was debated. Solly Zuckerman, a scientific advisor whose views carried great weight, stated: 'we should attempt to destroy the aircraft as well as the airfield facilities', and he estimated that 400 tons of bombs would need to be used against each airfield to achieve a reasonable result.

There were three groups of airfields to be targeted: firstly, those within 110 miles (180km) radius of the lodgement area, which comprised twelve main and fifteen secondary airfields; secondly, those within 130 miles (210km), a total of twenty-five main and twenty-four secondary airfields; and finally, those within 150 miles (240km), comprising thirty-five main and twenty-nine secondary airfields. The plan was for 'attacks to be launched against all airfields up to the maximum radius permitted by the effort available. This would deny the enemy the advantage of disposition that he would otherwise enjoy.' In Phase One of the plan, aircraft would target airfield maintenance, repair and servicing facilities; in Phase Two, attention would switch

*Medium bombers of 9th Air Force attacking a German airfield on 10 April, with a good concentration of bombs over a dispersal area.*

to runways and landing areas to 'render them unserviceable for two to three days or longer at the time of the assault'. The first concentrated attacks would be scheduled to commence on D minus 21, with the plan rolling into Phase Two 'not earlier than necessary because of the ease of repairing runway surfaces.'

The co-ordination of the mass of air power and its effective employment was a mammoth task, especially with the differences in doctrine between the British and Americans. As related above, many elements of air power doctrine had been tested in previous operations, but applying those lessons to the situation faced by the *Overlord* planners was no easy task. On 10 March, Eisenhower issued the following directive: 'The object of Operation *Overlord* is to secure a lodgement area on the Continent from which further offensive operations can be developed. The target date is 31 May.' The directive went on to outline the two air plans: Plan A, the Strategic Air Plan; and Plan B, the Tactical Air Plan; these simply reinforced the overall plan already issued, the first phase of which was almost complete. However, it was not until 15 April that SHAEF issued a final

version of the overall air plan, which included further changes in the chain of command, with provision for Coningham to have 'operational control of the planning and operation of both British and American tactical air forces'.

The gradual slipping of the invasion date was in large part due to the lack of landing craft, amongst the reasons for this being a desire by the US Navy to hold on to such vessels for operations in the Pacific. By postponing Operation *Anvil* and transferring landing craft to Britain, and by accelerating the building programme, it was hoped to have sufficient quantity by the end of May.

The overall air plan as of 7 February envisaged the provision of 171 fighter-type squadrons during the actual assault, with the following allocation or roles:

| | |
|---|---|
| Beach cover | 54 squadrons |
| Shipping cover | 15 squadrons |
| Direct air support | 36 squadrons |
| Offensive fighter ops (including bomber escort) | 33 squadrons |
| Striking force (including escort of airborne forces) | 33 squadrons |

 STE.MARGUERITE

TARGET

Light A.A.

From DIEPPE

ENGLISH CHANNEL

Photographed in February 1944, the site at Dieppe/Ste Marguerite was recorded in target folder XII/62 as comprising 'a Giant Wurzburg and Coastwatcher, the latter being on the lighthouse building nearest the cliff edge. The Coastwatcher stands on top of the square masonry tower in front of the lighthouse, and the Giant Wurzburg is on a low concrete structure to the west. There is a light AA site nearby.'

BELOW: German soldiers scatter as an Allied reconnaissance aircraft flies low over the beach to record the defences. Low-level photographs such as this were essential for planning the landings.

## The Preliminary Phase

It is almost impossible to define a start date for this phase of the air campaign, as the elements of which it comprised had been under way for many months – the *Pointblank* offensive, for example, being a key element of this phase. The overall requirements of this phase were the disruption of enemy communication routes, winning of air superiority, detailed air reconnaissance and the destruction of enemy naval forces. Attacks on enemy lines of communications had been an aspect of the Bomber Command bombing strategy, albeit as a bonus effect of destroying the centres of cities through which such major communications routes passed; however, it was now to be an objective in its own right, a directive to this effect being issued in early March.

Air reconnaissance has all too often been ignored when analysing aspects of air campaigns; with the *Overlord* campaign it played a central part, providing the data from which the planners chose the assault areas. The whole of the western European coastal belt was covered over a period of time to provide a detailed photographic record of beaches and terrain, information vital in the selection of the lodgement area. Extensive coverage behind the coastal fringe allowed selection of likely sites for airfield construction, a major factor in choosing the Cotentin peninsula. Added to this was the routine cover of German defence works and the compilation of target details for attack planning; from March onwards this latter task became of even greater importance.

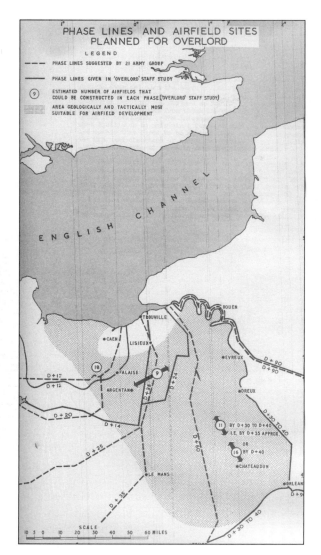

*Map showing planned phase lines (advance from the beach-head) and areas suitable for airfield construction.* (AHB)

construction personnel, RAF and Royal Engineers, with the ACS making up two-thirds of the total in five wings. The Americans had their own airfield engineers embedded in the command structure; as far as airfield construction in France was concerned, responsibility would lie with IXth Engineer Command. Another fear of the military planners was that the German Air Force would launch a major effort against the airfields of southern England in an attempt to disrupt the air support for the invasion: to meet this eventuality a mobile blitz repair scheme was implemented, involving 10,000 men of the ACS covering seventy-four airfields, including the twenty-three ALGs, in southern England. In the event, the Germans made no significant attempt to attack the airfields.

The planners realized that air power would play a major role in the breakout phase, and it was therefore vital that tactical aircraft be based as close to the front line as possible. The summary paper of February 1944 for Operation *Bigot*, the overall air plan, had outlined the minimum airfield requirements as:

D+3    4 refuel and re-arm strips (2 British,
       2 American)
D+10   10 ALGs (5 each)
D+14   18 airfields (10 British, 8 American)
D+24   27 airfields (15 British, 12 American)
D+40   43 airfields (25 British, 18 American)

The paper stated that:

> The extent to which these requirements can be met depends on the ability of airfield engineers to locate and develop suitable sites. In the initial stages the terrain of the British Sector is generally favourable, and that in the US Sector is not.

## March 1944

On 4 March, RAF Bomber Command received instructions to carry out a series of trial attacks on French marshalling yards, to provide

We have already alluded to the plans for airfield construction, and in February 1944 the RAF Airfield Construction Service (ACS) had formed its first mobile wing, No. 5357 Wing. The mobile Field Force Wing comprised a HQ unit and two construction squadrons, and was equipped with the machinery required for the 'rapid construction of airstrips in forward areas' (AP 3236). When the invasion took place it included over 16,000 British airfield

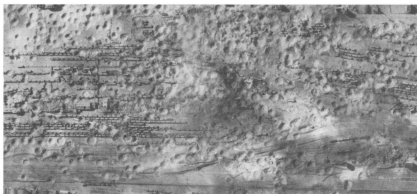

*The major rail yard and junction at Aulnoye in 'before' and 'after' views; the target was heavily attacked by Bomber Command on the night of 27/28 April.*

planning data for a series of such attacks planned in support of the *Overlord* Transportation Plan. The targets to be hit were Trappes, Aulnoye, Le Mans, Amiens/Longeau, Courtrai and Laon. The first of these attacks took place on the night of 6/7 March, when 261 Halifax aircraft, led by six Mosquitoes, attacked Trappes; weather conditions were excellent, with good visibility and little opposition. The attack was one of the most successful yet undertaken by the command, and there were no losses. Bomber Command analysts enthused over the results, concluding that: 'It is appreciated that this new-found ability to saturate with bomb strikes a given area of approx. 500 × 1,000yd [805 × 1,610m] square constitutes a weapon of war of enormous power.'

The following night a slightly larger force of Halifax and Lancaster bombers attacked Le Mans, again without loss and, despite cloud cover, with good results, although the number of French civilian casualties did cause concern. At least 300 bombs fell on the rail yards, causing several cuts and the destruction of 250 wagons, a number of locomotives and substantial damage to installations.

During the remainder of March several more such raids were carried out against marshalling yards: Le Mans (13th–14th), Amiens (15th–16th and 16th–17th), Laon (23rd–24th), Aulnoye (25th–26th) and Courtrai (26th–27th). But the question of bombing marshalling yards in towns where French civilian casualties might result, as had been the case with the Le Mans attack, continued to trouble some Allied planners and politicians, although many saw such casualties as a price that France would have to pay for liberation. Nevertheless, a conference took place on 5 April to discuss this subject, and with such powerful voices as Churchill's expressing concern, a revised target list was drawn up to include only those targets where French civilian casualties could be kept low. But as the date for the invasion grew closer this restriction was amended, and eventually lifted altogether.

Throughout March the American heavies attacked a variety of targets, having to cope with heavy cloud cover in the first part of the month, which greatly reduced their effectiveness, although the development of 'pathfinder' techniques along the lines of those employed by the RAF proved of great benefit. For the 8th Army Air Force, 6 March was significant as it brought the first daylight attack on Berlin: some 730 bombers took part in the mission, with sixty-nine failing to return; crew losses for this one mission were seventeen killed, 686 missing and thirty-one wounded. Fifteen of the missing B-17s were from the 100th BG, a unit that continued to suffer heavy losses and became known as the 'Bloody Hundredth'. In addition to claims made by the bombers' air

gunners, the 800 escort fighters claimed eighty-one enemy aircraft destroyed. Despite the success of the fighters, they were still unable to offer all-round protection for the entire route flown by the bombers. However, by the middle of March the combined fighter groups of the 8th and 9th Air Forces were able to put up around 1,000 fighters for a maximum effort.

On 25 March the Supreme Commander held a crucial conference to finalize the employment of air power in the two months leading up to the invasion and during the immediate post-invasion period. Much of the discussion centred around items that had already been given tacit approval in the outline air plans; the real arguments started when it came to the employment of the heavy bombers of the US 8th Air Force and RAF Bomber Command. The conference was presented with two very different proposals: from Tedder came the 'Transportation Plan', and from Spaatz the 'Oil Offensive'. Both had rehearsed their arguments, and both held very vehement opinions – it was to be a bitter

*Flak bursts around a B-17 formation. The 8th Air Force bomber chiefs were criticized for failing to dedicate resources to targets connected with* Overlord. (US National Archives)

struggle. Much of the basis of the Transportation Plan came from Tedder's experience in the Italian campaign, and he had enlisted the same scientific adviser, Solly Zuckerman. His proposals had been put forward in January in a paper entitled 'Delay and disorganization of enemy movement by rail', in which he ventured that if the seventy-six most important rail servicing and repair facilities in north-west Europe were destroyed, the effect would be to 'paralyse movements in the whole region they serve and render almost impossible the subsequent movement by rail of major reserves into France.'

The tactical employment of air power against line-of-communication targets, such as railways, had been an element of the air plan for some while, but what Zuckerman and Tedder now proposed was bringing this onto the strategic stage and letting loose the full weight of Bomber Command and the 8th Air Force, the trials undertaken in early March against major railway centres having proved successful. However, they considered that hitting small tactical targets such as bridges was far too difficult for the heavy bombers, and would have only a limited effect; far better, they argued, to hit a marshalling yard where every bomb would be likely to do damage and 'reduce traffic potential by the destruction of rolling stock and repair facilities.'

The view of the 21st Army was quite similar, and concentrated on the need to win the race to build up Allied strength ashore before major German reinforcements could be brought to bear: '... there is little doubt that unless we can disrupt the enemy's communications, the Germans have a 4 to 1 chance of winning the race. It is not too much to say that this would result in the failure of *Overlord* at a very early stage.' As railways were the main military transportation system, they were the key to the proposed strategy of isolating the invasion area.

The contrary argument put forward by the Enemy Objectives Unit (part of the Economic Warfare Division) on behalf of Spaatz was that the effects of such a transportation plan were overstated; they also disputed the Italian evidence, and in their view a far better target system was that of oil: 'No other target system holds such great promise of hastening German defeat ... the loss of 50 per cent of Axis output would directly and materially reduce German military capability through reducing tactical and strategic mobility and front-line delivery of supplies.' The USSTAF representative was quite forthright:

Our plan is to attack the German petroleum industry, along with the aircraft industry as a secondary objective. This plan has been studied in great detail by our scientific analysts, and one of its great attractions is that it involves deep penetration attacks into Germany, and we would be hitting at a weak link in the enemy war economy. We are quite certain that such attacks would produce constant air battles resulting in the progressive destruction of the enemy front-line fighters, and force him to retain his remaining fighters for defence of his industry. The shortage of fuel that would result from successful attacks would, we estimate, be felt on the battlefield, and so reduce his mobility, and his chances of staging a counter attack against our bridgehead.

There is insufficient space in this study to go into the pros and cons of the two standpoints, but the net result of the conference discussion was that Eisenhower came down in favour of the Transportation Plan, and this was duly adopted as a key element within the overall Air Plan. This was but one of many disagreements amongst the Allied senior commanders, and Montgomery later (with post-war hindsight) recorded his opinion that:

The fact that the Allied air forces were divided into commands held by parallel commanders-in-chief reacted on the speed of military planning because it frequently took long periods and many lengthy meetings in order to finalize, in a co-ordinated form, the plan of the various air forces in support of the land operation.

The Bec d'Ambes oil-storage depot under
attack by Bomber Command in a daylight
raid. Attacks on oil targets had been part of
the Allied air strategy for much of 1944,
especially by the American bombers.

## April 1944

A new directive was issued on 1 April, stating
that:

> The Supreme Allied Commander has decided that
> the time has come for the operations of AEAF to be
> directed more closely to the preparation for *Overlord*

and has agreed to release 9th Air Force from its over-
riding commitment of assisting 8th Air Force *Pointblank* operations. Until further notice 9th Air Force
and 2nd TAF will conduct bombing missions against
the following targets in order of priority as shown:

1. First priority – railway centres as listed in appendix A [target lists such as this were updated and

circulated on a regular basis]. These objectives are to be attacked whenever suitable weather conditions permit. It is important that attacks be made under conditions that will allow definite visual identification of the target, and precise visual bomb runs. A minimum of 10 per cent of the bomb load will be fused for delayed action, not in excess of twelve hours.

2. Second priority – *Noball* targets [V-weapon sites] in the priority listed by the Air Ministry, issued or amended weekly. A minimum of 20 per cent of the bomb load will be fused for delayed action.
3. Third priority – industrial targets selected from the latest Jockey signal.
4. Fourth priority – GAF, occupied airfields selected from the latest Jockey signal.

With the tactical and strategic bombers being tasked against railway centres, the Allies began a progressive degradation of the French railway network; it must be remembered, however, that the effort had to be widespread in order to maintain the deception policy of not focusing solely on targets within the proposed invasion area. In addition to the rail attacks and the continuing *Pointblank* campaign, there was a diversion of effort to other target categories. The *Noball* (or *Crossbow*) sites for the German V-weapon programme occupied an increasing amount of bomber effort, and despite the difficulties of attacking the launch sites – that were sometimes hard to find, and for which a comprehensive series of dummy sites had been provided – the overall effect of the bomber campaign was to delay the operational debut of this potentially decisive weapon until it was too late for it to have any real military impact.

Amidst all the offensive operations, the importance of strategic and tactical reconnaissance was recognized, and mission rates were intensified during the Preparatory Phase to cover the following:

1. Continual visual and photo recce of enemy dispositions and movements, particularly those that might affect the situation in the assault area.
2. Detailed recce of enemy coastal defences, to detect new constructions and/or strengthening of old installations.
3. Continuous observation of ports.
4. Comprehensive photographic survey of prospective airfield sites, to provide a basis for estimating requirements for constructional materials and for planning the future build-up of air forces on the Continent.

*Bomb craters dot a V-weapon site. The diversion of bomber effort against these* Crossbow *targets was considered inappropriate by many of the air planners.*

*This low, oblique shot of 8 April 1944 shows both radar installations very clearly at Dieppe/Ste Marguerite (target XII/62). The two radar arrays are arrowed just to the left of the lighthouse. As with most of these radar sites, there is a light anti-aircraft battery adjacent to the site, limiting the line of approach for attacking aircraft.*

*BELOW: Another classic low-level reconnaissance photo; target XII/63 was the navigation beam station at St Valéry-en-Caux/St Leger. Note also the beach defences in the foreground.*

*BELOW RIGHT: Calais/Sangatte (target XII/65) comprised a Giant Wurzburg plus a range-finder in an armoured cupola. The whole area, which included gun batteries, was defended by light and heavy anti-aircraft guns as well as extensive minefields and wire obstacles. This photo was taken on 25 April, looking south over the radar site.*

The 10th PR Group of the US 9th Air Force specialized in getting good beach photography – often flying at 15ft (4m) or so to get the correct angles! For its outstanding work during this period the 10th received a Distinguished Unit Citation.

Day by day the reconnaissance aircraft returned with detailed information about the increasing scale of German defences along the invasion coast. Since Rommel had taken over as commander of Army Group B in December 1943, he had instituted a programme of defence improvements, trying to create a hard crust along the coast upon which the invaders would expend themselves; he was a firm exponent of the strategy of defeating the enemy on the beaches – though fortunately for the Allies he was to a large extent over-ruled by Adolf Hitler and C-in-C West, Field Marshal von Runstedt.

Army Group B comprised 7th Army (Normandy and Brittany), 15th Army (Pas de Calais) and 88 Corps (Holland); the other major element was Panzer Group West (General von Schweppenburg), an independent organization reluctant to contribute its tanks to forward defence. Nevertheless, the presence of Rommel did inspire his troops with new confidence, and he managed to make some progress with his system of beach hazards, strongpoints, minefields, coastal artillery, flooding of the hinterland, constructing concrete emplacements for coastal batteries, and so on. He was also aware of the danger from airborne forces, and instructed that all suitable fields should be obstructed, the commonest method being by wooden poles, a technique dubbed 'Rommel's asparagus' by the Allies.

The German navy was by no means a spent force; although the Allies had the upper hand, constant pressure was essential to guarantee that German naval forces would not be able to interfere with the invasion during its vulnerable assault and build-up phases. Threats came primarily from U-boats and E-boats (fast-attack patrol boats), and to a lesser extent from other surface combatants, destroyers, as there were few German capital ships still in action. In addition, all coastal shipping was attacked to prevent movement of military and economic traffic. Enemy naval forces were targeted by all elements of Allied air power, but as the focus of Coastal Command's contribution to *Overlord* was centred on countering the U-boats, in April a directive was issued to the four main operational groups, setting out their tasks:

*No. 15 Group:*
1. Cover Atlantic shipping.
2. Cover entrances to the North Channel against the passage of U-boats.
3. Attack U-boat cover in North Transit area.

*No. 16 Group:*
1. Seek and destroy U-boats attempting to enter the English Channel from the east.
2. Provide air cover and close escort to the invasion convoy during passage from The Nore and Beachy Head.

*No. 18 Group:*
1. Provide anti U-boat cover in the North Transit Area.
2. Provide aircraft for Fleet reconnaissance duties.

*No. 19 Group:*
1. Provide air cover in the SW Approaches to protect the flank of the invasion convoy.
2. Provide air cover/close escort to the invasion convoy in the SW Approaches.
3. Seek and destroy U-boats attempting to attack the invasion convoy.

In addition to these tasks, aircraft of No. 16 and No. 19 Group would be called on to undertake anti-shipping strikes, including night operations by Albacores and Swordfish using GCI, or with the support of flare-dropping Wellingtons. There was also a standing task for Beaufighter units to carry out dawn and dusk sweeps to 'destroy enemy light surface craft when leaving and entering harbour'.

The pre-invasion bombing strategy was well under way by spring 1944, and in an April 1944 review paper the role of the heavy bombers was again discussed:

A major conclusion emerging from the air operations that have so far been undertaken in preparation for operation *Overlord*, is that outstanding bombing concentrations can now be achieved by

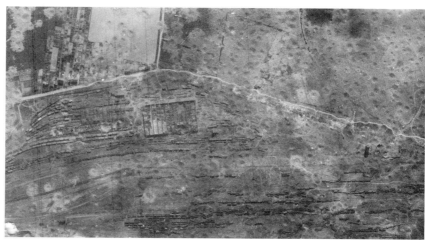

*'Before' and 'after' photographs of a railway centre, but despite such levels of destruction the Germans made rapid repairs to essential through lines and air planners had to re-target key points, eventually focusing on targets that were harder to repair, such as bridges.*

RAF Bomber Command upon any given objective of limited size within Oboe range, and in certain circumstances outside Oboe range. The density of bomb strikes per acre achieved upon, for example, Juvisy and Aulnoye railway centres or Mailly le Camp has much exceeded expectations. The area attacked has been reduced to a wilderness of bomb craters that in many cases are lip to lip, or actually overlapping. It is appreciated that this new-found ability to saturate with bomb strikes a given area of approximately 500 to 1,000yd [800 to 1,600m] square constitutes a weapon of war of enormous power.

Despite this initial triumphalist tone, the paper urged some caution with regard to 'limitations inherent in its use, and the tactical situations that must be anticipated immediately before and immediately after D-Day.' As we shall see later, this warning was not always adhered to. The paper went on to stress that:

It was generally accepted that the whole of the available Allied air power must, if necessary, be applied to direct support of the assault in the period immediately preceding and following D-Day. It is clearly preferable to arrange in advance to embrace, within a well prepared plan, all air resources that might afford direct support of the Army, rather than to await the arrival of an emergency in which (as at Salerno) direct tactical support has to be improvised at the last moment.

Three types of target were envisaged as being suitable for night attack by RAF Bomber Command, the first two in the period preceding the landings and the third following the landings:

1. Night attack by heavy bombers on airfields in lieu of proposed attacks by medium day bombers.
2. Night attacks on dumps by larger forces of heavy aircraft than have hitherto been used.
3. Close support for ground forces at the front by means of heavy night attacks by RAF Bomber Command.

On 8 April, the draft Joint Fire Plan was issued, in essence the 'fire-power' timetable for the assault, and all but one of its schedules concerned air bombardment, such was the importance of this aspect. Operational control of the strategic bomber forces finally passed to SHAEF on 14 April. The most powerful air armada ever assembled was now, in theory at least, under the operational control of the Supreme Commander.

The following day, 15 April, the definitive version of the overall air plan was issued, to act as a general guide for detailed planning; it stated that the overall object was to 'attain and maintain an air situation that would assure freedom of action for our forces without effective interference by enemy air forces, and to render air support to our land and naval forces in the achievement of this object.' The principal air tasks were stated as:

1. To attain and maintain an air situation whereby the German Air Force is rendered incapable of effective interference with Allied operations.

*28 April, and a visit by the RAF's Enemy Air Circus to the 390th BG.* (US National Archives)

2. To provide continuous air reconnaissance of the enemy's dispositions and movements.
3. To disrupt enemy communications and channels of supply by air attack.
4. To support the landing and subsequent advance of the Allied armies.
5. To deliver offensive strikes against enemy naval forces.
6. To provide airlift for airborne forces.

There was nothing new in this instruction, and many aspects of the associated air offensive were already well in hand as integral parts of the first two phases of the air campaign: Preliminary and Preparatory. What this directive did was to apply and stress the overall air strategy to all elements of the now integrated AEF air arms.

From this point onwards, almost the entire air effort launched from the UK was directed at targets in support of the *Overlord* objective, although the direct relevance of certain strategic bomber operations could be questioned.

## The Transportation Plan Brings Results

Meanwhile, on 17 April the Supreme Commander issued a new directive to the strategic bomber forces of USSTAF and RAF Bomber Command, although the overall mission remained the same, namely 'to provide targets, the attack of which is most likely to be of assistance to *Pointblank* and *Overlord*'. The immediate objective was to be the destruction of German air-combat strength, particularly fighters, the 'primary aim being to secure and maintain air superiority, whilst at the same time continuing attacks on rail targets'. The two-point directive gave the priorities as:

1. To deplete the GAF and particularly German fighter forces, and to destroy and disorganize the forces supporting them.
2. To destroy and disrupt the enemy rail communications, particularly those affecting the enemy movement towards the *Overlord* lodgement area.

*Aerial shot of Task B for 440 Squadron, two anti-aircraft sites (one heavy and one light).* (440 Squadron)

However, Harris was given a 'let-out clause' whereby he could continue his offensive against German cities: '... in view of the tactical difficulties of destroying precise targets by night, RAF Bomber Command will continue to be employed in accordance with their main aim of disorganizing German industry.' This was despite the fact that Bomber Command had demonstrated its ability to hit pinpoint targets. By the end of April, RAF Bomber Command

*Smoke rising from the marshalling yards at Cambrai from a 98 Squadron attack on 1 May.*
(98 Squadron)

BELOW: *Trains were high on the target list for the tactical aircraft; camera-gun film shows strikes on a supply train.*

had attacked 40 per cent of its designated rail targets, whereas USSTAF had only visited one of its forty-five targets; the latter's major effort had gone into oil targets and, for the US VIIIth Bomber Command, raids over Berlin.

A first for the RAF's fighter-bombers came on 24 April when the Typhoons of 438 Squadron were sent to attack bridges in northern France, the aircraft carrying two 1,000lb (2,200kg) bombs apiece – the first operational use of this weapon by single-seat aircraft. The eight aircraft were led by Wing Commander Davidson. Finding that the primary target was weathered out, they went for the secondary, the bridge at St Saveur: hits were claimed, and the squadron diarist recorded '... we are justly proud that we had the opportunity to pave the way in this sphere of operational warfare.' Fighter-bomber employment of such bombs became a standard procedure, and certainly increased the level of tactical firepower, albeit problems of accurate delivery remained whilst squadrons had little chance to undertake intensive training.

All previous restrictions on rail targets were removed on 5 May, with the strategic bombers being given clearance to bomb railyards in densely populated areas, including Paris. The decision was not taken lightly, but results up to this date had shown that the bombers were able to hit the targets with little or no collateral damage; also, for the overall strategy to be successful, all relevant areas of the target system simply had to be attacked. With the same overall concept in mind, from 21 May the tactical aircraft of 2nd TAF, US 8th and 9th Air Forces were given freedom to attack moving trains; up to this point such targets had been prohibited on the grounds that the train might be a civilian movement. It was now assessed that sufficient damage had been caused such that only military trains were active, and these were definitely regarded as fair game. Thus started an intense period of 'train busting', usually referred to as 'Chatanoogas' by the Americans, often in conjunction with a fighter sweep.

The American fighter-bombers proved particularly adept at this type of work, some units chalking up impressive scores; the 4th Fighter Group alone claimed twenty-eight locomotives on day one (21 May) of this offensive (along with seven barges and thirteen trucks). The total US 8th Air Force effort for the day was 552 sorties, during which 225 locomotives were attacked, and ninety-one claimed as destroyed – along with attacks on stations, bridges, level crossings, signal boxes, bridges, and other forms of transport. The fighters also put in a claim for 102 aircraft destroyed on the ground.

The RAF squadrons were also active this day: for example, Spitfires of 222 Squadron were airborne on *Ramrod* 905:

…train busting in the Somme-Seine area. The squadron, led by Squadron Leader Innes, proceeded to Freiston with 30-gallon [136ltr] slipper tanks to refuel and to be briefed. Take-off was at 1030 hours. The squadron crossed in at Ault at 10,000 feet [3,050m], and then split up into three sections. Cloud was 10/10ths, with base at 2,500 feet [760m]. Blue Section proceeded to the Amiens area, Red Section went to Gourney, and Yellow Section to the Forges area: Blue Section destroyed one loco and two trains damaged, two lorries destroyed and troops strafed. Red Section encountered flak, but located no targets. Yellow Section fired at a signal box and some goods wagons. Yellow Section had two aircraft damaged by flak. Warrant Officer Lenehan (MK833) lost most of his rudder. Pilot Officer Reid (MK830) had to make a belly landing as his wheels would not come down.

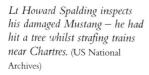

*Lt Howard Spalding inspects his damaged Mustang – he had hit a tree whilst strafing trains near Chartres.* (US National Archives)

ABOVE: *An understandably pensive-looking Flt Sgt Rush of 245 Squadron posing with his flak-damaged Typhoon. Effective ground attack was an essential element of Allied air power, but it was also the most hazardous of roles and losses were high.*

*Allied officers inspect the damage caused to the rail facilities at La Chappelle; the destruction included no fewer than eighty wrecked locomotives.*

The 4th Fighter Group seemed to have a flair for finding good targets and then making the most of them. During a patrol on 22 May, the CO, Lieutenant Colonel Don Blakeslee, spotted a large German convoy and promptly raced his formation back to base (Debden) to get bombed up with 500lb (225kg) bombs. This was achieved in record time, but on returning to the target area they found almost total undercast; but their luck held, and through the one reasonable hole in the cloud they identified their target: 'We didn't wipe it out completely, but we sure did shake hell out of 'em!' (Blakeslee).

The destruction of rail facilities and rolling stock, especially locomotives (and here we must also mention the part played in this campaign by the Resistance movements' sabotage efforts) soon had a crippling effect. The strain placed on the locomotive repair organization through the loss of facilities, and the destruction of the locomotives themselves, meant that the authorities were struggling to find enough motive power, the result being a virtual termination of all non-military rail movements. This had a double significance, in that it meant a huge reduction in economic traffic moving raw materials and supplies. Destruction of the actual rail lines themselves was of somewhat more limited effect because a through-line could usually be repaired in a matter of hours or days, and it would require far too much air effort to keep a line cut. However, any damage that required the attention of the construction or repair organization meant that personnel and resources could not be employed on other work – such as the Atlantic Wall.

Furthermore, the crippling of the rail network forced the Germans to make greater use of road transport, with an associated increase in the consumption of precious fuel oil, an aspect of the oil campaign interwoven with the Transportation Plan (a combination that would prove the successful one in 1945).

In the three-month period leading up to D-Day, some 33 per cent of the total strategic bomber effort had been expended against transportation targets (63,609 tons out of a total 182,729 tons); of the remainder, the majority was against the German aircraft industry, mainly by the US 8th Air Force, but with a fair degree of effort still going against German cities, especially Berlin, to keep up the pressure on the Nazi regime.

The final item with respect to shutting down the German ability to move reinforcements into the assault area by rail was to attempt a total, albeit temporary, closure of key lines. We have mentioned above how difficult this would be by simply cutting the line; however, to take out a more substantial element of the line, such as a bridge, would have longer-term implications. This, then, was to be the final element of the anti-rail campaign, an attempt to isolate the assault area by cutting a number of rail bridges. The bridge attacks also included road bridges as from mid-May; the Transportation Plan had started to pay more attention to the road transport situation as the Germans started to make greater use of this aspect. The strategic bombers would, in due course, be called upon to seal important road junctions – though this often meant the destruction of small towns in which such junctions were located.

Although some bridge-busting had already taken place, a concerted 'anti-bridge' campaign

*P-47 Thunderbolt pilots of the 9th Air Force became experts at destroying bridges.*

was delayed until a late phase as it was considered that to start it too early would be to give too many clues to the enemy; however, a number of trial attacks were carried out to determine the best method of destroying such targets. It was soon realized that bridges were not profitable targets for the medium or heavy bombers, their capabilities lying in other, equally important fields; instead, it was an ideal target for the increasing number of tactical fighter-bombers. Early trials suggested that it would take approximately 100 aircraft sorties to guarantee the destruction of a typical bridge, although this was later revised to a lower figure in the light of experience.

The campaign opened on 24 May, and by D-Day all twenty-four major bridges over the Seine between Paris and Rouen, plus a further twelve significant bridges, had been collapsed. The effort required had been 5,209 sorties (5,370 tons of bombs) by AEAF, with a further 445 sorties by 8th Air Force fighter-bombers. The American 9th Air Force low-level fighter-bombers proved particularly good at this work, and soon specialized on it to such an extent that they could nearly always guarantee to destroy bridges relatively cheaply in tonnage of bombs – though because of the considerable anti-aircraft protection often afforded to important bridges, at considerable cost in men and aircraft. Of all the Allied aircraft it was the rugged P-47 that was without doubt the exponent of this art.

The bridge-busting campaign also saw the trial of a special weapon, the Azon glider bomb. On 31 May, four modified B-24s of 753rd Bomb Squadron/458th Bomb Group attempted to attack the bridges at Beaumont-sur-Oise, Melun and Meulan. The aircraft carried three weapons, each being a 1,000lb bomb with radio-controlled tailfins, the bombardier steering the weapon by monitoring a smoke canister fitted to the bomb. But the formation failed to hit the targets, and similar experimental attacks were equally unsuccessful,

leading to the abandonment of what was, in reality, a promising idea.

It had been assessed that of the nine German divisions that might be brought to bear on the assault area, six would need to move into the area by rail; these divisions would comprise the immediate counter-attack force, and their ability to arrive in time as cohesive fighting units could be critical to the German ability to prevent the Allies gaining a firm foothold – to the Allies they simply had to be stopped, or the 'build-up race' would be lost. The Allied aim would be to make these units detrain 100–150 miles (160–240km) from the beach-head, and then to ensure that the rest of their journey was equally fraught.

## Coastal Defence Batteries

One of the major fears of the planners was the destruction that could be wrought by the coastal defence and field artillery batteries located along the stretch of coast selected for the landings. The 155mm guns in some of the sites had a range of 26,000yd (24,000m), and with the assault force only able to move at approximately 12,000yd (11,000m) an hour, this would mean a period of exposure of two and a half hours. It was considered essential that these sites be destroyed or at least damaged to such an extent as to limit their effectiveness. Early in 1943 discussions and trials took place to consider the best way to attack the coastal batteries, with options ranging from mass bombing to airborne assault. Detonation trials of heavy bombs on the ground close to concrete emplacements proved that only a direct hit would knock out the guns, and that the percentage of such hits in even a mass bombing raid would be small. With this type of attack it was considered that the best result would be the effect on crews that might make them incapable of operating the guns. In May trials were carried out with rocket projectiles (RPs) against open emplacements, and these showed promise, as did the accuracy being achieved by Typhoons in the

ABOVE: *10 May 1944, and the marshalling yards at Charleroi are under daylight attack by two boxes of Mitchells – 98 Squadron and 180 Squadron.* (98 Squadron)

*Bridge-busting was a difficult but essential task; this 8 June shot shows damage to bridges over the Seine.*

ABOVE: *On the eve of the invasion, Bomber Command despatched over 1,000 bombers against coastal batteries. These aircraft dropped over 5,000 tons of bombs, the highest total in a single night so far.*

RIGHT: *On 13 April twenty aircraft attacked the coastal battery at Nieuport, dropping eighty 1,000lb (450kg) bombs; this post-attack photo shows the fall of bombs, with the major concentration indicated by the hatched area.*

BELOW: *Rocket-projectiles (RPs) were a very effective weapon, and the RAF's Typhoons specialized in their delivery; PR-L was a 609 Squadron aircraft.*

DIRECTION OF ATTA

dive-bombing role against various types of target. It was considered that the most effective tactic was a three-pronged attack:

1. Heavy blitz bombing and low-flying attack by fighters to soften the defences and cause some damage.
2. Attack by RP aircraft, followed swiftly by
3. Airborne forces to destroy guns not already put out of action.

This was an incredible allocation of resources, and reflected the perceived threat that these heavy coastal batteries posed.

RIGHT: *Coastal guns near Le Havre under attack on 19 May.* (98 Squadron)

BELOW: *Coastal guns that never made it to their installations on the Atlantic Wall, but were held up in the destruction of rail facilities at Aulnoye.*

By spring 1944 all but one of the major sites in the assault area were still under construction and thus vulnerable to air attack, although the programme to provide concrete emplacements was well under way. There was much heated debate as to the employment of bombers against these sites, and so a trial raid was mounted by Marauders of the 9th Air Force against Le Grand Clos, Le Havre on 10 April. The attack went according to plan, but for a variety of reasons there was insufficient feedback as to the result. The bomber chiefs were reluctant to divert effort to what they still considered to be unprofitable targets, an opinion that was not changed following a further inconclusive trial on 13 May. One analysis claimed that it would take 420 tons of bombs to ensure damage to a single gun, and 2,500 bombs to secure one strike within 5yd (4.5m) of the aiming point – and that such bomb loads could be more profitably expended elsewhere, the bomber chiefs returning to their favourite argument of bombing the gun before it reached the site (that is, in the factory or in the rail siding en route). Nevertheless, attacks against coastal batteries were considered

to be essential and so they remained on the target list, with the now standard proviso that for every target attacked within the assault area two must be attacked outside of it.

By D-Day minus 10, Bomber Command had dropped 3,700 tons and AEAF 5,000 tons of bombs on such installations, the assessment being that eighteen of the fifty-one major guns within the assault area had been damaged. A later report by the Bombing Analysis Unit stated that 'bombing both delayed further construction and was very successful in reducing the efficiency of the batteries, not only because of the damage it caused but also because of the threat of further attacks'. The period 5–6 June saw a major effort against the batteries within the assault area, and we will return to look at this later.

## Blinding the Enemy

Amongst the other target systems chosen for intensive attack was the radar network. By 1944 the Germans had established a comprehensive and effective radar network along the coast of occupied Europe, a radar network that could observe all air and sea movements and thus must

*Softening up the Atlantic Wall: bombers attack gun positions at Longues, near Caen on 25 May.*

*Sompuis/Vouberbeau was an important target as it was also a day fighter control centre.*

be blinded by the Allies in order to achieve an element of surprise on D-Day. One Allied estimate put the total at sixty-six main radar stations between Dunkirk and Brest, plus a number of secondary installations. As most of the radar stations were also connected with the German fighter organization, this was an integral part of the air superiority campaign.

There are two ways to negate a radar: a 'soft kill' using electronic means to prevent accurate information being gained; and a 'hard kill' to physically destroy the site. The former operation was in the hands of the Radio Counter Measures (RCM) units of RAF Bomber Command's No. 100 Group, and comprised ground and airborne jamming equipment. Use of this equipment as part of offensive air operations was standard by spring 1944, helping to keep bomber losses, especially amongst the Command's night raiders, as low as possible. However, it was realized that certain types of equipment could be used for other deception

purposes, and specialist squadrons began to train for D-Day related missions. Anti-radar operations were scheduled to commence four weeks before D-Day; on 15 May a RCM Advisory Staff joined SHAEF under the direction of Air Vice-Marshal V. Tait, Director General of Signals, tasked with allocating targets and monitoring progress of the campaign.

In the meantime the offensive aircraft went out to attack the radar and communications sites, and instructions to the fighter-bomber units were quite clear: 'Destroy all enemy radar stations between Ostend and the Channel islands.' However, they were difficult targets, heavily defended and hard to kill.

The campaign officially opened on 10 May, with the first series of attacks against the long-range reporting stations, the principle being that these sites would be the hardest to repair and therefore could be knocked out first. A week later it was the turn of the night-fighter control and the coastal defence battery control radars. Attacks had in fact been made before this, the Typhoons of 198 Squadron hitting a Wassermann radar near Ostend as early as 16 March, four aircraft diving from 8,000ft (2,500m) and using 60lb (27kg) RPs, the others making low-level strafing runs to deal with flak installations.

A typical attack is related by Desmond Scott in his book *Typhoon Pilot*, the account coming from a German soldier who watched the attack on Cap de la Hague on 24 May:

> The Typhoons came in from the valley, flying very low. The second aircraft received a direct hit from 37mm flak, which practically shot off the tail. The pilot, however, managed to keep some sort of control and carried on, straight at the target. He dived below the level of the radar structure, fired his rockets into it and tried at the last moment to clear it. The third aircraft, in trying to avoid the damaged Typhoon, touched the latter's fuselage and both aircraft crashed into the installation. This radar site was never again serviceable.

**ABOVE LEFT:** Rhubarb *target XII/64, the coastwatcher radar at Bayeux/Le Mesnil as photographed in May 1944; the German coastal radar and reporting network was one of the main targets for the fighter-bombers (and RP Typhoons) in the weeks immediately prior to the invasion.*

**ABOVE:** *A very low-level recce pass of target XII/64!*

**RIGHT:** *Area target map for the coastwatcher installation at Bayeux/Le Mesnil.*

**BELOW:** *Plan and two photographs showing the extensive radar installation at St Valery-en-Caux/St Martin-aux-Buneaux. The vertical photograph was taken on 5 January, and the plan, constructed from photos such as this, provided pilots with all the information needed to plan an attack. Radars were not easy targets to destroy, and it was found that cannon fire and RPs were the most effective options.*

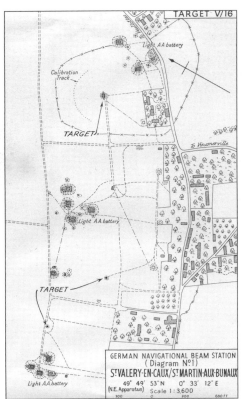

(The two aircraft were from No. 198 Squadron: MN410, Flying Officer Freeman and JR527, Flight Sergeant Vallely.)

The number of attacks was increased from 30 May, with forty-two major sites being scheduled for attack right up until D-Day. Not all damage to the enemy communications network was intentional, however; on 21 May, Spitfire BL646 of 234 Squadron had a 'small problem':'Lieutenant Bernard was successful in being able to tear away a good few feet of telephone communications in Belgium after having made his attack on a train, and retained the wire for use in this country by bringing it back wrapped around his kite' (234 Sqn ORB).

This was but one of many hazards faced by aircraft operating at ultra low level; this Spitfire came back, but many other Allied aircraft were not so lucky.

**Destruction of Airfields**

The strategic bomber forces had been conducting an anti-air campaign for some time, in the early part of 1944 being aided by tactical elements as the pressure was increased on German units in north-west Europe. During the March conference to discuss the combined Air Plan the AEAF Plans' representative stated:

> Until airfields are available on the Continent, we decided that the intention was to deny the enemy the use of airfields within 100 miles [160km] of the beach-head, and if possible 130 miles [210km]. This would make the distance from bases to beach-head the same for both sides. On past experience we believe that the answer is to divide the attacks into two phases. First, attacks against permanent airfield installations and depots a few weeks before D-Day; then, immediately before D-Day,

*Airfield attacks were a core part of the air campaign in the days either side of D-Day; according to a squadron diary, 'this morning the Squadron went to the airfield at Cormeilles-en-Vexin, NW of Paris. Weather was excellent and both boxes had good bombing runs from 8,500ft [2,600m] and 9,500ft [2,900m] respectively. Bombs fell on the target area from both boxes. No enemy opposition was encountered.'* (98 Squadron)

attacks to make the runways of operational airfields unserviceable.

With effect from 11 May, this campaign was intensified, emphasis being placed on airfields within 150 miles (240km) of the invasion beaches, the aim being the destruction of aircraft maintenance and repair facilities. When this had been achieved, attacks were mounted on airfield facilities such as hangars and operating surfaces.

Area One comprised a list of forty fighter airfields within the prescribed zone, and Area Two a list of fifty-nine bomber airfields outside of this zone. However, of the designated targets, only thirty-four had been attacked pre-D-Day, and the overall plan was far from achieved; with higher priority being given to other target systems, and an intelligence estimate of a reduced air threat, this was not considered critical.

In the period to 5 June, the total effort expended on this target system comprised:

*Airfield being strafed by P-51s.*
(US National Archives)

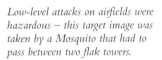

*Low-level attacks on airfields were hazardous – this target image was taken by a Mosquito that had to pass between two flak towers.*

US 9th Air Force    56 attacks/2,550 sorties dropping 3,197 tons

2nd TAF    12 attacks/312 sorties dropping 487 tons

RAF Bomber Command    6 attacks/119 sorties dropping 395 tons

US 8th Air Force    17 attacks/934 sorties dropping 2,638 tons

## Control of the Sea Lanes

As mentioned above, the four operational groups of RAF Coastal Command had been given directives relating to *Overlord* tasks, the primary duties involving air cover of the Atlantic convoys and the intensification of the anti-submarine war. During May the Germans attempted to move U-boats from Norway to the Bay of Biscay, so Coastal Command sent reinforcements to air bases in Scotland to permit a round-the-clock offensive. Many

*Beaufighters of the North Coates Strike Wing raking a German minesweeper with cannon fire.*

BELOW: *Coastal Command Beaufighters attacking a convoy.*

submarines tried to fight it out with their attackers, and aircraft losses certainly rose; but the determination of crews to 'get their boat' led to fierce battles – and many U-boat losses. Of seventy-five submarines spotted in northern waters, fifty-one were attacked, sixteen claimed as sunk, and a further twelve damaged.

On 24 May, a Catalina of 210 Squadron:

…sighted a fully surfaced U-boat off the port bow at a range of 5 miles [8km]. On the run–in for an attack, heavy but inaccurate flak was encountered, the aircraft suffering no damage. The attack was carried out from the starboard side abaft the beam, and six depth charges were dropped. The depth charges fell short, but the sixth was so close that the impact splash fell across the boat to the port side. It was seen to spin around on its stern for almost 360 degrees and then lie stopped on the surface. The U-boat then sank stern first until only the top of the conning tower was awash; then it pivoted at the conning tower, the stern sinking and the bows rising out of the water at a very acute angle. The whole U-boat disappeared for approximately one minute and then surfaced as though all tanks had been blown. It then sank slowly stern first.

(This was later confirmed as U-476, a Type VIIC.) There was also no let-up in the campaign against surface ships, military and merchant, Beaufighters and Mosquitoes being primarily charged with this role.

## Special Duties Operations

One final area of air operations that requires mention in association with the *Overlord* air campaign is that of 'special duties', in particular the support of Resistance movements in occupied Europe. During the first half of 1944 some 3–4,000 containers of equipment had been delivered in each moon period to France, with just over 50 per cent of all missions being considered a success. In May the total was more than 6,000 to France and 364 to Belgium, with the majority reaching the intended recipients. Most of this work was carried out by the RAF's special duties' squadrons, but since February there had been a small-scale American involvement with this task. The RAF narrative summarizes the results of this work:

So great a weight of supplies had been delivered to western Europe during the first months of 1944 that on the eve of the invasion of France, Resistance movements everywhere found themselves sufficiently well equipped to fulfil, even beyond SOE [Special Operations Executive] expectations, the role which they had been allotted. The D-Day plans were implemented on the receipt of the BBC messages, railways and roads were attacked, and the enemy found his lines of communication continually cut, while isolated German units were harassed by guerrilla bands.

## Air Reconnaissance

The reconnaissance units were particularly heavily tasked, and as D-Day approached the number of reconnaissance requests increased as army commanders sought low, oblique photography to show terrain configuration, the latest beach obstacles and defences, landing craft approach routes, and the routes inland from the beaches. There was particular concern as to the degree of flooding the Germans had achieved, and what impact this would have on movement away from the vulnerable beaches. Tens of thousands of prints were made and distributed (although all too few survive), and interpreters examined every print to glean as much information as possible for the planners and land commanders – a new pillbox here, a flooded field there. Mustangs, Spitfires, Mosquitoes and F-5 Lightnings (photo recce versions of the P-38, minus the nose guns) flew hundreds of sorties to ensure that the German defences held no secrets.

## The Position at the End of May

Although in April SHAEF had been given control of virtually all air assets, it is interesting to look at the percentage of total air effort that had been applied during the first half of May in support of *Overlord*:

| | |
|---|---|
| US 9th Air Force | 91.6% |
| 2nd TAF | 86.8% |
| RAF Bomber Command | 84.0% |
| US 8th Air Force | 52.7% |

It would appear that the 8th Air Force was not totally committed to the *Overlord* campaign – but this was only true of the VIIIth Bomber Command, indicating perhaps the reluctance of its commander to take assets away from his strategic campaign; however, the figures are also misleading in that much of the bombing effort was against targets in Germany that were related to the anti-air and transportation elements of the air offensive, but did not show as such in this AEAF summary.

As May progressed the number of commanders' conferences increased, some meetings being of a routine nature to discuss the progress of pre-invasion operations, primarily air operations, others being major briefings, such as that of 15 May to King George and Winston Churchill. Changes were still being made to the air plans on an almost daily basis, but overall the air campaign was assessed as being on schedule, and there was little cause for concern. The major cause of worry amongst the planners was that the enemy would discern which of the possible landing areas the Allies were aiming for – deception and trickery remained high on the

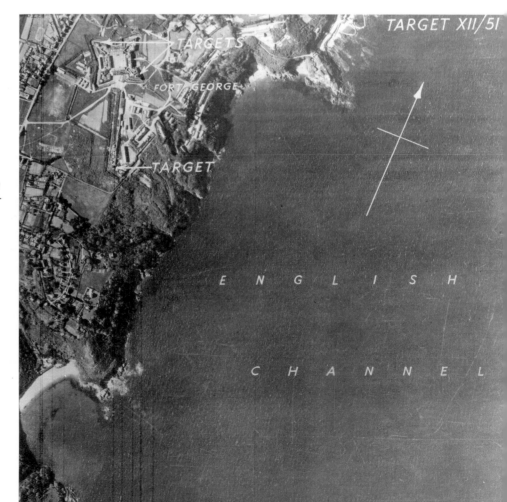

*Thousands of photographs, vertical and oblique, were taken in the months leading up to D-Day; requests for up-to-date imagery increased as D-Day approached.*

TARGET XII/51

TARGETS

FORT GEORGE

TARGET

E N G L I S H

C H A N N E L

list – and that the weather might deteriorate and affect air operations.

During May, the 8th Air Force gained a large increase in strength as an additional seven heavy bomber groups and one fighter group became operational, thus giving a total average (available) daily strength of 1,304 bombers and 856 fighters. The 66th Fighter Wing flew the most sorties (5,671), almost 1,000 more than the other two fighter wings, for the loss of fifty-eight aircraft. Bomber statistics were equally impressive: 36,075 sorties, dropping 36,344 tons of bombs and with the fighters alone claiming 622 destroyed, 31 probable and 252 damaged (622-31-252) against enemy aircraft for the loss of 171 of their own number, with additional bomber claims of 377-115-170; bomber losses were 361. If all the claims were valid, then the 8th Air Force alone had accounted for 999 enemy aircraft destroyed in one month!

To the command statistics officers, however, the most important aspect of May was

> ... the striking upward trend in intrinsic improvement of bombing accuracy. Excluding attacks on targets of opportunity, 38.8 per cent of the bombs dropped on visual bombing missions fell within 1,000ft [300m] of the pre-assigned aiming points. The average bombing altitude was 20,800ft [6,350m]. In prior months the percentage was 27.3 per cent.

The results certainly were impressive – but accurate bombing would be essential during the assault phase to prevent hitting the landing craft just offshore. Furthermore, the improvements in accuracy only applied to visual bombing – but would the weather be good enough?

According to the 15–20 May weekly situation report (Sitrep) of the German army commanders in Normandy:

> The enemy air forces attacked coastal defences with strong formations, and also transport targets and *Luftwaffe* installations, particularly in the area of northern France behind the line Calais-Dieppe, and in the area of Greater Paris. Considerable damage was caused to three transport installations and to airfields. Attacks continue to have little effect against coastal defences, and these raids cannot be considered yet as a systematic preparation for a large-scale attack.

It would appear from this that the Allied deception was working, and that the Germans were unaware of the imminence and location of the invasion. One of ADGB's major tasks was the prevention of German air reconnaissance, and it is true that the enemy were kept short of this vital intelligence, although a few successful photo missions were flown. The Sitrep for 24 May reports a 'photographic reconnaissance showed that there are sufficient landing craft in Poole, Weymouth and Portland to transport two and one-third landing divisions.' Much of the German defensive effort was being expended on construction of strongpoints and extensive minefields. On the latter, the air campaign was having an adverse effect, the 21–27 May Sitrep stating:

> Minelaying is proceeding according to plan on the Dutch coast, but has been made more difficult between Boulogne and Cherbourg owing to losses of torpedo boats, motor boats and barges. The naval depot at Dieppe has been destroyed. Operations by our U-boats off the northern coast of Brittany were unsuccessful because of prompt spotting by the enemy air forces.

*It had originally been intended that the invasion of southern France would take place at the same time, or even slightly earlier, than that in the north. However, in the event the Normandy assault went in first – but it was not long before Operation* Anvil, *the landings in the south, took place. Here, Spitfires sit on an advanced base in southern France.*

On the morning of 15 May 1944, the Force Commanders gathered in a lecture room at St Paul's School for a briefing to the king, Prime Minister Churchill and a number of other dignitaries. Eisenhower opened the proceedings:

> Here we are on the eve of a great battle, to deliver to you the various plans made by the different Force Commanders. I would emphasize but one thing, that I consider it to be the duty of anyone who sees a flaw in the plan not to hesitate to say so.

Montgomery then spoke for ten minutes, followed by Admiral Ramsay for a similar period, and then it was the turn of Leigh-Mallory – who had been given forty minutes for his part of the brief, a reflection of the importance of the air campaign. A record of notes taken at the meeting states that he spoke

> …confidently, and made it clear that he was absolutely convinced that he had the measure of the Luftwaffe, and that if they tried conclusions with us it could only end one way – with their destruction. His exposition of his plans left his hearers in no doubt not only of his intention, but also of his ability and determination to fulfil them.

During May the Allied air forces reached a pre-invasion peak of strength as the 9th Air Force received its final bomber unit, the 410th BG, and four additional fighter groups (36th, 373rd, 367th and 406th). This meant that the command had 7,800 aircraft in its eleven bomber, eighteen

*Throughout late 1943 and early 1944 the USAAF strength continued to increase as new units arrived in England. Of the other fighter types the P-51 and P-47 appeared in large numbers, and whilst new pilots lacked experience, they had plenty of enthusiasm.*
(US National Archives)

*The A-20 equipped a number of light bomber groups within 9th Air Force.*

fighter, fourteen troop carrier and two reconnaissance groups.

## June 1944

The German Sitrep for the week ending 3 June shows that at last the intensity of air attack had convinced them of an imminent attack:

> The continuation and systematic increase of enemy air attacks, and more intensive minelaying in our

harbours with improved mining equipment, indicate an advance in the enemy's readiness for invasion. Constructional work on the defence front is being impeded by a further deterioration in the transport situation and of fuel supplies (shortage of coal). Constant enemy air attacks obviously concentrated on bridges over the Seine, Oise, and to a certain extent over the Aisne, also coastal defences in the Dunkirk–Dieppe sector and on the northern and eastern sides of the Cotentin. Attempts to

*Servicing a P-38 Lightning of the 38th FS at Nuthampstead; the role of the groundcrew in keeping the maximum number of aircraft serviceable was critical to the maintenance of the air effort.*

cripple rail transport continue, with raids on marshalling yards and on locomotives. Whereas attacks on bridges have led to destruction or serious damage to all crossings over the Seine between Paris and Rouen, damage inflicted on coastal defences is comparatively small.

The invasion was now only days away, and at airfields throughout England the groundstaffs worked to keep the maximum number of aircraft serviceable. As with any air operation, it must be remembered that every aircraft that flew over enemy territory was supported by dozens of ground personnel in England. Whilst these men and women did not face the same dangers as the aircrew, although there were casualties caused by premature explosions of weapons, they certainly worked long hours in often inhospitable conditions and deserve more recognition than invariably they are granted.

# 3 June 1944

For the Typhoon pilots of 609 Squadron, 1 June proved to be a hectic day, as evidenced by this extract from the squadron's *Operations Record Book* (ORB):

> June, season of midsummer madness, starts with another red-letter day for the squadron with no less than 5 shows and 5 FW190s destroyed – the latter

through the medium of one sortie, F/Lt Wells and F/O Davies. The day's action starts at 0545 when 8 Typhoons take off on one of 'Ingles's Tours of the Dutch Islands'. 4 Typhoon fighters – the C.O., P/O de Moulin, F/O Smith and F/O Payne – reach land midway between Walcheren and Schouwen islands, where they find 2 coasters of 600 and 200 tons. All four attack the larger one, and all see strikes. It is left

*Typhoon* Tally Ho *complete with invasion stripes and an array of 'kill' marks – note the air-to-air victories (five) and an impressive line of symbols denoting destroyed locomotives.*

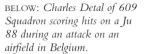

BELOW: *Charles Detal of 609 Squadron scoring hits on a Ju 88 during an attack on an airfield in Belgium.*

smoking. Proceeding SW the C.O. and P/O de Moulin follow with an attack on a stationary blunt-nosed vessel of 500 tons, while the other two go for a tender close by. The larger vessel turns out to be a Flak ship, and all its guns concentrate on S/L Ingle, forming such an intense cone of fire that evasive action proves useless, and he is struck by cannon shells, one piercing his spinner, another exploding in the port wheel bay, firing the priming fuel tank and exploding the spare starter cartridges. These in turn ignite the electrical wiring system and melt the port main tank breather pipe, which burns continuously till landing, the wing skin progressively blistering and buckling. Pulling up to 2,000ft [610m] and warning Hornchurch to stand by, the C.O. heads out to sea, more than half expecting his fuel tanks to blow up. Fortunately they don't, and he is escorted home by his loyal comrades.

Meanwhile the 2 fighters and 2 bombers – Kapt Haabjoern, F/Sgt Leslie, F/O Lallemand and F/O Geerts – have made landfall at Blakenberghe, and find a 200-ton trawler between Knocke and Niuwe Sluis. First Haabjoern attacks with cannon, seeing strikes all over and the vessel enveloped in smoke. Leslie's bombs then overshoot by 20yd, and Lallemand follows with cannon, reporting a burst of steam which hides the vessel from sight, and it is later seen to be stationary. Geerts attacks with cannon and bombs, the latter falling 10yd on near side. Haabjoern then sights six coasters of 600–1,000 tons between Westkapelle and Flushing. Calling 'Targets to port!' he prepares to attack. At the same time light Flak opens up from Niuwe Sluis, Flushing and all the ships. He opens fire at 1,000yd [1,600m], and thinking the other pilots are with him, presses home his attack on the leading vessel to 50yd [80m] in one long burst, seeing strikes, flashes and smoke, and silencing this vessel's Flak. In the last stages of the attack he is hit in the port nose tank, top of hood, main oil feed pipe and hydraulic pipe line. Crossing the coast behind the convoy, he uses the shore dykes as protection, and heads home, making a successful belly landing owing to his undercarriage being jammed. His oil supply is found to be exhausted!

At 1220 F/Lt Wells and F/O Davies take off as a precaution against enemy activity over the French coast. Instructed to orbit base they do so in wide circuits at 1,800ft, without further information, till 1305. At this time Wells sees 3 a/c flying south over Margate at 0ft. Making a steep diving turn towards them, he sees a bomb burst and a gas-holder blow up. Judging this to be hostile action, he calls 'Bandits!' and then sees 12 more a/c, identified as FW190s. He fires briefly at one over Broadstairs, and is promptly engaged by light A.A and hit (for the second time in two days). All E/A then turn on course 110 degrees and streak off at very 0ft. Deciding it is more important to bag the leaders, he closes on the first three, who are about a mile in front, and fires at long range to make his target weave, which it refuses to do. At this moment he notices members of the larger formation flying to either side of him. He fires again from 200yd [320m], whereupon the E/A dips its starboard wing and goes in. He flies through the spray, and finding he is overshooting, throttles back and selects the second victim of the three. This responds to long-range fire by a prolonged skid to starboard. Wells closes up, and firing again, sees this E/A go into the drink too. Red tracer meanwhile has opened up from behind, but ignoring this, he follows the third E/A, and fires, only to find his ammo exhausted. He therefore makes a steep climbing turn for home, and sees a number of E/A pass beneath him. Davies had not heard Wells' tally-ho and had his attention first attracted by bomb bursts in Margate, where he sees 4 E/A in line astern. He fires a brief burst at the last, but they gun the gas-holder and Broadstairs streets. He again attacks as they do so, then goes for a formation of 6 heading out to sea. As he crosses the coast he passes the 190 already attacked, and sees it jettison a black object, followed by apparently the pilot's legs (this aircraft was seen to crash just off the coast). The six which Davies now follows consist of 5 in vic and one in the box. He concentrates on the last, and as he is closing fast, fires from 500–600yd, and this E/A obliges by weaving. The range closes and he fires twice more, spattering the sea all round. At this

*The Transportation Plan was a comprehensive strategy to disrupt German military movements.*

moment he has to turn sharply to avoid red and yellow tracer which is flying over his wings, but not too soon to see his quarry crash into the sea with a great fountain of water. On completing his turns, Davies now finds himself alone, but pursuing his original course at max speed it isn't long before he comes upon a pair of 190s, with another to port. He selects the latter, which, as they approach Ostend, pulls up to 200ft [60m]. Davies closes to 150–200yd and fires his last one-second burst of ammo. Strikes are seen from the cockpit and wing, a large piece comes away, and the E/A bursts into flames. Meanwhile the remaining two E/A have turned to counter-attack, but Davies successfully avoids them and returns to base, having been airborne 1 hr and 12 min.

Other scrambles of the day occur at 0856 and 0933, and less hurried patrols of base at 1436, 1546 and 1700, with a Dover patrol at 2121.

This was, as the ORB writer suggests, somewhat of an exceptional day; nevertheless, in late May and the first few days of June, the tactical air forces were reaching a peak of activity, often with a free-roving commission to take on any targets within a given area.

As the Preparatory Phase reached its height, H-Hour for D-Day was confirmed as 04:00 GMT 5 June 1944, as low water would be soon after dawn and the previous night was one of a full moon. Low water was important to allow the landing craft to avoid the plethora of beach obstacles (most of them mined), and a full moon would give the bombers the best chance of identifying and hitting their targets.

On 2 June, Leigh-Mallory outlined to Eisenhower the bombing plan, aimed at establishing a belt cutting the major routes through towns and villages to prevent or slow down the passage of enemy reinforcements into the assault area. Once again the need to prevent the movement of German reinforcements was of such importance that objections regarding French civilian casualties and the destruction of important, and historic, buildings were over-ruled, once again, in the face of the pressing strategic need. Eisenhower approved the plan, and suitable targets joined the list for the medium and heavy bombers, for attack from D minus Two.

Leigh-Mallory saw the transportation campaign as crucial to the Allies in preventing the Germans concentrating in the invasion area

75

once they had identified where the landings had taken place:

> Any large-scale reinforcement of his troops near the invasion area could only be made if the railways behind are in good working order. My first object, therefore, in the preparatory stages, was to make such a mess of the railway system that the movement of reinforcements would be impossible. The railway experts whom I consulted when considering the programme urged the destruction of railway centres, that is to say, those places where servicing and maintenance shops exist, and also where signalling systems are concentrated. Moreover, to clobber junctions with a large number of points would be of immediate assistance, for they are not easily replaced when destroyed. I am quite sure that, speaking at this moment, the potential carrying power of the French and Belgian railways has been very considerably reduced, and that there are good prospects of being able to keep them in a state of paralysis. Of the eighty-two targets chosen, fifty have been completely destroyed, in eight of them one or two installations are still intact, and seventeen have been badly damaged but need further attention, which they will get. To accomplish this, the AEAF has made 8,000 sorties and dropped 5,600 tons; the American 8th Army Air Force 3,300 sorties and dropped 7,000 tons, and Bomber Command 4,600 sorties dropping 20,000 tons. Besides railway centres, bombs have been directed onto rail and road bridges. Of the ten rail and fourteen road bridges between Rouen and Paris, eight rail and ten road have been completely broken.

In these last few days the number of targets in need of attack was far greater than the available air resources, a problem made worse by the shortage of photographic reconnaissance (PR) aircraft to provide accurate and timely battle damage assessment (BDA). The net result was that some critical targets were attacked more than once, even though the threat they posed had been negated; others, however, should have been hit again, but were left through lack of intelligence updates. One cause of this was the unreliability of aiming-point photographs from the bombers and camera-gun film from the fighter-bombers. Whilst this material could prove that the attackers were hitting the correct target, the amount of obscuration by explosions (smoke and debris) made it impossible to assess the degree of damage being caused; thus, it could not be assumed that simply because the coastal gun site was covered with explosions the site was destroyed. To partially overcome this difficulty the Air Plan included provision to attack most critical targets at the assault beaches in the early hours of 6 June.

The Germans had constructed a number of decoy targets, and these were effective at drawing in some of the Allied attacks. Decoy, camouflage and protection of installations had become a fine art with the Germans, and a large amount of air effort had little direct effect. Leigh-Mallory in his eve-of-battle summary stated that:

> My tactical plan was to go for coastal batteries and for the enemy radar system. In order to deceive him as much as possible, I attacked two batteries outside the area for every one I attacked inside it. They are extremely difficult to bomb, but the results have not been unsatisfactory. Out of twelve batteries in the area listed for attack, five have been completely destroyed and seven have been badly damaged. The army is particularly pleased with these results, for they say that the attack was carried out at the right time before the enemy had completed the concrete casements for the guns. I have directed 4,400 tons on the batteries in the area and 8,800 tons outside it. The bombing has been done mostly by Marauders in daylight and Bomber Command at night. I do not maintain that all the batteries have been silenced, but I shall be surprised if they are able to produce anything like the volume of fire they might have laid on had they been left unbombed.

However, according to an 8th Air Force summary: 'Few of the coastal defences were seriously affected in proportion to the effort put

The B-26 Marauders were used for daylight attacks on coastal batteries in the days leading up to 6 June. (US National Archives)

BELOW: *Flying Fortress over a coastline that looks harmless from this height but that had been turned into a fortress by the Germans.* (US National Archives)

forth, but this had been anticipated [a planning estimate put the figure as low as 2 per cent effectiveness of total bomb tonnage], the more so since *Pathfinder* technique was necessary in most instances.' This reflected the views of other units, but the naval planners considered that any level of damage and disruption would prove of inestimable value. Furthermore, in view of the total tonnage dropped, it still equated to a reasonable effective total, and only the gun emplacements with concrete superstructures stood much chance of remaining undamaged. The 8th Air Force alone mounted 2,242 bomber sorties, dropping 6,679 tons of bombs on coastal defences during this four-day period. On 5 June the 8th Air Force sent 629 bombers to attack coastal defences, the major effort for the day, but a number of other targets were also attacked, including the V-l site at Wimereux.

Amongst those taking part in this latter raid was the deputy commander of the 498th Bomb Group, Lt Col Vance. During their first run over the target the bombs failed to release, and so they positioned for a second run with the bombardier attempting a manual release; all but two of the bombs fell away – but at that moment the B-24 Liberator was hit by flak, killing the pilot, injuring the co-pilot and damaging three of the engines. Vance lost his right foot, but moved forward to throttle back and feather the damaged engines whilst the co-pilot turned for home. It was a losing battle, and as the crippled bomber reached the coast the co-pilot ordered an abandon ship. Vance decided that the best chance lay with ditching the bomber and so climbed into the pilot's seat and put the B-24 down on the sea near the coast; he was blown clear as the remaining bombs exploded and was picked up by an Air-Sea Rescue (ASR) unit. In recognition of his actions, Vance was awarded the Medal of Honor.

RAF Bomber Command was also active in this period against the same type of targets: in the three nights from 2/3 June to 4/5 June, eleven gun batteries were attacked. The 9th Air Force meanwhile was primarily tasked against transportation targets, but did carry out a number of missions against coastal defences.

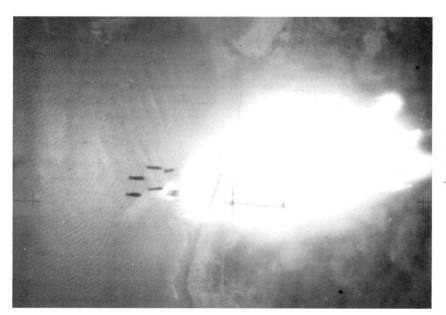

*The night of 30/31 May, and bombs go down on a coastal target at Boulogne from a 98 Squadron aircraft.* (98 Squadron)

ABOVE: *Another radar, again in the St Valery area, under attack.*

RIGHT: *Giant Wurzburg in Normandy.* (US National Archives)

BELOW: *Extensive aerial arrays at Boulogne/Boursin (target V/19) as photographed on 8 May.*

The diversion of effort to counter the V-weapon threat, the *Crossbow* targets, was a source of concern to some of the planners, but it was generally agreed that the potential threat from these weapons, should they become fully operational before a successful lodgement had been made on the Continent, was perhaps the greatest single pre-invasion risk. Whilst the V–1, and later the V–2, became primarily strategic weapons used by Hitler as revenge weapons against British cites, mainly London, the military planners were more concerned with the damage they could have inflicted on the staging and concentration areas in southern England.

The final series of Preparatory Phase attacks was made against the enemy radio and radar network, some forty-two major locations being targeted by fighter-bombers and, to a lesser extent, the mediums and heavies. To quote Leigh-Mallory:

> There is a network of radar stations all along the invasion coasts, and they are tiny and very difficult to hit. They are an absolute menace, because they locate our shipping and our aircraft; moreover, five of the largest radar stations (Giant Wurzburg) were discovered by our experts to be unjammable. These I attacked, and they have all been completely destroyed. Many secondary radar stations still exist, but I think that enemy radar activity has been reduced by at least 25 per cent. There is also good evidence that the morale and efficiency of the radar crews working the instruments has been considerably impaired. Of late, the fact that they switch off when our aircraft approach them has been noticed. The attacks on the big jamming stations are a triumph of precision bombing … the radar station near Boulogne, which measures 300yd by 150 (275m by 137m) received direct hits at night from seventy heavy bombs. In making attacks on radar targets, rocket projectiles have proved very useful.

Indeed, some of the most effective work was carried out by RP Typhoons that flew 694 sorties, firing 4,517 RPs. An additional 657 sorties were flown by Typhoons and Spitfires in the bombing and strafing role, with cannon and machine-gun fire proving effective against certain types of radar.

'Arrived at dispersal this morning to find all aircraft with their invasion markings painted on them. The groundcrew completed the job between 18:00 hours and 03:00 hours this morning. Word was received that only local flying was to be done with the marked aircraft.' Thus were the Typhoons of 438 Squadron given their special identification markings of black and white bands around wings and fuselage, a task that was completed for all tactical aircraft between 3–5 June. The decision to give the aircraft identification markings arose out of the experiences of similar major air-sea–land operations, notably Sicily, during which 'own goals', invariably ground to air, had taken too high a toll of aircraft; it was hoped that the new

*Spitfire of 308 Squadron; all Allied tactical aircraft were given black-and-white identification stripes on wings and fuselage in the few days immediately prior to the invasion.*

*With a map stretched out on the wing of the aircraft, P-47 pilots are briefed on their next target.* (US National Archives)

### Total Air Effort in the period 1 April to 5 June

| Unit | Sorties | Bomb tonnage | Losses | Claims |
|------|---------|--------------|--------|--------|
| 9th AF | 53,784 | 30,657 | 197 | 189 |
| 2nd TAF | 28,587 | 6,981 | 133 | 66 |
| ADGB | 18,639 | 0 | 46 | 111 |
| RAF BC | 24,621 | 87,238 | 557 | 77 |
| VIIIth BC | 37,804 | 69,857 | 763 | 724 |
| VIIIth FC | 31,820 | 647 | 291 | 1,488 |
| Total | 195,255 | 195,380 | 1,987 | 2,655 |

markings would prevent, or at least reduce this problem. Not all Allied aircraft were given the new scheme, the most notable exception being the strategic bombers.

On the eve of the invasion the statistics for total air effort in the period 1 April to 5 June were as shown in the box (*above*).

The scale of the effort is little short of remarkable, although the scale of losses is frightening, as these are aircraft losses and not casualties; the figure for claims is just that – claims, and it does not reflect actual German losses, although it is true that at this time losses amongst German fighter units were high. The above figures only cover those by offensive aircraft in the north-west European land area; they do not include thousands of sorties by, for example, Coastal Command units, these latter flying some 5,384 anti U-boat and anti-shipping missions during the same period.

In the critical period of the first week of June the inexact science of meteorology was very much under the spotlight, the invasion planners requiring a period of reasonable weather to ensure that effective use could be made of Allied air assets. Weather-reporting information, especially for the important Atlantic region, came primarily from ships and aircraft, including the unsung work, much of it hazardous, of the specialist weather reconnaissance units. There was, of course, a distinct lack of accurate data from the occupied countries. According to the meteorologists:

There was considerable difficulty in obtaining a clear synoptic picture of what was happening over

81

the NW Atlantic at the most crucial time; uncertainties in pressure distribution were such that the Central Forecasting Offices differed from each other by as much as 10 millibars in their interpretation of the pressure in an important area.

During the period 2–4 June, there was a lack of reports from the area 52–59 degrees North and 22–25 degrees West, an area crucial for predicting the progress and composition of Atlantic weather systems. The met. brief given by the chief meteorological officer, Group Captain Stagg, to the Supreme Commanders' briefing at 21:30 hours on 3 June, was pessimistic:

> The high pressure over the Azores is rapidly giving way, and a series of depressions across the Atlantic is moving rapidly eastward; these depressions will produce disturbed conditions in the Channel and assault area. Winds will be W-SW, Force 5 on the English coast, Force 3–4 on French coasts. From Sunday morning onwards cloud will probably be mainly 10/10 with base 500–1,000 feet [150–300m]. Visibility will be mainly 3–4 miles [5–6.5km], though 5–6 miles [8–9.5km] inland in the afternoon. There is a risk of fog spreading from the west up the Channel to sea and coastal areas.

This gloom of high winds and low cloud was predicted to last until sometime late Monday. With this in mind, Eisenhower delayed the invasion by twenty-four hours: D-Day was now scheduled for 6 June 1944.

According to some records, the question of weather requirements caused yet another conflict with Montgomery who, when told that the weather might mean a delay in the assault, stated that he was quite happy to go ahead with the original date – regardless of the level of air support. As so much planning and effort had been expended on the 'essential pre-requisite of air action to achieve a satisfactory situation', this statement could be seen as quite incredible and almost cavalier; however, one major fear of the army command was a longer-term delay (to the next tide and moon period), with consequent reduction of the campaigning season once safely ashore. It would, however, at this late stage have been almost impossible to have accepted more than a twenty-four-hour delay, as too much had already been set in motion; true, ships could have been recalled and units put on a lower readiness, but the question of maintaining the deception plan and keeping the Germans from guessing the location of the assault would have been impossible; add to this the negative effect on the morale of men keyed up, ready to go, and the result could have been a disaster.

The Air Commander-in-Chief held a short conference at 16:30 on 5 June in his HQ at Bentley Priory, and we have already quoted from this in the overview of the transportation,

*RPs inbound to a German barracks on 5 June.*

coastal defences and radar campaigns. This eve-of-battle conference is the first to be recorded in a remarkable 'diary' containing the daily impressions of Leigh-Mallory as recounted to Mr Hilary St-George Saunders. Extracts of this diary will be used over the next few pages of this account as they shed a unique light on the invasion as it unfolded. This first diary entry includes a description of the C-in-C's briefing room:

The room was one of the principal drawing rooms of the mansion housing the Headquarters. A tall, spacious room, with long French windows giving on to the grounds outside, reached from a balcony by means of a flight of steps. The main item of furniture in the room was a large desk facing a large-scale wall map of France and Belgium. Opposite the windows was a large board showing the number of British and American squadrons available. Behind the C-in-C's desk, on the mantelpiece, were a number of photographs of the Allied Commanders, and one of General Sperrle commanding the *Luftwaffe*. The carpet was of the standard Royal

Air Force pattern of pink and blue, as were most of the chairs. Outside, through the tall French windows, the rhododendron bushes and trees of the garden were in full bloom, and beyond them could be seen the landing strip for the puddle jumpers, light aircraft used for short journeys. It was a day of low cloud but no rain.

This is a marvellous piece of imagery, and seldom do we have such a picture of the places in which such key meetings and decisions took place.

Leigh-Mallory opened the conference with an overview:

I bore constantly in mind that we had a large preponderance of air strength over that of the enemy. My problem was, therefore, how to apply this to the best advantage in the air preparations for the assault. The point I want to reach is one where the enemy is forced to decide whether to fight it out till he wins or is destroyed, or to refuse to take that risk and adopt the course of preserving his strength for some

*Pilots of 245 Squadron with one of their aircraft at Holmsley South in May 1944. The squadron was part of No. 121 Wing under Wg Cdr C. S. Morice.*

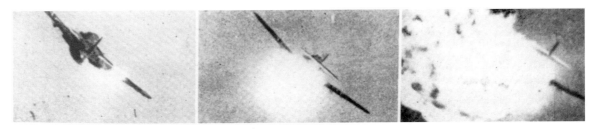

*Camera-gun film from a 9th Air Force fighter-bomber showing the demise of a German fighter.*

future effort to be made at a time when he judges the situation to be most suitable, or possibly most desperate. My own view for this battle which opens tomorrow has always been that the Hun would regard the second alternative as the proper course of action, and that he would keep back a considerable proportion of his fighter effort for use either immediately the battle was joined or shortly afterwards.

He surmised that as the American daylight raids had been meeting with little resistance in recent days, this was proof of a conservation policy by the Germans, but that it was his intention 'to take all possible steps to provoke the GAF into delivering battle by day. It will then be defeated and destroyed, and I shall have achieved air supremacy.' He then went on to explain part of the rationale behind the air campaign to date:

> It seems to me that the only way the Hun can force a stalemate at this stage of the war is by making a supreme effort to kick our armies back into the sea after we have got ashore. I think he may take a very big risk in order to achieve this object. He cannot, however, achieve it if his communications have been wrecked, or at any rate disrupted.

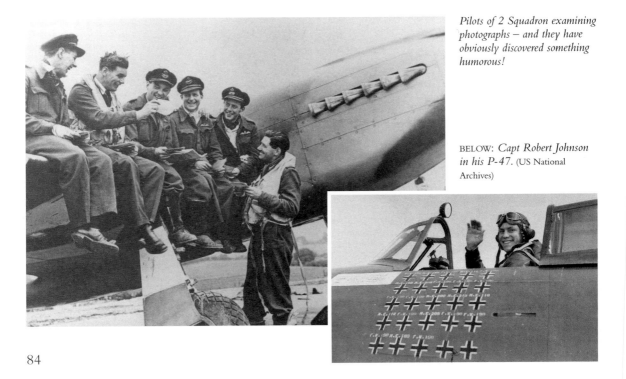

*Pilots of 2 Squadron examining photographs – and they have obviously discovered something humorous!*

BELOW: *Capt Robert Johnson in his P-47.* (US National Archives)

Leigh-Mallory concluded this first diary entry by saying:

It is my object, and I shall allow nothing to stand in its way, to make it as difficult as possible for the enemy to bring up his troops. As I have just said, I must redress the balance, and I will never be deflected from this purpose. I am going to use all my efforts to delay the German army. I shall make use of fighter-bombers for attacks on roads, and these will come into their own as soon as the German army is forced to take to them, not having railways at their disposal any longer.

The Allies had a massive superiority in air power – and every bit of it was going to be needed in the days to come, as the German army proved resilient, determined and adaptive.

## 6 June 1944: Operation *Neptune* – The Assault Phase of *Overlord*

The assault phase of the air campaign comprised six main elements:

1. Protection of cross-Channel movement.
2. Neutralization of coastal and beach defences.
3. Protection of beaches.
4. Dislocation of enemy communications and control.
5. Airborne operations.
6. Direct support of the land forces.

Although precise figures of Allied aircraft available vary from source to source, it is certain that they exceeded 10,000 aircraft, and the potential bomb lift was greater than any previously available. The statistics in the table below

| **Aircraft Availability** | | | | **Aircraft Availability –** **Bomb Lift (in short tons)** | |
|---|---|---|---|---|---|
| *Type* | *British* | *American* | *Total* | | |
| Strategic bomber | 1,248 | 1,980 | 3,228 | RAF Bomber Command | 34,400 |
| Medium bomber/F–B | 1,280 | 2,165 | 3,445 | US 8th AF | 21,000 |
| Fighter | 852 | 1,125 | 1,977 | US 9th AF | 12,150 |
| Maritime | 489 | 0 | 489 | No. 2 Group RAF | 3,900 |
| Transport | 337 | 876 | 1,213 | | |
| **Total** | **4,206** | **6,146** | **10,342** | Total | 71,450 |

The bomb lift figures do not include the additional bomb potential of the Spitfires and Typhoons (RP or bomber) of 2nd TAF.

*This reconnaissance photo gives some idea of the vast array of ships involved in the landings; the breakwater has been created by using landing ships.* (US National Archives)

| A/C. | PILOT. | NAVIGATOR. | W/OP (AIR). | AIR GUNNER. |
|---|---|---|---|---|
| | | NO 98 SQUADRON BATTLE ORDER FOR NIGHT OF 5/6th JUNE, 1944. | | |
| C. | W/C. PAUL. | P/O. WILLIAMS. | SGT. HARRIS. | P/O. KOKES & SGT. TURNER. |
| M. | S/L. BUNDOCK. | W/O. LEA. | SGT. VERDEN. | P/O. HUMPHRIS. |
| H. | F/L. GREGORY. | F/O. INGRAM. | F/O. VENABLES. | F/S. McINTYRE. |
| L. | F/O. CREEKE. | F/O. LEONARD. | F/O. JACOBS. | SGT. CONNOR. |
| ? | F/S. THURSTON. | F/S. DEAN. | F/S. GIRVIN. | F/S. ZADO. |
| D. | F/S. NEWELL. | F/S. BROWN. | F/S. COYEN. | SGT. FLETCHER. |
| K. | F/L. SPONG. | F/S. GOODWIN. | W/O. FENWICK. | F/O. WEBSTER. (GH) |
| F. | F/O. MacFARLANE. | F/O. DOYLE. | W/O. MOSSINGTON. | F/O. HORNE. |
| O. | W/C. LYNN. | Lt. WAADENBURG. | F/O. CUDLIPP. | F/O. PRITCHARD. |
| S. | S/L. EAGER. | F/S. PARRISH. | SGT. PAGE. | F/O. WEBBER. |
| P. | F/L. DAWES. | F/L. RICHARDSON. | F/O. GREEN. | W/O. JENKINSON. (GH |
| X. | F/L. BROWN. | P/O. EVANS. | F/O. GACE. | F/O. GRAHM. (GH |
| U. | F/O. MARSHALL. | F/O. GORDON. | F/S. NOTTLE. | F/O. WILFART. |
| V. | F/O. MARTIN. | F/O. CHAMMEN. | F/O. GORVIN. | F/S. LOBB. |
| T | F/S. FILBY. | F/S. HERMAN. | F/S. BIRD. | F/S. CAREY. |
| ? | F/O. HARRIS. | SGT. HARNDEN. | F/S. GLASER. | SGT. WILLIAMS. |

BRIEFING TIMES ETC: TO BE DETAILED LATER.

DISTRIBUTION: AS USUAL.

(Signed) C. J. C. PAUL,
Wing Commander,
Commanding No 98 Squadron,
Royal     Air     Force.

appear to be amongst the most reliable (Appendix I gives the Order of Battle for the Allied Air Forces).

The operational commitment had been kept to a reduced level of around 50 per cent of total potential for the two days prior to the evening of 5 June to enable units to conserve their strength for the maximum effort operations that would need to be mounted during the assault phase. Operation *Neptune* was planned to run on the tightest of schedules and to a complex co-ordinated plan whereby all air–sea–land elements had rigid time constraints and the failure of any one could spell disaster. As with all such major military operations, there was much that went awry.

Amongst the operations taking place on the night of 5/6 June was a variety of 'nuisance' raids by Mosquitoes and Mitchells; many of these sorties were airborne in the late hours of 5 June, but actually attacked their targets on the 6th: D-Day. Mosquito missions included forty-eight aircraft to various airfields (Rennes, Florennes, Venlo), gun positions, searchlight sites, bridges and any trains they happened to find; a further ninety-eight Mosquitoes patrolled the area

Rennes–Le Mans–Lisieux between 22:00 and 05:56 hours, with instructions to attack road and rail junctions; one aircraft failed to return. The final operation during this period by Allied Expeditionary Air Force (AEAF) aircraft was an attack on Caen by thirty-six Mitchells and nine Mosquitoes, of which fifteen and four respectively found the target and made bombing runs.

During the evening of 5 June, air bases throughout England became a hive of activity as aircraft were prepared for the first missions for D-Day; meanwhile, crews filed into hushed briefing rooms to receive long, complex and detailed briefings – designed to ensure that all aspects of the air offensive went smoothly. At Bungay, the crews of the 446th Bomb Group learnt that they were to be the first US 8th Air Force bombers into the attack: 'You are to strike the beach defences at Pointe de la Percée, dropping your bombs not later than two minutes before Zero Hour [06:30]. Landing craft and troops will be 400yd [365m] to 1 mile [1.6km] offshore as we attack, and naval ships will be shelling our targets onshore.'

At last the long-awaited invasion had arrived, and it brought a sense of satisfaction:

This morning at 4am when the boys were getting ready for their first patrol, the groundcrew were told and they cheered. The uplift in morale was good to see. All pilots and groundcrew realized the big day had arrived, and they seemed to take a new lease of life, and went about their work with renewed keenness.     (ORB of No. 402 Squadron RAF)

It was the same story at most bases: the aircrew knew by late on the 5th and the groundcrew – those who had not already guessed – by early morning the following day. All knew that it would be the prelude to days of intense effort, and that there would be losses – but all also knew that the war was a step nearer ending.

The same analysis of aircraft availability gave German strength as 1,286 on the Western Front,

of which 703 were fighters, plus an additional 1,168 fighters for the defence of the Reich. German statistics suggest that this was a gross overestimate, and that the number of operational aircraft was nearer 800, of which only just over 300 were fighters. Indeed, Luftflotte 3, whose area this was, had major problems not only in terms of its overall air assets, but also in predicting the likely point of attack by the Allies. The staff of Luftflotte 3 were convinced that the Allied blow would fall between Le Havre and Cherbourg, and they also knew that the air assets

*Mosquitoes were heavily involved in intruder operations attacking airfields, and a variety of other targets including trains.*

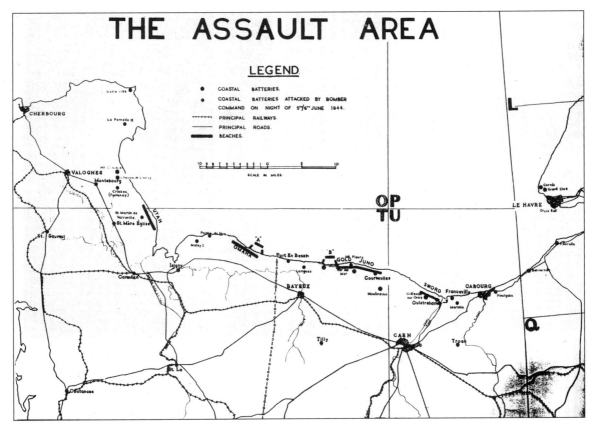

# THE ASSAULT AREA

### LEGEND

- ● COASTAL BATTERIES.
- ● COASTAL BATTERIES ATTACKED BY BOMBER COMMAND ON NIGHT OF 5TH/6TH JUNE 1944.
- ┼┼┼┼ PRINCIPAL RAILWAYS.
- ──── PRINCIPAL ROADS.
- ▬▬▬ BEACHES.

*Map of the assault area showing the beach codenames and general operational area.*

under command were totally inadequate; however, any call for reinforcements would fall on deaf ears, as the situation in Italy, Russia and the Home Front had priority – at least until the invasion. It would be the fighters of Jagdkorps II and the bombers of Fliegerkorps II that would bear the brunt of initial combat, as they were stationed in the north-west of France, along with the long-range bombers of Fliegerkorps IX. Most of the anti-shipping units, including some armed with the new radio-controlled missiles, were with Fliegerkorps X in the south-west of France.

## Deception Operations

Deception had been one of the key planning considerations throughout the discussions on the invasion; as already mentioned, air effort

had been expended in the ratio of two targets outside of the planned landing area to one inside it. The final part of the deception plan involved RAF Bomber Command in a number of special operations. In addition to these missions, aircraft from No. 100 Group performed two other special tasks, providing a 'Mandrel' screen and carrying out ABC (Airborne Cigar) jamming. Ground-jamming stations were also active against the German radar and communications network.

## Operation *Titanic*

There were three elements to this 'airborne diversion' operation:

1. *Titanic I*, Yvetot area – eleven Halifax and four Stirling

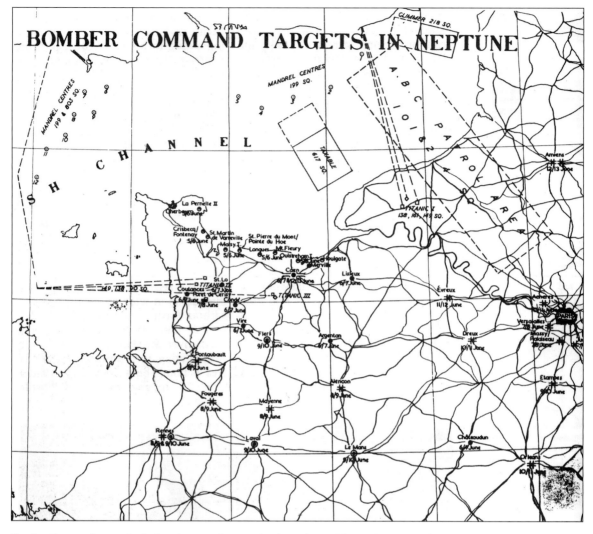

*Bomber Command targets in the invasion area; the map also shows the special operations race-tracks.*

2. *Titanic III*, Maltot area – three Stirlings of No. 149 Squadron
3. *Titanic IV*, Marigny area – fifteen Stirlings and one Halifax

These operations involved dropping hundreds of dummy paratroopers through a screen of 'Window', the latter being to draw the enemy radar's attention to what was going on. To make it appear as if real troops had landed, the dummies were equipped with sound and light simulators to mimic a small-arms battle. The whole idea was to confuse the enemy and draw him away from the real paratroop drop zones (DZs) and landing zones (LZs). The first *Titanic* drop was made in the early hours of 6 June between Coutances and St Lô, but was soon followed by others over a wide area.

### *Glimmer* and *Taxable*

As early as March, the Operational Research Section (ORS) had carried out a study to determine the best way of providing the screening, using 'Window' (strips of foil used to produce false radar reflections), proposed by AEAF; this study was followed by another, in April, of the feasibility of using Window to simulate a slow-moving convoy:'...the intention is to produce the illusion that a mass of shipping is approaching the coast at a rate of 5kts at each of two areas.'The conclusion was that each area would require twenty-four aircraft, working in boxes of eight, and that no less than 40,000 bundles of narrow, standard-type Window of 26cm (10in) in length would be required. To make the deception effective required accurate flying and precise dropping of the Window; anything less and the picture on the enemy radar screens would not look right.

*Glimmer* was a task involving eight Stirlings of 218 Squadron, simulating a convoy near Boulogne, the deception being enhanced by nine naval and RAF launches towing special balloons. *Taxable* involved sixteen Lancasters from 617 Squadron simulating a convoy off Cap d'Antifer, the deception being enhanced as for *Glimmer*. Both appear to have been remarkably successful, and radar units within 15th Army began reporting a large fleet between Boulogne and Etretat. Naval units put to sea and the whole area was on alert.

## The Mandrel System

The Mandrel system was developed to jam German ground radars such as the Freya, Hoarding, Chimney and Wassermann, there being a number of variants of the Mandrel equipment to cover specific frequencies which, through a combination of jammers, provided a complete screen, blinding the German radar defences. The Mandrel screen for *Neptune* was provided by nineteen Stirlings from 199 Squadron RAF and B-17 Flying Fortresses from the 803rd Squadron of the US VIIIth Bomber Command (attached to No. 100 Group RAF). However, the B-17s were limited in the frequency coverage of their equipment. This screen had to be in place from the night of 4/5 June in order to cover the invasion fleet, and pairs of aircraft flew a race-track pattern.

## The ABC Equipment

The Airborne Cigar (ABC) equipment was developed to disrupt, through noise and audio-jamming, enemy fighter control frequencies, the system being operated by a German-speaking special operator. As part of No. 100 Group, the Lancasters of No. 101 Squadron specialized in this role, and twenty-four of their aircraft were airborne in the early hours of 6 June. One aircraft (LL833) lost power and had to ditch in the Channel just off the beach-head, but the crew were picked up, making them some of the first air-crew to be rescued from a D-Day mission.

## Coastal Defences

Although the strategic bombers had paid numerous visits to the various coastal defence batteries in and around the assault area, the lethal potential that these sites possessed continued to cause grave concern amongst the planners. One of the initial air operations for 6 June was to be a series of attacks against the major gun sites. On the night of 5/6 June, RAF Bomber Command despatched 1,335 bombers to attack ten of the gun batteries, five in the eastern assault area and five in the western assault area: La Pernelle, Mont Fleury, St Pierre-du-Mont, Maissy, Houlgate, Ouistreham, Merville, Crisbecq and Longues. One of the primary aims was to drive the gun crews into their shelters and cause severe disruption, and with luck actually destroy some of the guns. Naval bombardment would then take up the attack against the guns as soon as it was light enough to allow accurate spotting. Fall-of-shot reporting would be carried out mainly by aircraft of the specially formed Aircraft Spotting Pool, a mix of Fleet Air Arm and RAF squadrons. All this would be taking place as the assault was heading into the beaches.

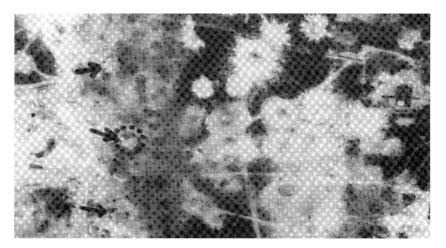

*Despite what looks like comprehensive damage to the coastal battery at Longues, the Allies knew that it was all but impossible to destroy the guns within the emplacements.*

*B-24* Ford's Folly *of the 392nd BG being readied for a mission on D-Day.*

The first bombs actually fell on Crisbecq just before midnight on 5 June as two Mosquito marker aircraft led ninety-two Lancasters of No. 1 Group in to the attack. Although the target was covered by cloud, the bombers were able to distinguish the glow from the target markers, and so, in a ten-minute period from 23:31 hours, released 533 tons of bombs. A few minutes later and the second Lancaster force from No. 1 Group was releasing its load over a cloud-covered St Martin-de-Varaville. Meanwhile a Halifax/Lancaster force from No. 6 (RCAF) Group was making its way to the site at Merville, the first bombs going down at 00:25 hours on 6 June. There was then

a gap of some hours before the next Bomber Command raid, by 100 Halifaxes of No. 4 Group, appeared over Maissy at 03:14 hours, dropping 525 tons of bombs in just fourteen minutes. At 03:31 hours the Lancasters of No. 5 Group began their attack on La Pernelle; the bombing was somewhat erratic in the first few minutes, but was quickly corrected by the master bomber after the target was re-marked from low level by a Mosquito. Because of the need to re-mark the target this was one of the longest raids of the night, the bombing taking over thirty minutes.

As this raid was taking place, so another force of Halifaxes from No. 6 Group dropped on

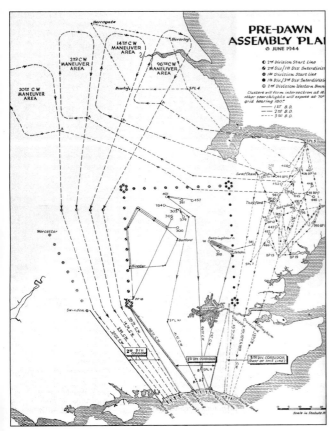

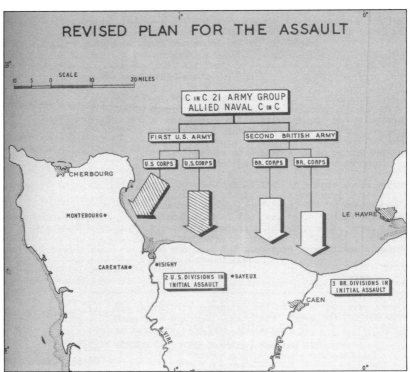

ABOVE: *Bomber assembly plan for VIIIth Bomber Command.* (USAAF)

*Map showing the revised assault plan for the American and British/Canadian sectors.* (AHB)

Houlgate. Next was Longues, where ninety-two Lancasters dropped 537 tons of bombs through complete cloud cover, the target, like most of the others this night, having been marked by Oboe-equipped Mosquitoes of 105 and 109 Squadrons. Within one minute of the bombers leaving this target at 04:28 hours, the first bombs were falling on Mont Fleury and, shortly afterwards, St Pierre-du-Mont. The final attack of the series was made by 110 Lancasters against Ouistreham from 05:02 to 05:15 hours.

Most crews reported that flak had been either light or non-existent, and there were very few reports of fighter activity. Losses amongst the bombers had also been very light: two Halifaxes from the Mont Fleury mission one Lancaster from the Longues mission and three Lancasters from that to St Pierre-du-Mont. Many of the missions involved a daylight withdrawal from the target areas with the associated danger from German fighters, and to counter this, US 8th Air Force provided large-scale fighter escort.

According to the RAF narrative: '... there was no real opposition from these batteries during the landing phase – Bomber Command had successfully accomplished the first major air task in the assault.' Whilst this statement is in general terms accurate, some gun sites did engage Allied shipping, albeit with little result, and had to be neutralized through a combination of naval gunfire and land assault.

Bomber Command mounted a number of smaller operations outside the invasion area on the night of the 5/6th, thirty-one Mosquitoes going to Osnabruck without loss; also, forty-eight Mosquitoes undertook bomber support missions, losing two of their number and claiming one Bf110 in the Aachen area.

The American bombers had been given the task of suppressing the beach defences as the landing craft were going in on the assault. The potential for a major 'own goal' disaster of bombing the assault craft was prevented by strict adherence to a bomb line, whereby the landing craft were not to proceed within 1,000yd (900m) of the beaches until a certain time; the bomber crews had express instructions not to bomb unless they were absolutely certain as to their target. However,

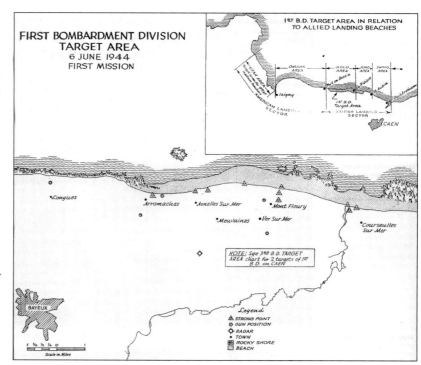

ABOVE: *Target area for 1st Bombardment Division.* (USAAF)

BELOW: *Target area for 2nd Bombardment Division.* (USAAF)

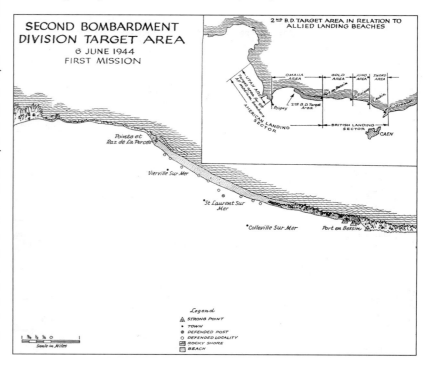

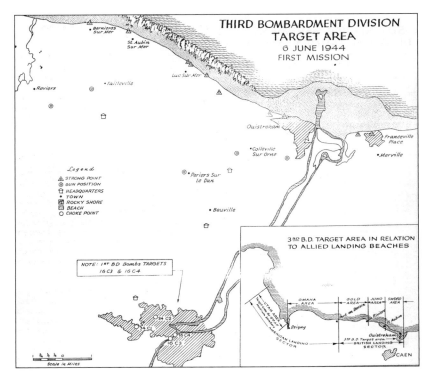

Target area for 3rd Bombardment Division. (USAAF)

The most important and by far the most elaborate D-Day plans concerned the first mission of the day, involving attacks immediately prior to H-Hour [the time of the seaborne assault – this varied from beach to beach] against forty-five coastal installations between the Orne and the Vire estuaries on the Normandy coast. The six-mile coastal strip included all the assault beaches except an adjacent beach, Utah, which was the responsibility of the US 9th Air Force.

The aim of the attacks was the 'demoralization of the enemy frontline defenders and the disruption of communication lines for reserve forces'. This air assault was an integral part of the complex Joint Fire Plan that had been worked out by the SHAEF planners, on which the success of *Neptune* depended. The Joint Fire Plan laid down timetables and procedures for medium bombers, fighter-bombers and naval gunfire support.

the results were not always appreciated by the troops on the ground; one Ranger company commander on the ill-fated Omaha beach commented: 'The Air Corps might have done better if they had landed their planes on the beach and chased the enemy out with bayonets.'

In general terms, however, this part of the air campaign was seen as being of critical import, the 8th Air Force analysis being that:

The British landing sector ('Gold', 'Juno', 'Sword') was to be covered by the US 8th Air Force's 1st and 3rd Bombardment Divisions, the American 'Omaha' area being allocated to the 2nd Bombardment Division, and the remaining American sector, 'Utah', going to the US 9th Air Force. It must be remembered that the bombers were working under severe constraints, not least of which was a restriction on bombing certain locations where it was considered that the problems created by bomb craters would outweigh any benefit in the reduction of enemy defensive capability. To this end, most bombs were given instantaneous fuses and only bombs of less than 1,000lb (450kg) were employed. The beach defences that the bombers attacked were often

Crew briefing 381st BG, D-Day. (US National Archives)

of a type not suitable for medium-level bombing – for example, concrete pillboxes set into sand dunes, and where there was very little chance of the bombing doing any physical damage; rather, the intention was that the bombing would send the defenders to shelter, and the assault troops would then land before the enemy had time to recover – it was all very much a matter of strict timing.

The first of what were to be four major operations by US 8th Air Force bombers got under way at 01:15 hours, with the B-17s and B-24s leaving their East Anglian airfields to follow a complex assembly plan – with searchlights, beacons and various radar navigation aids to ensure that timings and positions were exactly right – leading to the air corridors established over the Allied fleet. Each formation was led by H2X-equipped pathfinder aircraft so that blind bombing could be carried out if weather conditions so dictated; selected pathfinder navigators had been given special training in such H2X tactics to ensure success. This same consideration required a standby plan so that the 8th Air Force could attack the Utah beach targets, because the 9th Air Force bombers had no blind-bombing capability. In the event of cloud cover preventing visual bombing, the intention was to release when the pathfinder aircraft in the centre of the formation released a smoke marker.

Of the 1,365 bombers (543 B-24s and 822 B-17s) despatched by the 8th Air Force, 1,076 made attacks, the lowest percentage of attackers being amongst the 3rd Bombardment Division covering the eastern end of the assault area. These aircraft dropped almost 3,000 tons of bombs onto the beach defences. Lieutenant Litwiller was aboard B-24 *Liberty Run* of the 446th Bomb Group/20th Combat Wing heading for Omaha beach, the first aircraft of the US VIIIth Bomber Command to make an attack this day:

> We took off at 02:20, climbed to 10,000 feet and circled our prescribed forming area while our engineer fired the specific coloured signal flares as Col

Brogger, the formation commander, and the 446th assembled behind us. The mission went precisely as planned, with the briefed undercast necessitating bombing by H2X radar. As we approached the French coast the radar navigator called me over to look at his PFF scope. It indicated the vast armada of the invasion fleet standing just off the coast of Normandy – a thrilling sight even on radar. Bombs were away at 06:00.

The 95th Bomb Group, as part of the 3rd Bombardment Division, was tasked against the beaches in the British sector.

> Our group of about forty B-17s in close formation began to ease its way into the narrow corridor for the bomb run. As we reached the beach the lead plane released a smoke bomb, which was the signal for all forty aircraft to drop their bombs simultaneously. Thus, more than 100 tons of bombs exploded in a matter of a few seconds. The explosions caused our aircraft to bounce and vibrate.

War correspondents aboard the ships reported the attacks:

> … the air power that we have seen most forcibly was the final attack by the American 8th Air Force. Immediately before H-Hour they dropped a vast weight of bombs on the beaches. The beaches shook and seemed to rise into the air, and ships well out at sea quivered and shook. (Robin Duff)

Only one B-24 was lost to enemy action, an aircraft from the 487th Bomb Group, but a number of other aircrew were killed and wounded by flak. The entire event appeared to have taken the German defences by surprise. Two other B-24s, from the 493rd Bomb Group, collided in mid-air and both went down.

The task of escorting the bomber missions fell to the P-51 Mustangs and P-47 Thunderbolts of the US VIIIth Fighter Command, although as the day wore on with virtually no German air opposition, most of these aircraft

*Leigh-Mallory briefing US paratroops — none of whom look very impressed! As Air Commander he expressed reservations over the American airborne plan.*

undertook armed recce or bombing and strafing missions. The bombers would return three more times during the day, but even before the seaborne landings, which they supported, took place, the first Allied troops were already fighting in Normandy.

## Airborne Operations

Before the bombers made an appearance the first air operations of D-Day were already under way on the important yet much-debated airborne assault. This was one aspect of the Assault Phase that caused some air commanders, Leigh-Mallory in particular, great concern:

> Yesterday (June 5th) I confess that I was very apprehensive about the American Airborne Division. I felt they had a task that might be beyond them, and I say quite frankly that I was against this part of the plan. It seemed to me that to fly in so large a force at 500ft [150m] over almost the whole of the Cherbourg peninsula was extremely hazardous. If the enemy were alert and vigorous it looked as though American casualties would be far too high and could not, therefore, be justified. I went round

to several Groups and talked with them. I would describe their demeanour as grim and not frightfully gay, but there was no doubt in my mind of their determination to do the job.

D-Day was actually under way on 5 June, as the early morning airborne assault meant that aircraft were en route that evening; for many in Britain the sight and sound of this airborne armada was the first real indication that the invasion was a reality. The Headquarters history of the 474th FG was one of many documents to record these first impressions; it is also one of the most prosaic, and the author could have been a film scriptwriter, he paints the picture so well:

> We daubed on our war paint — big white stripes on our ships so our own ground troops wouldn't shoot them down. Grim-faced, high-ranking officers gathered for secret councils. Enlisted men sat around aircraft reading letters from home, wondering when they would get back. Planes sat waiting on the ground. The MPs stopped soldiers at the gate. The radio operator sat reading a comic book in the sudden hushed silence of his shack. We dug our fox holes and waited …

*Invasion preparation –
assembling gliders for
US airborne forces.*
(US National Archives)

At first it was just a fuzzy spot of light, a dim glow, hovering like a cloud-obscured star on the northern horizon. The briefing room clock said 11:20, the S-2 calendar said June 5, 1944. It was quiet. The dim blob of light didn't move – it just grew. It grew too big to be a star. And then it just hung there, taking on colour. First there were little pin-pricks of amber, then red, then green. Still nothing happened. There wasn't a sound. Still it grew. Larger, and larger. Then hung there like a little toy Christmas tree in the clouds … red, amber and green.

Here and there a grease-stained mechanic glanced carelessly across the low, dark valley to the north, then started, paused, stood transfixed on the dew-wet wing of his airplane and stared like a pilgrim beholding a vision …

'For Chrissake, Joe! What's that?'

Joe took his hands from the cold, oily womb of an engine and squinted intently at the still night sky.

'What's what?'

'There – right there!'

Then Joe saw it too … 'Oh-h … I'll be … I'll be a son-of-a-bitch!'

Slowly men arose from their work and turned tired faces to the wonder in the northern sky. Still it was quiet. Still it grew. Bigger. Brighter. It didn't appear to move, just grew. Grew until it looked like a great big Christmas tree floating in the clouds. Still there wasn't a sound. It grew until it looked like a huge, magic city floating in the sky. Then you could see it move – slowly, majestically. Then you could hear it move. Or maybe felt it first. The whole sky, the soft night air, alive with a tremendous throb – the low, deep throb of countless churning engines. Then you could see them – planes! Dozens of planes! Great big lumbering C-47s. Troop transports. Scores of them. This is IT! D-Day! Invasion!

They came right over the field at 500ft; ours was their last airfield this side of France. We knew they couldn't hear us, but we shouted anyway – 'Go get 'em, Yank!' We waved, we shouted, we even prayed. For three solid hours they came. Wave after wave. After the Yanks came the British, towing big Horsa gliders behind them.

A thousand planes that were going to fly over the coast of France at 500ft – with their lights on. God, what a target! Oh, what a sight!

*Part of the airborne assault approaching the enemy coast on 6 June.*

BELOW: *A C-47 carries out a snap pick-up of a CG-4 glider.* (US National Archives)

## The British Airborne Operation

The British plan had four main aims:

1. Secure and hold the two bridges over the Caen canal and River Orne.
2. Neutralize the coastal battery at Merville.
3. Secure a base area including bridgeheads east of the River Orne.
4. Prevent enemy reinforcements moving towards the British flank from the south-east.

At 22:49 hours on 5 June, seven Dakotas of 271 Squadron left Down Ampney towing Horsa gliders of 'E' Squadron, Glider Pilot Regiment (GPR), destined for LZ 'V' and the assault on the Merville battery. Over the next twenty minutes Dakota, Halifax and Albemarle tugs lifted Horsas from Blakehill Farm, Tarrant Rushton, Harwell and Brize Norton as advance parties for the various assault elements. Two groups of transport aircraft carried paratroops to act as pathfinders, dropping on the LZs and marking them for the subsequent glider assault parties.

Amongst these advanced units was that tasked with seizing the two bridges. Three gliders were

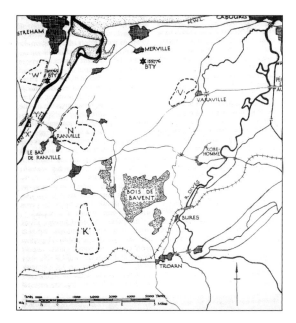

*The British airborne operation.*

allocated to each of the bridges, the intention being to land as close to the targets as possible, in the dark, and, with the benefit of surprise, overpower the defenders and remove any demolition charges. Of the six gliders involved in this *coup de main* operation, five landed spot on their assigned positions, but the sixth, due to an error by the tug aircraft, ended up some 8 miles (13km) away (although the soldiers managed to fight their way back to the bridges). The assaults went well with few casualties, and both bridges were seized.

The other advanced groups, all of whom had left their home airfields late on 5 June, comprised eleven gliders of 'A' and 'E' Squadrons GPR, and six gliders of 'T' Squadron GPR. The first group was destined for LZ 'V' with support equipment for the assault on the Merville battery, but because of the smoke and dust raised by bombing they had difficulty in locating their target area, and so landed somewhat south of the LZ. Unfortunately the anti-glider defences, known as 'Rommel's asparagus', caused a great deal of damage, and seven of the glider pilots were killed. The Horsas of 'F' Squadron suffered

*RAF Dakotas were used for paratroop dropping and re-supply missions.*

similar difficulties in trying to land at LZ 'K' – only two landed on the site.

Whilst this was going on, the Merville battery assault party of three gliders was preparing to cast off from its Albemarle tugs, the glider pilots' aim being to land virtually on top of the gun site. As with so much of the airborne operation, this did not go according to plan, although two of the Horsas landed reasonably close to the site, one ending up in an orchard just 50yd (45m) away, and the men of 9th Parachute Battalion were able to seize their objective. However, it was only after hours of fighting that the battery fell to the attackers (at 04:45 hours), and with heavy casualties.

During the early hours of 6 June, a further seventy-two gliders, including four Hamilcars

*British Horsa gliders on the ground, 8 June.*

each carrying a 17-pounder gun and associated support equipment, left England to take much-needed reinforcements and heavy equipment to the air lodgement established around the Orne river bridges. The codename for this phase of the operation was Operation *Tonga*, and the lead aircraft, Albemarle V1749 of 570 Squadron, was airborne from Harwell at 01:28 hours. The remaining gliders were taken under tow by Albemarles of 295 and 570 Squadrons from Harwell, Albemarles of 296 and 297 Squadrons from Brize Norton, and Halifaxes of 298 and 644 Squadrons from Tarrant Rushton. Whilst the combinations formed up over England, the engineers of 5th Parachute Brigade were still working on clearing four landing strips at the LZ in Normandy.

Five of the combinations turned back for a variety of reasons, but the rest pressed on, even though the weather was not good. As soon as they crossed the enemy coast they came under anti-aircraft fire; some had already been fired on in mid-Channel by the Navy, and twenty-five gliders were damaged. Eventually fifty-seven Horsas and two Hamilcars reached the LZ, and despite low cloud and a crosswind, most landed without too much difficulty. The Halifax tugs went on to bomb various targets, partly as a diversion to suggest to the Germans that the aircraft were simply a routine bombing force. Overall casualties in this phase of the operation were considered to be reasonably light with the loss of seven tugs; the highest casualty rate was amongst the glider pilots, with thirty-four being killed (17 per cent of the total involved). Nevertheless, they had delivered sufficient men and material to the LZ to ensure that it could be held until the arrival of ground forces from the seaborne assault.

In addition to the glider losses, some eight towing aircraft were lost: five Stirlings, one Albemarle, one Halifax and two Dakotas.

The final British part of the airborne assault took place on the evening of the 6th when, under Operation *Mallard*, 256 combinations

*British paratroops prepare to board Stirlings.*

took off from seven airfields in southern England en route to Normandy. The first aircraft airborne were Dakotas of 271 Squadron from Down Ampney at 18:40 hours towing Horsa gliders; over the next one hour and twenty minutes the remainder of the force, comprising thirty Hamilcar and 226 Horsa gliders, took to the air behind their tows, these comprising seventy-four Dakotas from 48 and 271 Squadrons (Down Ampney), 512 Squadron (Broadwell) and 575 Squadron (Broadwell); sixty-nine Stirlings from 190 and 620 Squadrons (Fairford), and 196 and 299 Squadrons (Keevil); eighty-one Albemarles from 296 and 297 Squadrons (Brize Norton), and 295 and 570 Squadrons (Harwell); and finally, thirty-two Halifaxes from 298 and 644 Squadrons (Tarrant Rushton). Out of this air armada one Horsa crashed on take-off, three broke their tows en route, and three were forced to ditch in the Channel; the remaining gliders, including all the Hamilcars with their precious heavy weapons and armoured vehicles, made it safely down to the LZs, the first landings taking place around 20:51 hours. A further fifty RAF Dakotas undertook supply-dropping missions. The overall air escort for British and American missions comprised 110 Spitfires, seventy-two RAF and ninety-eight American P-51 Mustangs, and ninety-six P-47 Thunderbolts. Losses in this second phase were thirteen aircraft: nine Dakotas, two Albemarles, one Halifax and one Stirling – which, considering the scale of the attack and the intensity of flak, were surprisingly light.

**The American Operation**

The American plan was similar, reflecting the same desire to secure routes away from the beaches to ensure that Allied forces would not be trapped in a confined area and vulnerable to counter-attack or bombardment: 'Both airborne divisions were to land by parachute and glider in advance of the main seaborne landings, seize ground and hold it to protect the flanks of the seaborne troops, and also to prevent German reinforcements reaching the

*Horsa gliders of IXth Troop Carrier Command, 6 June.*
(US National Archives)

invasion beaches.' There were four main operations planned for D-Day, and a further two for D plus One:

1. Operations *Detroit* and *Elmira* – 82nd Airborne
2. Operations *Chicago* and *Keokuk* – 101st Airborne
3. Operations *Galveston* and *Hackensack* – 82nd Airborne (7 June)

As with the British operation, the plan was for pathfinder forces to drop in advance and mark the DZs and LZs. The first group was airborne at 00:20 hours, but on arrival in the target area could not identify the precise locations and so the initial parties of the main force had to drop without the markers. This was to lead to a wide dispersal of both paratroop and glider forces, often with severe consequences in the face of concerted opposition; however, the wide dispersal also caused confusion amongst German commanders, as reports came in of paratroops dropping 'throughout Normandy'.

Under *Detroit* the 82nd was to take the town of Ste-Mère-Église, secure bridgeheads over the Merderet River, and give cover to the invasion beaches. But the dropping of the 82nd

onto the town has entered legend, as the unit suffered fearful casualties.

At 01:19 hours the *Chicago* main force of the 101st Airborne, in fifty-two Waco gliders, left Aldermaston behind C-47 Skytrain tugs of the 434th Troop Carrier Group (TCG) for the target area at the village of Hiesville, 10 miles (16km) inland; of these, forty-nine made it to the approximate area, the initial landings taking place around 04:10 hours; of the other three, one was shot down, one broke its tow, and one landed 8 miles (13km) away. However, it was a scattered landing, only six landing on the LZ, and in many instances the landings caused heavy casualties as gliders smashed into obstructions. Despite the problems, sufficient troops had assembled by early afternoon to achieve the primary objective of seizing the causeways.

Meanwhile, the 82nd's *Detroit* operation was airborne at 01:59 hours, with fifty-two Wacos behind C-47s of the 437th Troop Carrier Group from Ramsbury. Of these, only twenty-three landed on, or near, the LZ, again with heavy losses, whilst of the remaining gliders, fourteen either broke their tows or were released early. During these operations the 9th Troop Carrier Command lost sixteen aircraft in addition to glider losses.

*Most gliders were damaged in landing and would never be used again.* (US National Archives)

The same 474th FG historical record quoted above is equally dramatic when talking of the first returning aircraft, comparing the ragged formations with the neat wingtip-to-wingtip formations witnessed only a few hours previously:

> The flights coming back strung lights all over the sky in sharp contrast to the perfect wingtip patterns of outgoing craft. Warmwell was the first stop on the way home for crippled aircraft. Here they brought in their wounded and dead. They landed aircraft that by every law of man and God could not be flying. They flew back looking like sieves, trailing control cables and flopping ailerons, engines coughing and flaming, flat tires making a soggy slapping sound on the runway. Yet they came back. The dead man's ship circled the airfield in an eerie halocast of red and white flares. It groped down through the darkness and hit the runway. The big ship turned on the runway, wheeled towards us … it suddenly stopped. 'Doc' Collins was talking to the co-pilot. His voice was soft and calm. 'He's dead,' he said matter of factly, 'I didn't have time to examine the wound too closely, but it was a big chest wound.' One of the crew members came up. 'We had to go around twice, two paratroops wouldn't jump. We had to go round again for them. We talked to 'em. One guy said the slipstream was too strong. I helped to shove him out the door. The German fire was coming up thick as hell. Just after the last man jumped, the pilot caught it.' His face was bitter. 'If those goddam guys had jumped it wouldn't have happened.' He must have been the first casualty to return … this dead man.

Amidst all the facts and figures of sorties flown, bombs dropped and so on, it is the human aspects such as this one story that are often lost.

The first of the reinforcement missions was airborne at 18:48 hours, fifty gliders (thirty-six Horsa and fourteen Waco) from Greenham Common, and twenty-six gliders (eighteen Horsa and eight Waco) from Ramsbury, this comprising the two waves of the 82nd Airborne with troops, heavy weapons and supplies. C-47s for Operation *Elmira* were provided by the 438th and 434th Troop Carrier Groups respectively. The first wave landed at 21:04 hours and was met with intense small-arms fire, as part of the LZ was still in enemy hands; the second wave, arriving about thirty minutes later, had the same problem but suffered most of its casualties through heavy landings.

Operation *Keokuk* to reinforce the 101st was on a smaller scale, thirty-two Horsa gliders leaving Aldermaston at 18:30 hours behind C-47s of the 434th TCG. The main payload comprised the divisional staff and various support units, and all but two of the gliders made it to within a reasonable distance of the LZ. Losses amounted to six Dakotas.

Additional supply drops took place for the 82nd (*Freeport*) and 101st (*Memphis*). The *Freeport* mission went wrong from the start, when low cloud and rain squalls developed over central England shortly after take off. Of the 206 aircraft despatched, fifty-three returned early and landed at various airfields, and about 140 dropped their supplies near the DZ 1 mile (1.5km) north-east of Ste-Mère-Église. Only one of the 'lost' aircraft crashed in the UK; the other twelve were presumed lost to anti-aircraft fire, although a number were thought to have ditched in the Channel (*see* box left).

The airborne assault missions were provided with fighter escort, and typical of this was a mission flown by the 363rd FG. This unit sent fifty Mustangs on a transport and glider escort mission to Ste-Mère-Église:

Up 21:03, 6 June; down 00:30, 7 June. R/V with transports about 8 miles [13km] south of Bill of Portland [*sic*] at 22:05, fighters at 3,000ft [915m], transports at 600ft [180m]. Escorted to area over Ste-Mère-Église where gliders were released,

## American Airborne Operation

| Mission/unit | Troop Carrier unit | No of aircraft | | |
|---|---|---|---|---|
| | | SENT | GLIDERS | LOSSES |
| Pathfinders | PF Group | 20 | 0 | 1 |
| *Albany* 101st | 50th/53rd TCW | 432 | 0 | 12 |
| *Boston* 82nd | 52nd TCW | 368 | 0 | 8 |
| *Chicago* 101st | 534th TCG | 51 | 51 | 1 |
| *Detroit* 82nd | 437th TCG | 52 | 52 | 1 |
| *Keokuk* 101st | 434th TCG | 32 | 32 | 0 |
| *Elmira* 82nd | 53rd TCW | 176 | 176 | 6 |
| *Galveston* 82nd | 434th/435t TCG | 99 | 99 | 0 |
| *Hackensack* 82nd | 439th/441st TCG | 100 | 100 | 0 |
| *Freeport* 82nd | 52nd TCW | 206 | 0 | 13 |
| *Memphis* 101st | 50th TCW | 118 | 0 | 4 |

**Total sorties** 1,656, of which 822 were para-drop, 324 supply drop, 510 aircraft with gliders (395 CG-4A plus 115 Horsa); losses forty-six aircraft (2.78 per cent).

BELOW: *Gliders on a partially built airstrip in northern France, 15 June.* (US National Archives)

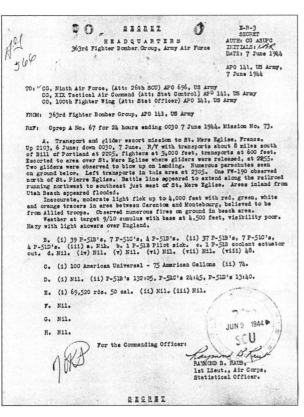

*363rd Fighter Group Oprep for 6 June, detailing the group's escort mission for the paratroop and glider operation to Ste-Mère-Église.*

at 22:55. Two gliders were observed to blow up on landing. Numerous parachutes seen on ground below. Left transports in this area at 23:05. One Fw 190 observed north of St Pierre Église. Battle line appeared to extend along the railroad running northwest to southeast just west of Ste-Mère-Église. Areas inland from Utah beach appeared flooded. Inaccurate light flak up to 4,000ft [1,220m] with red, green, white and orange tracers in area between Carenton and Montebourg, believed to be from Allied troops. Observed numerous fires on ground in beach area. Weather at target 9/10 cumulus with base at 4,500ft [1,370m], visibility poor.

(Oprep 363rd FBG)

The group had a similar escort mission airborne at 05:56 on 7 June, but they failed to link up with the transport on the outbound route. Flying the planned route they eventually picked them up on the return leg, and 'several stragglers were escorted in'.

We have now run a little ahead of ourselves in the timetable of events, and must return to the beaches.

**Battering the Defenders**

After the first waves of heavy and medium bombers cleared their targets, it was the turn of naval gunfire and the fighter-bombers to batter the defenders. The bombardment ships were to be on station at 05:00 hours, having moved into position under the cover of a smoke-screen laid by RAF Bostons. These ships were capable of laying down a massive amount of firepower, the accuracy and effectiveness of which was down to the aircraft of the Air Spotting Pool (ASP), a specialist organization based at Lee-on-Solent and comprising four Fleet Air Arm Seafire squadrons of No. 3 Naval Wing (808, 885, 886, 897), five RAF squadrons (26, 63, 2, 268, 144 – although the latter three of these were only available up to midday), plus a number of Spitfires operated by US Naval Squadron VCS-7. These latter had been recruited in May from naval pilots in the UK, mostly ex-Kingfisher pilots, who were then given a rapid Spitfire conversion course at Middle Wallop, followed by an even shorter course detailing shoot procedures.

Aircraft usually operated in pairs, and pilots were given either details of two pre-arranged targets to engage, or a specific area in which to look for targets of opportunity. The majority of sorties, certainly in the early phase, consisted of counter-battery work against coastal guns, field artillery and flak positions. Aircraft of the ASP flew over 400 sorties during the day on 135 shoots, about 50 per cent being considered successful, many of the others being aborted due to problems with communications or, in a few instances, lack of suitable

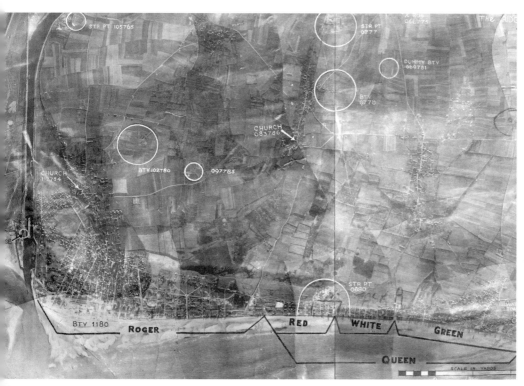

Target photographs used by 440 Squadron for briefing their missions for the morning of 6 June. Task A, with a 'time on target' of 07:20, was strongpoint 0880 – marked in red chinagraph on the photo. (440 Squadron)

targets. They performed their vital task for the loss of seven aircraft.

The first waves of fighter-bombers were given pre-arranged targets to hit at H-Hour, the majority being on or just behind the beaches, and all based upon the latest air reconnaissance information. However, some squadrons were instructed to check in with the relevant Head-quarters' ship to see if a higher priority target had been detected. Each assault beach was allo-cated an HQ ship:

### Eastern Area

| Beach | HQ Ship | Call-sign |
| --- | --- | --- |
| Juno | HMS *Hilary* | Herod |
| Sword | HMS *Largs* | Boatman |
| Gold | HMS *Bulolo* | Baldwin |

### Western Area

| | | |
| --- | --- | --- |
| Omaha | USS *Ancon* | Bullett |
| Utah | USS *Bayfield* | Gimlet |

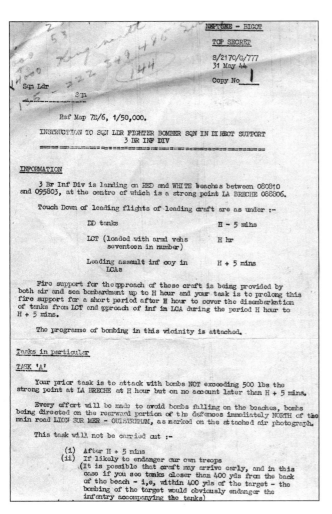

Sqn Ldr
Sn

Ref Map 7E/6, 1/50,000.

INSTRUCTION TO SQN LDR FIGHTER BOMBER SQN IN DIRECT SUPPORT
3 BR INF DIV

INFORMATION

3 Br Inf Div is landing on RED and WHITE beaches between 080810 and 095803, at the centre of which is a strong point LA BRECHE 088806.

Touch Down of leading flights of leading craft are as under :-

| DD tanks | H – 5 mins |
| LCT (loaded with armd vehs seventeen in number) | H hr |
| Leading assault inf coy in LCAs | H + 5 mins |

Fire support for the approach of these craft is being provided by both air and sea bombardment up to H hour and your task is to prolong this fire support for a short period after H hour to cover the disembarkation of tanks from LCT and approach of inf in LCA during the period H hour to H + 5 mins.

The programme of bombing in this vicinity is attached.

Tasks in particular

TASK 'A'

Your prior task is to attack with bombs NOT exceeding 500 lbs the strong point at LA BRECHE at H hour but on no account later than H + 5 mins.

Every effort will be made to avoid bombs falling on the beaches, bombs being directed on the rearward portion of the defences immediately NORTH of the main road LION SUR MER – OUISTREHAM, as marked on the attached air photograph.

This task will not be carried out :-

    (i)   After H + 5 mins
    (ii)  If likely to endanger our own troops
         (It is possible that craft may arrive early, and in this case if you see tanks closer than 400 yds from the back of the beach – i,e, within 400 yds of the target – the bombing of the target would obviously endanger the infantry accompanying the tanks)

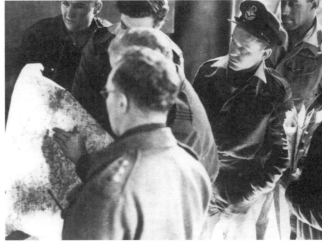

ABOVE: *RAF pilots gather round a map to discuss the next army support targets.*

LEFT: *Extract of the briefing instruction for 440 Squadron's mission of 6 June.*

*Mitchell in action over Normandy.*

The contact parties or army tentacles/US air support parties went ashore with the assault brigades/US regimental combat teams of the initial waves, the intention being that they could radio for air support from on-call aircraft. Such requests were sent to the HQ ship that would then relay it, via 21st Army Group G (Air) at Portsmouth, to Advanced HQ AEAF for analysis and allocation of resources. It might sound a long-winded procedure, but the theory was that it would be a maximum of two hours from a request being made, to the air attack being carried out. To the soldier in the field facing an enemy pillbox this could be an eternity, but in the overall scheme of air–sea–land co-ordination it was a necessary routine. Later in the campaign the technique would change to that of a cab-rank of fighter-bombers that could respond in minutes.

All Allied land forces were meant to display recognition markers to prevent friendly air attack; unfortunately, in the confusion of battle these were sometimes lost or forgotten, and casualties were incurred. With clearance to attack any enemy movement, or suspected enemy movement not displaying recognition markers, the fighter-bombers harassed every road in Normandy. The 2nd TAF's medium bombers were tasked to harass enemy road and rail movement, and to destroy/disrupt movement through road and rail choke-points. The role of the three Mitchell squadrons of No. 139 Wing at Dunsfold was typical, the general instruction having been expressed in Operational Order No. 3: '… to cause the maximum delay to the movement by road and rail, by enemy forces at night, in the area prescribed … Lessay-Caen-Lisieux-Argentan-Domfont-Fougères-Avranches… any movement is to be attacked whenever seen in the area.'

For the early hours of 6 June, each of the squadrons had a specific target. Running towards their target of a road/rail crossing north of Argentan, the twelve Mitchells of 180 Squadron found weather conditions worse than forecast; nevertheless, eight aircraft managed to identify and bomb the target. Meanwhile, the twelve aircraft of 320 Squadron were having great

difficulty in finding their road bridge over the Dives river, and almost total cloud cover led to this target being aborted. The final wing operation was that of 98 Squadron's eleven Mitchells to a road defile south of Thury-Harcourt; here, five aircraft found and bombed the target, whilst the other six went to the secondary target of Conde-sur-Vire airfield, although only one actually made an attack. The thoughts of one RAF crewman were included in a press broadcast later that day:

> We're going across to bomb a target that is a railway bridge, which may help those good fellows down below in those boats … every little bit that the RAF can do to help is going to mean something. We're just going in to drop our bombs: it's a very tense moment – just the dawn of the moment when our troops are going in on the beaches.

In the British sector, twelve squadrons of Typhoons were tasked with attacking strongpoints, beach defences, batteries and HQs at H-Hour, the intention being to keep the enemy in his bunkers as the initial assault troops hit the beaches. Typically, No. 146 Wing was tasked

*Omaha beach, D-Day.*
(US National Archives)

*Whilst the Typhoon is best remembered for operating with RPs, the bomb-armed 'Bombphoons' were equally active.*

against a tank concentration area near Bayeux, claiming four tanks destroyed and five damaged, whilst No. 121 Wing attacked gun batteries overlooking Omaha beach.

Hitting the troops in the front lines was only one element of the fighter-bomber plan; an equally important task was to keep the enemy commanders confused, and what better way than attacking HQs and communications sites. Many such locations were given as pre-planned targets. At 07:45 hours, eight Typhoon bombers attacked a HQ complex at Ste Croix-Grand-Tonne (Caen) with reasonable results; another HQ, at Meauffe Château, St Lô, was attacked by RP Typhoons an hour or so later. Numerous other installations were attacked on an opportunity basis, and great confusion was caused – the German 'fog of war' was very much a result of Allied air power, and critical command decisions were delayed or made in error.

Air power had thus played three distinct direct parts in the initial assault phase: bombardment by the medium/heavy bombers, naval gunfire spotting and close support. What effect did this have on the first phase of landings?

On Sword beach the plan worked well, and the troops of the 3rd British Division faced

little opposition from the German 716th Division (and 711th Division on the eastern flank). The defences appeared to be stunned, as intended, although they quickly recovered as the assault forces raced to seize their objectives. A few strongpoints came to life again and could have caused serious problems but, fortunately, enough tanks had made it ashore to provide the necessary firepower. The air assault had, however, caused sufficient disruption and uncertainty to keep the 21st Panzer Division in its positions around Caen. Although this formation was to cause serious difficulties to the British sector in subsequent days, it played no part in the initial phase.

At Gold the Typhoons failed to neutralize the strongpoint on the left flank at Le Hamel, although some damage had been caused. Troops of the 50th Division were faced with a strong part of the Atlantic Wall defences manned by the 352nd Division, at Le Hamel, and the 716th Division (a poor quality formation). It was unfortunate that the B-17s had also missed their aiming points, the bombs falling too far inland. By the time the assault waves hit the beaches the defences were almost fully manned, and casualties rose in the face of

*Marauder over one of the landing beaches.* (US National Archives)

determined opposition. Without firepower the strongpoints at Le Hamel could not be taken, there was no air control party to call down an air attack, and the situation was eventually saved by a solitary tank!

Of the British-sector beaches, most confusion occurred at Juno, where the Canadian troops were late in landing, thus giving the defenders time in which to partially recover. Although this beach was defended by the second-rate 716th Division, they were strongly entrenched and supported by artillery, and took a heavy toll of the landing craft as they approached the beaches. However, the 3rd Division fire-control teams were able to call up air and naval firepower to counter the artillery to give just enough breathing space for them to achieve a foothold.

It was a mixed story in the western, American, sector. At Utah the air bombardment by Marauders and fighter-bombers had worked well, and the assault troops were able to achieve their objectives with little opposition. Here the

4th Infantry Division faced two low-grade German units – the 709th and 243rd – both of whom were already engaged with chasing American airborne forces. The major difficulty was that the initial waves landed in the wrong place, although this was soon corrected. Severe flooding of the hinterland forced the advancing troops to use the causeways, and these soon became choked with men and vehicles – an easy target if German air power had been a player, and a prime example of how much the Allies relied upon, and had confidence in, their air superiority.

However, at Omaha it was a different story. This beach was to see the bloodiest action of the day when a combination of stronger-than-expected German defences, manned by the first-rate 352nd Division, relatively ineffective bombing and difficult landing conditions in rough seas, meant that the men of the 1st and 29th Infantry Divisions faced concerted and effective German opposition. Those troops who made it ashore were caught on the beach because the limited number of exits were dominated by German strongpoints, and it took some while and many casualties until these were neutralized. 'Bloody Omaha' cost 3,000 Americans killed or wounded, and was a salutary indication of what could have happened if the assault phase, and its air campaign, had been less well planned and executed.

Overall it was mixed fortunes for the initial assault; at most beaches the problems were no worse than anticipated, and the defences, whilst severe, had been sufficiently weakened. There was no major interference by the heavy coastal guns, the guns that could have wrecked the entire invasion, and on those beaches where the defences caused particular problems this was often because the assault troops were late, thus allowing the defenders time to recover from the air bombardment. The skies over the battlefield remained dominated by Allied air power, and many squadrons were on their second, or in some cases, third mission by early afternoon.

Just after midday, at 12:38 hours, four RP Typhoons attacked the radar site at Le Havre, although from late morning onwards, most fighter-bomber tasking involved armed recce –

often referred to as tactical 'Rhubarbs' – to search out road and rail movement. Suitable targets were passed to one of the forward air-control units, who would then allocate attacking aircraft; this would invariably be the formation that had reported the target, although sometimes the task was passed to another on-call formation that had more suitable weaponry.

Roving Typhoons were responsible for one of the most devastating attacks of the day when aircraft from No. 123 Wing spotted German armour moving along the roads towards Caen. This was Panzer Lehr Division, and despite objections from its commander, Lieutenant General Bayerlein, it had been ordered to move by daylight. As the Typhoons moved to attack they found conditions ideal: good weather, no enemy fighters and, for once, poor and unco-ordinated flak defences. Such a promising target was too good to waste, and it was attacked by relays of aircraft throughout the daylight hours, an attack that was renewed the following day. During one of the attacks the Typhoons of 183 Squadron were bounced by Bf 109s and had to jettison their bombs; nevertheless, three aircraft were quickly shot down. Flying Officer Taylor (R8973), Flight Lieutenant Evans

*Coastal radar station under attack on D-Day.*

*Interpretation of the thousands of reconnaissance and target photographs and the preparation of intelligence reports was one of many behind-the-scenes tasks that played an important role.*

BELOW: *With its 20mm cannon and RP armament, the Typhoon was one of the most effective ground-attack types.*

(MN432), Flying Officer Gee (MN478) and all three pilots were killed.

Total losses to Panzer Lehr amounted to five Mk IV tanks, eighty-four self-propelled guns/ armoured personnel carriers, forty fuel bowsers, and ninety other vehicles; added to this was the psychological trauma to inexperienced soldiers from such an aerial onslaught. However, the low loss rate amongst tanks confirmed the view that the RP was not an ideal weapon against such targets – it was difficult to aim and required extensive practice. One analysis suggested that it required 308 RPs to kill one tank! However, if the squadrons had been given more time and appropriate training targets, this average could have been greatly improved. Many squadrons, of course, did achieve better results than this average.

General Bayerlein was captured and interrogated on 4 May 1945, and the report of this interrogation includes numerous references to the problems caused by Allied air power:

In Normandy, railheads were much further than 150km [90 miles] to the rear, due to the destruction of railway sidings and lines in the heart of the

*Thunderbolt (note the shadow of the aircraft on the right) strafing a lone vehicle; daytime movement on roads was very hazardous, and many senior officers, including Rommel, fell victim to Allied fighter aircraft.*
(US National Archives)

combat area. Troop movements could not be carried out in daytime when the weather was favourable for flying. Movements were therefore always dependent on the weather. It was no longer possible to fix a definite time for a movement. Nevertheless if marches had to be carried out, they were very expensive in casualties and material. Necessary night marches required more time than day marches. No long distances could be covered during the short summer nights. All troop movements were, therefore, delayed and rendered very difficult by Allied fighters so that Headquarters were unable to make any definite time calculations and troops often arrived at the decisive place too late.

The general also made the point that the long distance from railheads, and the need to detour around obstructions, meant increased use of fuel, a resource that was in short supply.

It was a similar story with the American fighter-bomber units. Dive-bombing was the most accurate way to deliver the standard bombs, but it required training and practice. The P-47 units tended to use this technique against static permanent targets (such as bridges) whilst the standard fighter-bomber delivery against most other targets was a level or shallow-dive attack. The level first-pass attack was the least accurate but had the advantage of minimum exposure to the defences; however, there were added problems if inadequate arming time was allowed for the weapon if released from too low (thus giving a higher percentage of unexploded bombs) plus the possibility of self-damage from bombs that did explode. The Thunderbolts employed a variety of other bombs, fragmentation weapons being very effective against personnel and soft-skinned (rather than armoured) vehicles. They also used a rocket-tube system with three rockets mounted under each wing.

The US VIIIth Bomber Command flew three more operations during the day, all with the task of keeping German reinforcements away from the beach-head areas. The first of these took place as the initial waves that had attacked coastal defences were returning to England: 508 bombers, mainly B-24s, were airborne to attack towns and villages on main roads to the south and south-west of Caen, to create road blocks; however, weather conditions were poor and only thirty-seven B-24s attacked a target, Argentan, using pathfinder techniques. The afternoon missions involved seventy-one B-24s going to Caen, where fifty-six managed to complete attacks, dropping 156 tons of bombs, and 738 bombers, of which 362

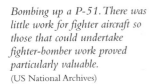

*Bombing up a P-51. There was little work for fighter aircraft so those that could undertake fighter-bomber work proved particularly valuable.*
(US National Archives)

*Fragmentation bombs on a P-47.* (US National Archives)

*Rocket installation under the wings of a P-47; the combination of weapons (bombs and guns) and the rugged nature of the Thunderbolt made it an ideal ground-attack aircraft.* (US National Archives)

RIGHT: *Under-fuselage bomb racks with a variety of bombs.* (US National Archives)

were B-17s, attacking targets in the Laval area and, again, the road junctions around Argentan. In continuing poor weather, 553 aircraft carried out attacks, although the assessment of results was only 'fair'.

The medium bombers of the 9th Air Force were also tasked against towns and villages that afternoon, forty-five Bostons attacking Carentan at 14:30 hours, followed by twenty-four Marauders to Falaise at 15:20 hours, and an

hour later, seventy-three Marauders to Caen, the latter attack resulting in the loss of one aircraft.

This latter series of missions was a result of concern at 21st Army Group HQ that enemy armour was still able to move towards the beach areas because not all the vital bridges had been destroyed. If substantial numbers of German tanks appeared on the battlefield at this critical juncture, then the entire invasion was in jeopardy. Initial plans to attack the major road routes at St Lô, Vire, Coutances, Conde, Argentan, Lisieux, Caen, Thury-Harcourt and Pontaubault using medium bombers had to be amended, as bad weather seemed likely to prevent success. Low cloud meant that the only possible air operation likely to be effective was that by low-flying fighter-bombers; so, in the area outlined above, Typhoon patrols were ordered to cover every major route, whilst in bordering areas this same task was to be performed by P-51s and P-47s. The P-47s also mounted offensive patrols in the immediate beach-head area looking for troublesome enemy strongpoints, working with control teams on the ground and attacking a number of targets of opportunity. On 139 sorties of this sort in the late afternoon period, some 60 tons of bombs were dropped, and two aircraft were lost to anti-aircraft fire. Such bombing and strafing missions were given poker names by the VIIIth, such as *Stud*, *Royal Flush* and *Full House*.

An evening sweep by forty-eight Typhoons and fifteen P-38 Lightnings in the Caen–Argentan–Lisieux–Bayeux areas paid dividends, the aircraft attacking a wide range of targets with bomb, rocket and cannon, claiming the

destruction of twenty-three armoured vehicles, one signal box, a variety of soft-skinned transport and a number of sections of railway line! Three Typhoons and one P-38 failed to return.

This patrol routine did not prevent all enemy road movement, but it certainly caused many delays, and forced the German commanders to disperse and camouflage. The need to protect road moves led to the employment of a small number of defensive fighter patrols by the *Luftwaffe.*

In the late afternoon of 6 June, nine Typhoons of 266 Squadron were airborne out of Needs Oar Point, one of them being flown by Sgt Edward Donne; in his words:

I took off with eight other Typhoons at about 17:00 hours on an armed recce, looking for tanks in the area SE of Caen. When we were about 25km [15 miles] south of Caen we saw a column of German transport and bombed it. When I dropped my bomb there was an explosion and I went up with it. The engine was still running and we carried out another attack, but when returning home about five minutes later I had no other option but to bale out. This was about 18:00 hours. I landed in a field 5km [3 miles] west of Caen. I stuffed my parachute,

Mae West and gauntlets into the hedge, and ran north for about 2 miles. I then hid between two hedges till about 20:30 hours. Whilst there I saw four German tanks going south. Some of our own aircraft were dive-bombing a wood next to me.

Sgt Donne continued to move north and tried to elicit help from two French civilians, who refused to get involved. He carried on, and at dusk saw a number of Sherman tanks, the commander of which sent him by motorcycle to the HQ area. Taken by jeep to the beach-head, he left Normandy on an LCT the following night.

During the late afternoon, P-47s of the 9th Air Force made two accurate attacks on bridges: eighteen aircraft attacked and damaged a road bridge at Vire, whilst a short time later, thirty-six aircraft attacked the rail bridge at Oissel (Rouen) and demolished the southern span.

Other sweeps by Spitfire and P-47 formations along the coast later in the evening failed to produce any result in the air or on the ground.

The majority of the evening effort by the 9th Air Force was against rail targets and coastal defences. At 17:30 hours, a force of forty-eight P-47s attacked coastal defences at Cherbourg; thirty minutes later two formations of

*Typhoon of 193 Squadron operating from Needs Oar Point, as part of No. 146 Wing – one of the largest wings, with four typhoon squadrons.*

*Vehicles are starting to make their way off the beach as more landing craft arrive; bomb craters are visible all along the dune line.* (US National Archives)

Marauders attacked Caen (seventy-three air-craft) and Trouville (thirty-eight aircraft); whilst sometime later a larger force of P-47s (ninety-nine aircraft) returned to the coastal defence sites at Cherbourg. Between 21:00 and 21:13 hours, five attacks were made against rail targets in the assault area, Marauders attacking Amiens and a rail bridge at Caen, and Bostons going against Abancourt, Serqueux and Longpré-les-Corps-Saints (Abbeville). Each formation comprised around thirty-six aircraft, and total losses were four Bostons.

### Fighter Operations
For the fighter squadrons D-Day was hectic but fairly unproductive, the day's events being summarized in the Fighter Command intelligence summary:

> No major encounters took place throughout the first day of the launching of the invasion of Normandy. Enemy air activity was negligible. It is estimated that both escorting and protective fighters over the assault areas and defensive fighters over France did not exceed 50 to 70 [enemy] sorties.

The AEAF squadrons and US VIIIth Fighter Command had a somewhat busier day, but certainly not the great air battles that Leigh-Mallory had predicted (and planned for). The Allied expectation had been somewhat different, the directive issued to the fighter forces stating that:

> The intention of the British and American fighter forces is to attain and maintain an air situation that will assure freedom of action for our forces without effective interference by the German Air Force, and to render maximum air protection to the land and naval forces in the common object of assaulting, securing and developing the bridgehead.

SHAEF anticipated a major German air reaction along the lines of that encountered over Dieppe in 1942, and although the air campaign had spent much effort on attacking German airfields and the fighter control system,

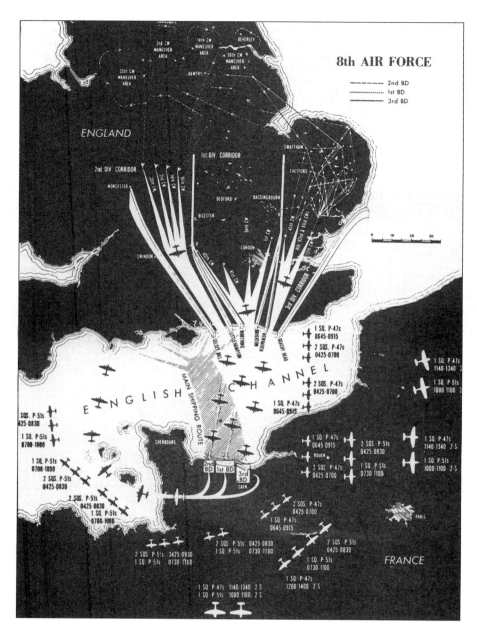

*The overall 8th Air Force air plan for D-Day.*

the fighter plan for D-Day was complex and comprehensive.

The fighter boys were prepared for a hard fight. Lieutenant Colonel Don Blakeslee, commander of the 4th Fighter Group, briefed his pilots at 03:00 hours on 6 June, and left them in no doubt as to what he expected when he said: 'I am prepared to lose the whole Group.' In the event he almost did, as they came close to colliding with a P-47 Group in bad weather!

The American Fighter Commands provided the bulk of the escort and high cover patrols throughout the day, the low cover patrols being provided by RAF Spitfires. The plan was to provide a screen of fighters around the entire invasion area, the first squadrons to be in position by

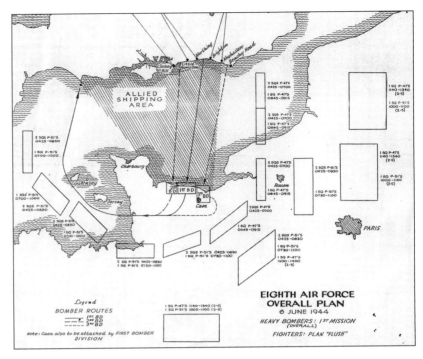

*The overall 8th Air Force plan for 6 June. (USAAF)*

*Naval gunners were responsible for shooting down a number of Allied aircraft.*

04:25 hours. This fighter screen was to be in operation for what was considered to be the 'peak operational period' from 05:00 to 10:00 hours, and then at two further periods during the day; fixed patrol lines were given to the P-51s and P-47s of the VIIIth Fighter Command. At the end of each patrol, once relieved by the next group of fighters, the pilots were clear to attack ground targets. Should enemy aircraft make it through the outer fighter screen, then in the actual beach area additional high cover was provided by three squadrons of P-47s, with six squadrons of Spitfires acting as low 'beach cover'. Meanwhile, shipping cover over the invasion convoys and Normandy anchorages was provided by six P-38 groups, patrols to be

A 9th Air Force Mustang turns off the grass runway of an ALG.

of four-squadron strength, starting at 16:00 hours on 5 June. The reason for the choice of aircraft was the distinctive shape of the P-38, it being like no German aircraft, and thus it was hoped the naval gunners would leave it alone!

The problem of 'own goals' was the motivation behind the special identification marks on Allied aircraft, naval gunners having an established reputation for letting loose at almost any aircraft. Efforts to reduce this likelihood included not only the use of special markings and 'unique' aircraft (P-38), but also the attachment of members of the Royal Observer Corps (known as 'sea observers') to merchant ships within the Allied fleet. However, as the report by the Allied Naval C-in-C Expeditionary Force was to state:

> The SHAEF rules for restriction to flying and to AA fire are considered to have worked well, but unfortunately casualties to our own aircraft were caused by naval gunfire in the early stages of the operation, particularly in the US sector. Fire discipline and aircraft recognition in such a diverse fleet of ships and craft as was at any one time in the assault area was obviously extremely difficult to achieve; and the situation was much aggravated by the low cloud base that prevailed on most days which, by forcing aircraft to fly very low, gave the minimum of time for their recognition.

Despite efforts made to reduce the risks, the problem remained, and throughout June there were numerous references to friendly fire; on 22 June, Leigh-Mallory wrote a terse note to the Allied Naval Commander:

> You will appreciate that feelings run high not only in those squadrons which have lost pilots to naval action, but in the Service as a whole – a feeling which absence of apology from those responsible for firing has not helped to dissipate … it is clear that the only answer to this problem is a higher standard of aircraft recognition, a better signalling system between ships and better discipline amongst ships' gunners.

In theory, anti-aircraft fire was banned by night because of night fighter operations; however, a number of these aircrew found time to admire the multi-coloured pyrotechnics that lit up the night!

The P-51 Mustangs of the 355th Fighter Group had a quiet first *Full House* mission, taking off at 02:51 hours led by Lieutenant Colonel Dix:

> For the first mission of D-Day, the 355th Fighter Group was divided into two parts, 'A' Group composed of the 354th and 357th Fighter Squadrons, and 'B' Group consisting of the 358th Squadron. Actually, this first mission of the Big Day turned

*This is a particularly good shot to illustrate the size and rugged nature of the P-47 Thunderbolt.*
(US National Archives)

out to be a Milk Run, for neither division of the Group saw any enemy planes. The 'A' Group patrolled an area, labelled 'M', in the forefront of a giant U-shaped shield behind which the mammoth ground and heavy bomber operations were taking place. The geographical co-ordinates were 4810N–0020E to 4830N–0020E to 4850N–0100E to 4030N–0100E. This area was southwest of Paris. Handicapped by weather and the darkness, the Group was soon split up into sections and flights. It was impossible to orientate the outfit definitely over its assigned area. They flew through it, around it, and around Paris. However, since the Group was flying under Type 16 control and were rather freelancing it, they could still have taken care of any bandits reported in their vicinity. All told, it seems that not one member of the *Luftwaffe* was on hand to offer resistance to the first phase of the invasion.

Control of Allied fighter aircraft operating over the ships and beaches was exercised by Ventnor ground-controlled interception (GCI) site, for the area (William) nearest to the English coast, and by three fighter director tenders (FDTs). Of the latter, FDT 13 covered areas Victor, Yoke, X-Ray plus additional cover of William,

and was stationed in mid-Channel in the main shipping route; FDT 216 was responsible for low cover over the American beaches; and FDT 217, acting as the co-ordinating vessel under Air Commodore C. A. Bouchier, was stationed in the eastern area. The other elements of the air control network were the air operations centres on the various 'flagships' plus the HQ ships, although, as mentioned above, the primary role for these vessels was co-ordination of the close air support missions. The intention was for shore-based GCI to take over from FDT 217 as soon as possible.

In addition to the standing patrols outlined above, almost every other air mission – bombing and airborne assault – was given strong fighter escort. The total fighter strength of almost 2,000 aircraft was impressive, but the sheer number and scale of the tasks it was called upon to perform meant that units were heavily committed.

Other fighter units were given specific tasks. The P-47s of 405th Fighter Group were put under operational control of RAF Coastal Command to provide fighter cover for the anti-submarine patrols in the English Channel western approaches; the Mustangs of the RAF's 133 Wing at Coolham were on standby to provide similar cover in the eastern approaches. This latter unit was one element of the 'Pool of Readiness' squadrons, which also comprised five American fighter groups (354, 358, 362, 363 and 371, and a variety of RAF units), 122 Wing and 150 Wing, plus three squadrons each at Detling and Lympne (*see* Order of Battle appendix, page 159). As it became apparent that no real weak links existed in the air plan and that the requirement for a rapid reaction force to counter the GAF was not required, so these reserve units were fed into the battle. The all-important task of preventing German reconnaissance was given to the Spitfire XIVs of 91 and 322 Squadrons, along with the Spitfire VIIs of 124 Squadron. In addition, the Typhoons of 137 Squadron were allocated the standing task of *Channel Stop*.

At the planning stage it was considered that German aircraft posed a major offensive threat, and that airfields in England would be profitable targets. Each airfield, therefore, was required to maintain one section at high readiness for base defence. During the day these readiness aircraft were involved with a number of scrambles, the majority of which turned out to be spurious targets, or friendlies returning without suitable identification. This requirement and the decision to hold the 'Pool of Readiness' squadrons in the UK reduced significantly the tactical air assets available for the early hours of the assault. Some commentators, with the benefit of hindsight, have argued that every available aircraft should have been employed in the hours either side of H-Hour.

In his book, *The Big Show*, Pierre Clostermann, then with 602 Squadron, records an evening patrol:

> We flew along the Cotentin peninsula. There were fires all along the coast, and a destroyer surrounded by small boats was sinking near a little island. Our patrol zone was the area between Montebourg and Carentan. We were covering the 101st and 82nd American Airborne Divisions, while the 4th Division, which had just landed, marched on Ste-Mère-Église. We couldn't see much. A few houses were in flames. A few jeeps on the roads. The sky was full of American fighters, in pairs. They were wandering about rather haphazard, and showed a tendency to come and sniff at us from very close to; when they seemed too aggressive we showed our teeth and faced them. One Mustang coming out of a cloud actually fired a burst at Graham. Graham, whose shooting was as good as his temper was bad, opened fire on him, but luckily for the Mustang, he missed.

One reason for the lack of German air effort was the continued pressure being placed upon their airfields. However, from mid-afternoon onwards the *Luftwaffe* made a few sorties, usually tip-and-run attacks against either naval targets or troops coming ashore. German records detail no more than 100 offensive missions flown on this day. However, as soon as the location and scale of the invasion was clear, the German commanders attempted to move air reinforcements into pre-prepared bases. One such move was by III Gruppe Schlachtgeschwader 4 with their Fw 190s from southern France to bases at Laval and Tours. A round-about route was flown in an effort to avoid Allied fighter patrols, as each Fw 190 carried a mechanic in the cramped space behind the pilot's seat. Some formations were out of luck and were bounced by American fighters; at least five of the German aircraft were lost en route to their new bases. Of those that reached their new locations, some were active over the beach-heads later that afternoon, flying hit-and-run bombing attacks.

Most combats took place late in the day, the most successful being that of the 355th Fighter Group, which jumped a formation of Ju 87s and rapidly claimed fifteen of them. Two squadrons had taken off on a *Royal Flush* mission at 18:10 hours, and the first formation went to the area of Châteaudun:

> Then dropping through the clouds onto the deck, the Squadron sighted three trains in the Chartres

area. All flights fired, with the results that four oil cars were set afire and the other two trains were damaged. Four trucks were also damaged. At 21:15 in the Chartres-Dreux area approximately fifteen Ju 87s were encountered. In this encounter some of the enemy aircraft tried to crash-land in the open fields. This attempt accounts for the squadron's ground claims:

| | |
|---|---|
| Capt Marshal | one Ju 87 |
| Lt Fortier | one Ju 87 |
| Lt Perry | one Ju 87 |
| Lt Ray | one Ju 87 (shared with Lt Morris and Lt Floyd) |
| Lt Col Dix | one Ju 87 (plus one on the ground). |

The second formation fared even better, spotting a similar formation near Janville:

Flying in V formation of three-plane Vics, and going westward toward the beach-head and flying on the deck. The formation was bounced, with claims as listed below. Lt Douglas was hit by flak near Calais coming out and is missing in action:

| | |
|---|---|
| Capt Kelley | two Ju 87 |
| Lt Bernoske | one Ju 87 |
| Lt James | three Ju 87 |
| Lt Fuller | one Ju 87 plus one probable and one damaged |
| Lt Cotter | one Ju 87 |
| Capt Wilson | one Ju 87 damaged |
| Lt Minchow | one Ju 87 damaged |
| Squadron shared | one Ju87. |

Statistical summaries by the US VIIIth Fighter Command do not distinguish between defensive and offensive missions; the overall account for the day states:

| | |
|---|---|
| P-38 Lightning | 555 sorties, no losses |
| P-51 Mustang | 505 sorties, 22 missing |
| P-47 Thunderbolt | 287 sorties, 4 missing |

Loss rates are interesting, and reflect the employment of the various aircraft; the P-38s flew cover patrols and saw no action, whilst the other two types were engaged on a mix of fighter cover and ground attack. It was during the latter that aircraft were lost, primarily to anti-aircraft fire. The reason for the high loss rate of Mustangs was the unsuitability of this aircraft for ground-attack work; it had already been appreciated by the planners that the Mustang was not rugged enough for this task, the engine being particularly vulnerable to ground fire, whereas the Thunderbolt was a far more rugged aircraft. The Mustangs were certainly effective, and large numbers of targets were destroyed or damaged, but, as with the Spitfire, ground attack was not a role for which the aircraft was best suited. However, the need to have a maximum number of fighter-type aircraft operating against ground targets — and the desire of pilots to take on whatever targets they could find — kept the P-51s in this role.

The total claims made by the VIIIth's fighter pilots ran to twenty-six destroyed and eight damaged in the air, plus four destroyed and nine damaged in ground attacks. However, an alternative VIIIth Fighter Command statistic gives somewhat different figures, of nine destroyed and two damaged, for the loss of eleven aircraft — which does not fit with the claims of the 355th alone, or the losses mentioned above! As night fell, only one of the planned GCI sites was operational ashore, that in the British sector at Arromanches, and this undertook limited control of defensive fighter operations. Aircraft of No. 85 Group maintained constant patrols and made claims for twelve of the forty enemy aircraft (out of an estimated total of 175 enemy sorties that night) plotted in the beach-head area. Amongst these aircraft were specialist bombers of Fliegerkorps X using guided bombs, although on this occasion the bombers were unsuccessful. Other attacks were mounted by Fliegerkorps IX, which claimed no real successes but did lose aircraft to night fighters and to German flak units. According to Allied naval records, however, the German aircraft scored some success, hitting three ships and sinking one LST.

German attempts at moving air assets into the area had started almost as soon as the landings had been confirmed, and within thirty-six hours over 200 fighters had flown in from Germany, being taken from the Defence of the Reich, along with a number of torpedo and bomber aircraft. However, the Germans were now fighting a war on four fronts – Normandy, Italy, Russia and the Homeland (against the bomber offensive) – so there was little flexibility left to them in respect of transferring aircraft between theatres. And within weeks they would have yet another front on which to fight, when the Allies landed in southern France. Nevertheless, by 10 June, the *Luftwaffe* forces in this region reached a maximum strength of around 1,000 aircraft – though from that point on, as we shall see, the decline in numbers was steady and inevitable.

### Reconnaissance Missions

The PR units had provided hundreds of thousands of prints during the planning stages of *Overlord*; now it would be their task to keep the commanders informed of developments on and around the battlefield. Although every Allied aircraft would, in the course of making its mission report, provide intelligence data, it was the trained reconnaissance crews who, with visual reports and photographic confirmation, would be the key elements in trying to unravel the so-called 'fog of war' that pervaded every battlefield. But despite the best attempts of pilots to obtain photographs, Allied commanders were to complain of a lack of information.

'The success of any bombing policy depends upon our ability to acquire and interpret quickly and accurately a constant flow of photographs of our targets.' This official statement concerning the value, and problems, of air reconnaissance may sound somewhat obvious, but it does highlight both the integral nature of air recce in the overall air campaign, and the huge task performed behind the scenes by photographic interpreters and intelligence officers. It was essential for tactical recce information to be as near real-time as possible: more than a few hours old and it would be almost useless. Great reliance was placed upon the visual report made by the pilot, and initial action was often taken on this while the photographic interpretation was still under way; the whole operation became very slick, with the first prints being available within minutes of the film arriving. Mobile units were organized to take to the field with the squadrons, thus ensuring that rapid interpretation was available.

### Coastal Command Operations

Aircraft of Coastal Command continued their anti-submarine patrols in the expectation that the Germans would attempt to attack the flanks of the invasion fleet. Early on 6 June a number of U-boats were spotted on the surface to the south-west of Brest and making towards the invasion area. Although the Germans did not have a large surface fleet in this area, the few available destroyers did pose a threat, as did the rather larger number of fast-attack craft such as the 'E' boats. The potential of this type of ship against landing craft had been proven some time previously, when a small force of E-boats had attacked an amphibious landing training exercise off the coast of South Devon.

The squadrons of Nos 16 and 19 Groups, including attached Fleet Air Arm units, were poised for action from the early hours of D-Day, some units having moved to airfields further south to be nearer any potential action. But for most of them it was to be a day of waiting, and yet more waiting, as the 'great day' passed them by. Other squadrons flew armed patrols on the flanks of the invasion fleet, but saw little movement by enemy forces. However, when a force of three enemy destroyers was spotted heading from the

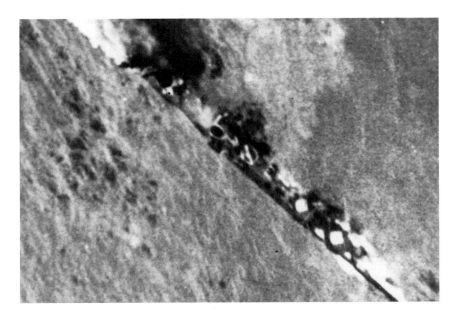

*A beached and burning German destroyer following an attack by Coastal Command Beaufighters.*

Gironde estuary towards the fleet, a strike force of Beaufighters, with Mosquito escort, was soon on the scene. Thirty Beaufighters, fourteen RP aircraft from 404 Squadron, and sixteen cannon-firers as anti-flak from 248 Squadron, were led into the attack by Wing Commander Lumsden.

One destroyer was damaged, and all three made for the nearest port. The intense flak had, however, caused some damage to the Allied aircraft, and one Beaufighter was forced to ditch on the way home and another had to make a wheels-up landing at Davidstow Moor. The Mosquito escort claimed one Ju 88. Another Beaufighter force went in search of the ships just after midnight, some aircraft attacking ships that they took to be the targets, but no results were observed. The destroyers tried to move out of port a few days later, and two were sunk by the Navy.

A major U-boat movement from the Bay of Biscay ports was reported later in the day, and various units were tasked with hunting them down. However, it was not until the night hours of 6 June that contact was made, the submarines having surfaced in an attempt to make

a high-speed dash into the Channel. During the night at least twenty-two sightings were reported, the aircraft of 53 Squadron proving particularly alert; but only seven of these sightings culminated in attacks, and only two submarines were claimed destroyed (Type VIICs, U-955 and U-970).

It was not only Coastal Command aircraft that took part in anti-shipping operations: just after dawn a force of Whirlwind bombers ('Whirlibombers') of 137 Squadron, with a Typhoon escort from 609 Squadron, went after a group of four Class M minesweepers off Ambleteuse. All the aircraft made successful attacks against the enemy ships, despite heavy flak from the targets and from shore installations. The German surface forces were given no opportunity during the daylight hours of making attacks against the flanks of the invasion fleet. In contrast to this failure the Germans did have some success with a minelaying effort, by aircraft and boat, in which they let the mines loose to drift down into the packed Allied shipping. Countering this threat was to prove very difficult, and was never fully accomplished.

## Air-Sea Rescue

With so many Allied aircraft crossing the Channel it was inevitable that some would end up ditching, either through battle damage or mechanical trouble. The Air-Sea Rescue (ASR) network was ready to deal with any eventuality, having been re-organized prior to the invasion. Responsibility for ASR work within the assault area was transferred to ADGB, with effect from 15 April. The four main RAF ASR squadrons were given increased establishments and changes of location: for example, 276 Squadron moved its Warwick flight to Portreath and its Spitfire/

Walrus flights to Bolthead. The four squadrons together mustered eighty aircraft to cover the assault area; responsibility outside this region fell to the P-47s of the ASR squadron of the 65th Wing based at Boxted, and four Coastal Command deep search squadrons. However, aircraft were only one part of the RAF's ASR team, the other main element being the high speed launches (HSLs) of the Marine Craft Units (MCUs). By late May the RAF had ninety HSLs to cover this area, including fourteen of the brand-new 68ft (20m) launches with No. 32 ASR MCU at Calshot. Additional cover was

*Spitfires of 276 Squadron were part of the Air-Sea Rescue network; here, survival equipment, including a dinghy, is being loaded into a compartment in the belly of the aircraft.*

BELOW: *The RAF's high speed launches (HSL) were an essential part of the ASR network.*

provided by the Royal Navy rescue launches (forty), seaplane tenders (six) and American coastguard cutters (sixty) of the Coastguard Rescue Flotilla. Two HSLs were moored alongside each of the fighter director tenders (FDTs), whilst others were stationed at regular intervals throughout the area.

As with other aspects of the invasion plan, these vessels were given identification markings, in this case a five-pointed white star on the foredeck, to prevent Allied aircrew mistaking them for enemy patrol boats. Likewise, aircrew were to follow a specific ditching procedure (if they could, in the heat of the moment and in a damaged aircraft) whereby single-seat fighter pilots should bale out rather than ditch, preferably ahead of a surface craft heading north; they were instructed not to ditch *beside* any vessel in case they were taken as being an enemy glide bomb.

In the early hours of 6 June the launches took up their positions and waited; the Spitfire and Walrus patrols started before dawn. During the day a total of sixty aircrew were rescued; reaction times were so quick that one Spitfire pilot was picked up within minutes of baling out, the HSL crew watching him float down and getting as close as they could. The total rescued in the first ten days of *Overlord* was an impressive 163 aircrew.

### A Successful First Day

The battle continued overnight. Whilst the tactical aircraft rested, the heavies were in action again. Amongst the sorties this night were twelve by the US 8th Air Force's Special Leaflet Unit, the B-17s flying routes covering at least thirty towns and cities in northern France, Holland and Belgium. This unit had been operating most nights since 1 June, and would continue to do so throughout the month.

Some 1,034 RAF Bomber Command aircraft went against road and rail targets at Achères, Vire, Caen, Châteaudun, St Lô, Argentan, Lisieux, Coutances and Conde-sur-Noireau, with other Command aircraft carrying out

mine laying, Resistance supply drops and bomber support, plus a force of thirty-two Mosquitoes going to Ludwigshafen. The raids against targets in Germany were important in order to keep enemy defensive fighters confined to the Defence of the Reich.

Typical of the squadrons active that night was 460 Squadron from Binbrook. Twenty-four Lancasters took off at 22:00 hours to attack the rail bridges at Vire – one over the main road by the station, and the other over the river. The bombers arrived over the target just after midnight and, despite a good deal of smoke, were able to distinguish the markers and drop their loads with what appeared to be good results. Some crews reported seeing enemy night fighters and one aircraft, JB700, failed to return. A second Lancaster, ME811 of 576 Squadron, was lost on this same raid. At some targets the raids achieved their objectives, blocking rail and road routes through these built-up areas, but despite attempts to ensure accuracy, there was a fair degree of damage to the towns and casualties amongst the French population. Total aircraft losses for the night were ten Lancasters and one Halifax, five of the Lancasters being lost on the attack against Caen. This town had become the lynchpin of the German defences in the British sector and was to become a major stumbling block for almost two months – despite the fact that its capture had been scheduled for Day One of the invasion.

## Summary of Operations for 6 June

As with almost every statistical element involved with this air campaign, it is difficult to obtain an exact figure for the total number of Allied air sorties for 6 June. The following table (*see opposite*) is constructed from various contemporary command reports, and whilst it may not be accurate to the last sortie, it certainly provides the general picture, and gives a reasonable breakdown of sortie types (a more detailed analysis of sorties is given in Appendix V).

| Operations for 6 June 1944 | | | |
|---|---|---|---|
| *2nd TAF* | *Sorties* | *Coastal Command* | |
| Medium bombers | 190 | Anti U-boat and ship patrols | 353 |
| Smoke-screen cover | 31 | | |
| Convoy/beach cover | 848 | *No. 38 Group* | |
| Escort of airborne forces | 72 | Transport para/glider tug | 391 |
| Close air support | 519 | Glider | 265 |
| Reconnaissance | 110 | | |
| Artillery spotting | 435 | *No. 46 Group* | |
| Other | 44 | Transport para/glider tug | 270 |
| Total | 2,249 | Glider | 87 |
| | | | |
| *ADGB* | | *VIIIth Bomber Command* | |
| Beach-head cover | 273 | Coastal defences and | 2,656 |
| Shipping protection | 194 | transportation | |
| Offensive sweeps | 100 | | |
| Defensive patrols | 207 | *VIIIth Fighter Command* | |
| Anti-shipping patrols | 38 | Patrols/sweeps | 1,072 |
| ASR patrols | 63 | Area support/F-B | 511 |
| Other | 37 | | |
| Total | 912 | *9th Air Force* | |
| | | Bomber, fighter, TCC | 3,587 |
| *Bomber Command* | | | |
| Coastal defences and | 1,335 | **Grand Total** | 13,688 |
| transportation | | | |

The main problem areas lie with the overall figures for the US 8th and 9th Air Forces, figures for the former being either 4,239 (as above) or 4,704; the 9th Air Force's statistics are even more confusing, with many sorties not being accounted for; this is because the statisticians of the 9th worked most of their figures for the Normandy period (6 June to 25 July), rather than the twenty-four hours of 6 June.

The AEAF statistics for Allied losses were calculated for the period 21:00 hours 5 June to sunrise 7 June – this being taken as the assault phase – thus incorporating both nights of the assault; overall losses were given as:

| | |
|---|---|
| 2nd TAF | 24 |
| ADGB | 8 |
| 9th AF | 26 |
| IXth TCC | 22 |
| No. 38/46 Group | 20 |
| Bomber Command | 11 |
| 8th AF | approx. 20 |

However, this total of 131 aircraft is by no means certain, and there has been much debate as to the actual losses. Regardless of what the actual figure was, it was certainly a very small percentage of the total sorties flown during the period. The total number of sorties flown between midnight on 5 June and midnight on 6 June was around 14,000, of which 60 per cent were flown by American air assets; some 12 per cent of the total was by night, mainly by Bomber Command and the night fighters of No. 11 and No. 85 Groups.

## Conclusions for 6 June

'The unsuitable weather nullified, to a large extent, the advantage enjoyed by the Allies of overwhelming air superiority. This was largely because the heavy day bombers could not operate effectively in such conditions.' This statement features in the official RAF history of the invasion of Normandy, and requires some explanation. Despite the best efforts of Allied intelligence officers to uncover the facts and figures that would disclose the effectiveness of the air effort, there was much debate regarding its overall contribution to the day's events. Although the operational research sections and the bombing analysis units endeavoured to be impartial in their conclusions, it was inevitable that 'politics' should creep in to the studies; for example, to US VIIIth Bomber Command officers their efforts were seldom found wanting, and yet they came in for most criticism from senior air commanders; to a lesser extent the same applied in RAF Bomber Command and to each of the other air elements. Thus there is always the problem of determining what percentage of the overall effort was truly effective, and what was 'wasted'. I have no simple answer;

having studied dozens of such reports and summaries, it is impossible to come up with a firm set of figures that prove or disprove the effectiveness of Allied air power on 6 June. The only statement that can be made with certainty is that it was not as effective as it could have been, given better weather conditions!

By close of play on D-Day the Allied armies were ashore and reasonably well established, and Operation *Neptune* had been a success; true, there had been difficulties, not everything had gone according to plan, but overall it had gone well and losses had been light. The part played by the air campaign, not just on this first day but in the days, weeks and months leading up to the 6th, is what really should be analysed.

However, the story does not end at midnight on D-Day: at that hour the Allied forces were reasonably well established ashore, and most of the objectives for Day One had been achieved; but it was by no means certain that the hold on Normandy could be maintained. It all depended now on the 'build-up race', and in this, air power had a very distinct part to play, and our conclusions as to the air campaign must wait a little while longer.

*Bulletin board at 391st BG, 6 June 1944. At bases back in the UK, aircrew and groundcrew studied whatever intelligence was to hand on the progress of the invasion.* (US National Archives)

Combat reports, 379th BG.

# The Follow-Up, Phase One: Linking the Bridgeheads (7–12 June)

Montgomery assessed the immediate post-landing tasks as:

1. Linking the bridgeheads.
2. Retaining the initiative.
3. Guarding against any setbacks or reverses.

He also praised the task performed by the air forces:

> The Allied Air Forces had laid the foundation of success by winning the air battle before the invasion was launched, and by applying their whole striking power, with magnificent results, to assist the landings … the disruption of enemy communications caused by our bombing, and the breakdown of his radar caused by our counter-measures, left the enemy for a considerable time in doubt about the actual extent and strength of our assault.

These are useful comments to bear in mind for our overall conclusions – but in the meantime the battle is still going on. 'Enemy movement was difficult and dangerous, but it was carried out under cover of darkness, bad weather and with elaborate camouflage arrangements. Fortunately, it was much slower than it might have been, thanks to the success which had attended the preparatory air operations.' With these words the RAF's official account stated the true value of Allied air power in the *Overlord*

Armourers load ammunition belts ready for fitting to the Spitfires of 56 (US) and 411 (DB) squadrons.

BELOW LEFT: Bazenville (B2) was one of the B-series airfields allocated for RAF aircraft in Normandy. No. 3207 SCU moved in, having landed at Gold beach on 7 June.

BELOW: The airfield at Cardonville (A3) was given the standard single landing strip, along with fifty SMT hardstands.

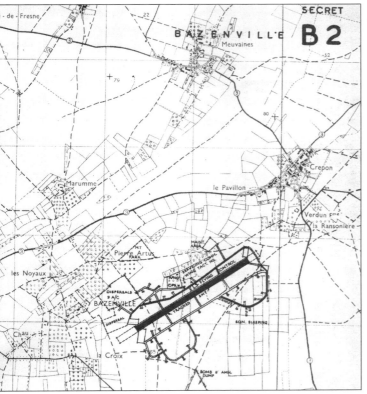

campaign; much of the effort had gone into not only securing the immediate aim of getting ashore, but more importantly, of making sure that once the ground forces were ashore, they could stay there. If all the available firepower had been expended on the coastal belt, it is possible that the landings would have been easier – but it is certain that the German response would have been swifter and more effective without the interdiction campaign.

Inevitably the interdiction air campaign could make no detailed plan for the post-invasion period, because it would be a case of reacting to the situation; however, it was certain that 'the primary aim will be to compel the enemy to detrain at a considerable distance, and continue by road with consequent delay and increased vulnerability.' A great deal of air effort had already been expended on this task; it would now become the key to overall success or failure. It was also considered essential to establish air bases on the Continent at the earliest opportunity; the need for suitable locations had indeed been one of the considerations in choosing the invasion location. According to AP 3397:

> The immediate and overriding task of the RAF administrative organisation in the days following the initial assault on the beaches was, to put it simply, to maintain in fighting condition as many aircraft as the operational plan required, and to ensure that no hitch occurred through a breakdown in the chain of supply and maintenance.

The vital role of logistics is often ignored in studies of military campaigns, except in instances of failure when it is used as one of the reasons for a lost battle or campaign. But it is an inescapable truism that without fuel and weapons, combat aircraft are useless, as indeed they are if they have nowhere from which to operate, and if they cannot be fixed when they break. Sounds obvious, but those self-evident facts require a massive administration and logistics organization, and it was one of the great successes of the invasion that seldom did this organization fail in any critical way.

The RAF had allocated six Servicing Commando Units (SCU) for *Overlord*, four to go ashore at D plus One, the remaining two at D plus Seven. It is worth noting here that the first servicing commandos had been formed early in 1942 (Nos 3201, 3202 and 3203), and they had subsequently gained operational experience during operations in North Africa: their recommendations based on this experience proved invaluable in developing the role and capability of the SCUs. One of the first ashore in Normandy was No. 3207 SCU, landing at Gold beach early on 7 June, and moving inland to B2 Bazenville. Meanwhile, No. 3205 SCU had arrived and moved to B3, and was tasked with building up petrol, oil and ammunition

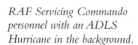
*RAF Servicing Commando personnel with an ADLS Hurricane in the background.*

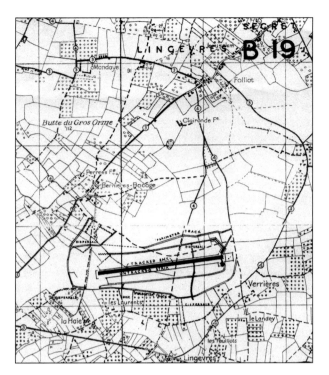

*Plan of airfield B19, the first to be built by the RAF Airfield Construction Service.*

dumps ready to receive the first Allied aircraft. Before long the SCUs were working flat out looking after Spitfires, Typhoons, Mustangs and any other stray aircraft that came their way. Life could be very hectic, a 'typical' day's trade, 13 June, comprising seventy-seven Spitfires, one Mustang, two Thunderbolts, four Typhoons and one Halifax.

The general plan called for eighteen airfields by D plus Fourteen, and twenty-seven by D plus Twenty-four, but with two R&R (refuel and re-arm) strips to be available in each sector as soon as possible after the landings. The first of the true airfields within the American sector to become operational was A3 Cardonville, with effect from 19 June. It was somewhat later that the first airstrip on the Continent was built by the RAF's ACS: the site that became B19 (Lingèvres) was visited by a survey party from the Wing HQ, and in five days all the essentials were ready and the first aircraft were using the strip – 'The selected

site was on agricultural land, and the first oper-ation was to clear the crops. Men of the ACS drove horses and reapers, harvesting the corn and hay, and as the crops were cleared, bulldoz-ers began operating over the stubble' (AP3236).

## 7 June 1944

The day after the landings proved to be a qui-eter day, as the forecast weather deterioration started to have an impact – although the full force of this deterioration would not hit Nor-mandy until two days later. After the intense activity of the 6th, many units found them-selves sitting waiting, albeit maintaining a high state of readiness either in the aircraft or at dis-persal. No. 438 Squadron at Hurn kept four aircraft at runway readiness, and a further six on three-minute readiness in dispersal for most of the day – and yet the only activity was a scramble by two aircraft late in the evening to undertake a convoy patrol.

The next phases of the airborne operations were en route early in the morning. Operation *Galveston*, comprising two waves of fifty glid-ers apiece to reinforce the 82nd Airborne, suf-fered similar problems to those of the previous day, with early releases causing some gliders to miss their LZs. However, casualties were light, and most of the sixty-eight Horsa and thirty-two Waco gliders made it down safely. Two hours later, Operation *Hackensack* brought a further 100 gliders, in two waves, to LZ 'W'. In addition to towing gliders, the C-47s of the IXth Troop Carrier Command were heavily involved in the air drop of supplies to the two airborne divisions; on D plus One these air-craft flew 208 missions to the 82nd and 126 missions to the 101st. Unfortunately, poor weather caused many aircraft to turn back, and only 155 of the planned 250 tons of supplies made it to the 82nd. The 101st drop had a higher success rate, 118 against 156 tons, but in this instance the troops had not requested the drop and so were not ready to receive it.

Pressure was maintained against German airfields to ensure that enemy air effort was restricted to the lowest possible level. The effectiveness of this tactic is confirmed by the war diary of III Gruppe Schlachtgeschwader 4:

In spite of favourable weather our operations achieved little, because successful operations were impossible without effective fighter protection. The losses in pilots and aircraft on this day can be blamed on the absence of any flak defence at the airfield.

Those German aircraft that did manage to get airborne found an overwhelming Allied fighter umbrella eager to take them on. Allied claims for the day amounted to fifty-eight, the P-47s of the 56th and 353rd Fighter Groups having a particularly successful day, claiming twelve and eleven respectively. However, there was an increase in German intruder activity over England, as the 34th Bomb Group found to its cost, losing three B-24s shot down near Mendlesham.

Bayeux fell on 7 June, as the Allied land forces pressed forward to their objectives, and gradually the beach-heads were linked up. There were a few minor German counter-attacks, but none presented any serious problem; the German command network was still in chaos as a result of the air assault. A coup for the direction finding (DF) intelligence network was locating the HQ of Panzer Group West; details were passed to AEAF, and a series of attacks were mounted in which command vehicles were destroyed, General von Schweppenburg was wounded, and many other Staff officers were either killed or wounded.

The situation at the beaches still required air support, as German artillery was continuing to harass the landing operations; the aircraft of the air-spotting pool proved their worth, providing counter-battery control that was able to engage and negate the threat. The overall Allied land strategy was for a break-out to be attempted on the east flank, towards Caen, to draw into this battle all available German resources. Once these had been committed, then the main break-out, by the US armies of General Omar Bradley, would pivot the front at Caen and advance down to the Loire and Paris, to cut off all enemy forces south of the Seine, all the bridges having been destroyed by the Allied interdiction campaign.

Thus the major air effort for this and subsequent days was tasked against enemy lines of

Chatanooga *mission as a P-51 lets loose at a train.*

communication, to create, in the words of the Bombing Analysis Unit (BAU) '... a cycle of breakage and repair'. The general plan was to attack bridges, rather than rail centres, in an attempt to cut all the rail and road bridges over the lower Loire, west of Orleans, and in the Seine–Loire gap, west of Paris – this being considered as the '1st line of interdiction'. Assuming that this was a success and that the Allied advance remained on schedule, then the '2nd line of interdiction', bridges south of Staples, would come into force in mid-June. Each attack was to have a follow-up PR mission to assess damage, and attacks were to continue until the target had been destroyed. Recce aircraft would then monitor the target to determine if, and when, it required re-attack. Attacking road and rail movements was also a high priority for the tactical aircraft, and on average 500–600 sorties a day were tasked

*Massy Palaiseau was one of four rail centres attacked by Bomber Command on the night of 7 June.*

against trains, approximately 50 per cent of this effort being in the tactical operations area, the remainder being in the interdiction band on its fringes. During the period 7–17 June, VIIIth Fighter Command flew numerous attacks against such targets, their tally being:

| Type | Destroyed | Damaged |
|---|---|---|
| Locomotives | 118 | 70 |
| Rolling stock | 375 | 1,258 |
| MT | 607 | 533 |
| Tanks | 16 | 31 |
| Armoured cars | 12 | 15 |
| Staff cars | 7 | 10 |
| Other vehicles | 80 | 36 |

The 9th Air Force statistics cover a longer period (6 June–25 July), but are in rough proportion the numbers are similar to the above. If 2nd TAF and ADGB figures are included, then the overall impact of this element of the air campaign becomes significant. In its post-war report, based on French records, the Bombing Analysis Unit concluded that:

> It is perfectly plain from the records that both civilian and military [rail] traffic had been very seriously affected by the end of the first phase of the attack, and that attacks on rail centres were responsible for by far the larger part of the overall decline in traffic originating in France. Apparently the unanimous view of French railway officials is that the determining factor in these attacks was the destruction of the depots in which locomotives were housed, serviced and repaired.

The air situation changed slightly on the 7th, with the *Luftwaffe* making more of an appearance:'Enemy air activity was on a considerably increased scale. The single-engine fighter scale of effort is estimated at between 200 and 250 sorties, the majority operating in the Le Havre–Cherbourg area. In addition, some 40–50 fighter-bomber aircraft, in two operations, attacked troops in the Caen and beach-head

*Invasion barge with barrage balloon; Allied air supremacy ensured little interference from the* Luftwaffe.

is being reinforced and I cannot bomb the reinforcements in daylight. I have a feeling that we are losing precious time at the moment when the main movements of the enemy are beginning ... on the other hand, we have had a very easy run as far as the *Luftwaffe* is concerned; but I want to knock the German Air Force for six, for then we shall have absolute freedom in the air.

In other correspondence he mentions that the German air threat cannot be ignored, and that the great air battle he predicted may yet occur, hence the need to maintain the fighter shield and preserve fighter assets. Indeed, he concluded his 7 June diary entry with the comment that 'it may be that the Hun is trying to lull us into a false sense of security. We shall soon know.' Tactical and fighter aircraft had had a busy day, and the explanation of the comment 'badly affected by weather' refers primarily to the weather hampering use of the heavy bomber forces with their huge destructive potential. It was these forces that were tasked with the interdiction campaign against rail centres, and without them the air commander considered that his overall strategy was weakened.

Some commentators have argued that greater results would have been obtained by launching all available tactical aircraft into the direct land battle, and in the absence of accurate application of the tonnage from the medium and heavy bombers, an increase in tactical fire-power would have been of benefit. Whilst the number of sorties flown on 6 and 7 June was impressive, it was little more than one sortie per available aircraft, although some aircraft and pilots flew three or four times in one day. Whilst losses to enemy action remained at a low rate, the problems of 'own goals' continued to plague the Allied air effort – not air-on-air, although there had been a few close calls – but still, anti-aircraft fire from the army and navy. The situation was perhaps made worse by reports of German aircraft being seen wearing RAF markings and the use of captured Allied aircraft – 9th Air Force

areas.' Leigh-Mallory recorded in his diary on 7 June:

So far the German reaction has not been great, but he is now bringing more troops into the area. He has also moved a number of aircraft to Lorient, which may indicate that he intends to increase his submarine activity. His reserves seem to be coming into the beach-head area in bits and pieces, and it doesn't look as though he can launch a big attack yet. ...The weather has interfered with my air programme all day and is seriously upsetting me. The German army

*Large numbers of L-birds, American and British, deployed to Normandy and performed a number of key roles.* (US National Archives)

*Visit to the beachhead on 7 June by Sir Charles Portal (third from the left), Chief of Air Staff, and Sir Archibald Sinclair.*

fighter pilots claimed to have shot down a number of 'German' P-47s and a Mosquito.

Not all aircraft required airfields, and amongst the earliest types to forward deploy were the liaison aircraft. There were around 350 liaison aircraft, mainly the L-4 'Grasshopper' but with a number of L-5 Sentinels in support of US 1st Army, most of these being deployed as air sections with the Field Artillery battalions to act as air observation posts (AOPs). Whilst some aircraft were scheduled to fly over from bases in England, others had been stripped down and placed on trucks, the idea being that once driven ashore – in the first wave of the assault – they

would be reassembled and be ready for action. According to one American L-4 pilot, 'We all knew that our mission was doomed, even before we left England.' With two L-4s of his squadron loaded on to an LCT, Lt Tom Turner of the 58th Armoured FA Battalion had a hazardous arrival at Omaha beach: 'As we approached the beach, enemy air bursts were exploding overhead. We got a few holes in the wings and fuselage of the aircraft, but sustained no major damage.' The LCT grounded some way off the beach, and during the attempt to drive ashore, one L-4 went to the bottom and the other aircraft only made it to the beach with some difficulty – thus becoming the first American aircraft ashore. However, it did not survive for long, as it was targeted and destroyed by German artillery.

Many L-4 pilots believed that the best solution would have been to deploy the aircraft on a small carrier just offshore, which they could have used as a base until the beach-head was secure. However, the possibility of using one or more carriers had been investigated by the planners and rejected for a number of reasons, not least the crowded nature of the waterway and the desire not to risk an aircraft carrier no matter how small. To this set of arguments could be added the ever-present danger of naval gunners, engaging any aircraft that flew near any ship!

## 8 June 1944

The following extract from Leigh Mallory's diary again graphically expresses the unfolding situation:

> The situation is changing as the German reinforcements come up. The weather is still bad, but our fighter-bombers have certainly delayed their movements, and I think that the Germans are 24 hours behind their schedule. My problem, as I see it, is two-fold. First, to hold the ring outside the invasion area; secondly, to try to stop railway movement towards the area, particularly from the south-east. What I must try hard to do is to stop the trains as far back as possible. I want to take the bridges out and thus force the enemy onto the roads. If this succeeds, the rapid movement of reinforcements will become impossible.

For the 400 bomber sorties by the 9th Air Force, and the 1,178 by the 8th Air Force, the primary targets were lines of communications, railway centres, bridges and marshalling yards: these were to be heavily hit, although a variety of tactical targets, such as supply dumps and strongpoints, also received attention.

Leigh-Mallory was also concerned about increased *Luftwaffe* activity, and his diary continued:

*Le Mans was attacked by heavy bombers of the 8th Air Forces as part of the on-going campaign against airfields.*

> The German Air Force is beginning to thicken up, and about half the fighters in Germany are now, I think, moving against us. I have put the American 8th Army Air Force on to the bombing of enemy airfields. Now is the moment to mess them up. I am therefore going to make heavy attacks on Flers, Laval, Le Mans and Rennes, and for this purpose I am going to use my heavies. I want to catch the German Air Force while they are moving in.

The attacks by British and American heavy bombers on these targets did not take place until two days later; on the night of 9/10 June, Bomber Command sent 400 bombers against the four airfields, with the 8th Air Force attacking five airfields during daylight on 10 June.

Meanwhile, German air activity continued to increase, and more Allied fighter squadrons

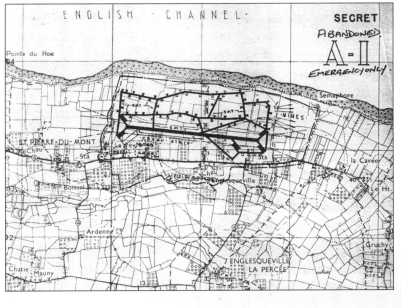

LEFT: *St Pierre-du-Mont (A1) was constructed by IXth Engineer Command as one of the first landing grounds in Normandy; this plan is dated 23 July, by which time the strip had been abandoned.*

BELOW: *Dakota being used to evacuate casualties from the bridgehead; the establishment of an efficient casualty evacuation system had begun in late 1943, and eventually included a number of special units in addition to the requirement that all returning transport aircraft should perform a casevac role.*

*This C-47 was the first American aircraft to (officially) land at a permanent airfield (rather than an R&R strip).*
(US National Archives)

reported combats; 222 Squadron's Spitfires flew four missions on 8 June, the final one taking off at 18:50 hours to patrol Sword beach. Some thirty minutes after commencing the patrol, the Spitfires were warned of enemy aircraft in the area, and soon visually acquired a gaggle of Fw 190s. Battle was joined, and in the space of a few minutes the squadron claimed three enemy aircraft shot down, one probable and a further four damaged – all for no loss.

The American fighters were also busy this day: VIIIth Fighter Command flew 1,353 missions of various types, during which they lost twenty-two aircraft and claimed thirty-one aerial victories and twenty-one ground victories. Most of the losses were to flak during attacks on ground targets, including the loss of one of the leading aces – 1st Lt Robert Booth of the 359th FG, a P-51 pilot with eight victories, who was shot down by flak near La Flèche and taken prisoner. Major Rockford Gray of the 371st FG was the most successful pilot on the day, claiming three Fw 190s near Cabourg, which also raised him to ace status. The 9th Air Force's fighter pilots put in claims for seven aerial victories, but the bulk of their missions were against ground targets, often on roving patrols.

Air drop of supplies also continued, including a few special missions – such as that on 8 June to drop 15lb (7kg) of ether to a field hospital between the beach and Carentan. The C-47s were amongst the first aircraft to operate out of Normandy, landing to pick up 'casevac' cases for return to the UK. The scale of this medical evacuation increased as more landing facilities became available, and was at once a great morale-booster to the soldiers. Two weeks prior to D-Day an exercise had been conducted to test the air evacuation system, and the results had indicated that the organization that had been created earlier in the year worked reasonably well. The 'air evacuation of casualties' policy had been decided in February, when AEAF Instruction No. 8 detailed four types of airfield:

1. Advanced landing strip (ALS) – close to the front line, usually a single strip for use by light aircraft.
2. Forward delivery airfield (FDA) – a terminal airfield allotted by the TAF for transport aircraft, possibly as much as 50 miles (80km) from the ALS.
3. Advanced base airfield (ABA) – similar to the FDA, but with better facilities.
4. Main base airfield (MBA) – for the RAF these were nominated as Broadwell, Blakehill Farm, Down Ampney and Watchfield. Only in an emergency were 'casevac' aircraft to land at any other airfield. Once a casualty had arrived at an MBA, he would be transferred by road to an appropriate medical facility.

Whilst all transport aircraft operating into the beach-head were tasked with bringing back casualties, there were also dedicated units for this task; shortly before D-Day, seventy Ansons were transferred from Training Command and fitted out to carry stretchers. However, one of the main RAF units was 271 Squadron, whose Sparrow aircraft formed an ambulance flight. The Casualty Air Evacuation Units (CAEU) had been integrated with the forward staging posts, and it would be their responsibility to prepare casualties for air evacuation from the battle area. The first casualties flown out of the beach-head were fifteen US Army personnel aboard Dakotas on 10 June; the first British air evacuation took place a few days later.

Also amongst the unsung aircraft of the war were those performing the air observation post (AOP) and liaison roles, already briefly mentioned with the L-4s brought ashore from landing craft on D-Day. These aircraft were not perhaps as glamorous as their more offensive-oriented brethren, but they were nevertheless a vital asset to the land force commander. The British Auster squadrons invariably operated as an integrated element within an army corps; for instance, on 8 June, the first two squadrons moved to France, 652

Squadron to support 1st Corps and 662 Squadron to support XXX Corps. There was an increasing demand for air photography as the battle developed, and this would often be best met by the AOP units; each squadron formed a PR flight to cover this task. However, they also provided artillery spotting, usually counter-battery work to engage hidden targets, as well as other functions such as communications. As an officer of the 10th SS Panzer said: 'The biggest nuisance, though, are the slow-flying spotter planes, which in utter calmness fly over our positions and direct fire, while our infantry weapons cannot reach them.' Within a matter of weeks, a further five RAF AOP squadrons had deployed to France.

**9 June 1944**
On the evening of the 9 June, Leigh-Mallory wrote as follows in his diary:

> I am feeling a bit depressed today. It seems to me that the German armies are moving up against the beach-head and I am unable to do anything against them because of this perfectly bloody weather. Yet I need not be really depressed, for even with the limited number of sorties we have been able to fly, we have done well. The German armies are not moving up as fast as was anticipated. We have undoubtedly slowed them down in the strategical area, but I repeat, the air is the weapon which we must use against the German army to prevent their quick build-up; all the more so because the Germans do not have the power to use the air against us. I am absolutely satisfied with the air defences, no serious damage has been done to ships or military units, and that is a comforting thought. I have had several comments from our own army wounded, which seem to show that the army is delighted with the RAF and consider that the air cover over the beach-head is marvellous. Admiral Vian has actually gone so far as to complain of the number of British aircraft flying over his ships; I suppose they disturb him in his bath.

The major Bomber Command effort on the night of 8/9 June involved 483 bombers attacking the rail centres of Alençon, Fougères, Mayenne, Pontabault and Rennes, for the loss of four aircraft. One of the most significant attacks that night was made by 617 Squadron and involved the first operational use of the 12,000lb (545kg) 'Tallboy' bomb. This special earthquake-effect bomb had been designed by Barnes Wallis to destroy targets that had proved resistant to the usual air-dropped bombs. A force of twenty-five Lancasters from 617 Squadron attacked the railway tunnel at Saumur to block a route through which a Panzer division was reported to be heading. The target was marked by Mosquitoes and illuminated by flares dropped by Lancasters of 83 Squadron. The attack was incredibly accurate, with one bomb actually penetrating the roof of the tunnel, and the route was blocked for some time.

However, the weather on the 9th was bad enough to hamper the strategic bomber effort; indeed no missions were flown by the 8th and 9th Air Force bombers.

The need for aerial reconnaissance meant that aircraft tasked with these missions flew even when other types were grounded. This was a bad day for the 67th TRG, with four of their F-6 Mustangs being shot down by Allied naval gunfire; only one pilot was rescued.

One significant development of 9 June was the establishment of a forward command post by the 70th FG in the beach-head at Criqueville; and over the next few days aircraft began to forward deploy. The following day the advanced HQ of IXth TAC moved from England to Au Guay.

As the battle developed, so the routine tasks of re-supply and air support continued, and even expanded. For example, the 436th Troop Carrier Group flew a number of small-scale operations into the Ste-Mère-Église area between 9–13 June as part of the continued build-up of the 82nd Airborne Division.

Leigh-Mallory closed his daily entry thus:

They promise me a temporary [weather] improvement tomorrow, but I am doubtful. It is depressing to think that I have more than 11,000 aircraft and cannot make full use of them, and I confess to experiencing a certain sense of frustration. Today seemed to me a crucial day, and very little has been done in the air.

## 10 June 1944

In contrast to his gloom of the previous day, the Air Commander had this to say as 10 June came to a close:

Today has been a grand day and I feel a different man. The weather made a complete gap in my information, but things started to build early today, and movement on the road was noticed from points west of Paris and Dreux. Only a few trains have been seen; I think they have been clobbered too badly to move much. By bombing Amiens, Beauvais and Abbeville I hope to create a bombing barrier round the battlefield, and inside it to reduce and possibly destroy all railway movement. The American heavies have done very well and I have a feeling that there is little build-up on the enemy's side. Bomber Command did good shows last night on railways in Brittany.

The overnight attacks of 8/9 June against rail targets were followed on this night by a concentrated raid by No. 5 Group against the important rail junction at Étampes, south of Paris. Target marking was average, and the bombers hit the junction, although the bomb pattern spread over parts of the town. Later reports indicated that about a quarter of the town was hit by bombs, with the loss of over 100 civilian lives. The Allied commanders were very aware of the risks of such bombing missions, and every effort was made to minimize French casualties.

The American heavy bomber operations for this day have been mentioned above; for the light and medium types of the 9th Air Force,

targets in the battle area were the focus of attention. Overnight on the 10/11 June the RAF's bombers were again in action against railway targets, with 432 aircraft, mainly Lancasters, attacking Achères, Dreux, Orleans and Versailles. It was a relatively costly night, and eighteen bombers were lost.

On the air side: 'The *Luftwaffe* is beginning to operate. Contact was made with them this afternoon (but) he seems scared stiff of poking his nose in. We gave him such a bloody nose at Dieppe that I should not be surprised if he has learnt that lesson, and is not going to risk the same fate over the Normandy beaches.' For the fighters of VIIIth Fighter Command it was business as usual, and they flew 1,491 sorties for the loss of twenty-four aircraft. Claims for twenty-nine German aircraft were made by 8th and 9th Air Force fighter pilots.

*Sqn Ldr Stoner was the first RAF pilot to (officially) land in France – 10 June.*

*10 June, and the first RAF fighter aircraft land in France; as each aircraft came to a halt it was quickly re-armed and re-fuelled by the servicing commandos.*

*The Allied fighter-bombers played a major role in the establishment of the bridgehead: Spitfires of 132 Squadron being armed with bombs.*

*Spitfires of the Polish 308 Squadron at an ALG in Normandy.*

The Spitfires of 222 Squadron, having completed their patrol of Sword beach on 10 June, landed at 16:30 hours at airfield B3 (Ste-Croix-sur-Mer), the first time that this squadron had landed in Europe. The servicing commandos refuelled and re-armed the aircraft whilst the pilots went on a quick souvenir hunt, and the Spitfires were back on patrol at 18:00 hours. These quick turn-rounds on airfields in Normandy meant that greater use could be made of the available tactical aircraft.

On the same day, Pilot Officer Bavis of 402 Squadron had to force-land his Spitfire, having been damaged in a tangle with enemy fighters; however, he had no time to admire the French countryside, as he was whisked away to the beach, taken by motor torpedo boat (MTB) to England, put on a train to Horley, and was back on the squadron the day following his incident!

Immediately a suitable airfield site had been selected a construction party would '... rush in to prepare a grass landing strip so that fighters and fighter-bombers could operate with the minimum of delay. In the beach-head the greatest handicap to flying was dust. Clouds of it streamed from the roads and airfields, making quick "scrambles" by the fighters almost impossible' (AP 3236). The Royal Engineers tried using watering systems to suppress the dust, but with rapid drying this was not very effective; an experiment by the airfield construction units using an oil spray, with oil salvaged from a beached destroyer, was more successful, and this became the standard technique.

Rommel's daily *Sitrep* again stressed the effect of Allied air power:

> In the battle area over the SS Corps, numerous enemy fighter-bomber formations circled uninterruptedly over the battlefield, and strong formations bombarded troops, villages, bridges, and road junctions as heavily as possible and without consideration for the population. Neither our flak nor the *Luftwaffe* seems to be in a position to check this crippling and destructive operation of the enemy air forces. The army and SS troops are defending themselves as well as they can, but ammunition is scarce and can be replaced only under the most difficult conditions.

The latter point is an important one, and the part played by logistics in military operations –

*RAF Mustangs operating from an ALG in France; dust was a major problem at these strips, and at times clouds of dust made formation take-offs very difficult.*

BELOW: *Rocket-armed Typhoons sit ready for the next mission.*

keeping the troops supplied with the means to fight – is critical. Disruption of this logistics is a vital part of any battlefield campaign, and whilst it is, of course, crucial to prevent reinforcements reaching the battle area, it is equally important to prevent re-supply. Disruption of re-supply also involves destruction of military stores stockpiled in the battle area, and the location and destruction of such sites was one of the many tasks of the fighter-bombers.

A formation of eighteen Typhoons from 164 and 183 Squadrons was tasked with army support in the Evrecy, Aunay and Noyers area, and were on task at 15:25. The first target spotted and attacked was a group of vehicles southwest of Evrecy, the result of which, according to the AEAF operations summary was: 'eight AFVs believed destroyed, three lorries damaged. A second opportunity target was attacked, during which five vehicles were destroyed and one damaged. A final attack near Noyers destroyed ten trucks – with impressive explosions.' The same summary noted that forty-four Thunderbolts of the 373rd FG undertook a successful armed reconnaissance

in the Avranches–Villedieu–St Lô area, during which they dropped sixty 500lb GP bombs. Units of the AEAF flew 3,693 sorties on 10 June for the loss of twenty-eight aircraft, whilst a further 2,374 were flown by 8th Air Force and 474 by Bomber Command. In addition to the air combat claims made by the fighters, units of VIIIth Fighter Command also recorded an impressive ground tally, claiming 8-0-14 (destroyed-probable-damaged) locomotives, 54-0-115 rail cars, 136-0-98 trucks, 6-0-2 tanks and 17-0-7 assorted motor transport.

ABOVE: *A P-47 flies low over a group of tanks.*

*The Germans relied on the extensive and efficient French railway network to move large numbers of troops and heavy equipment; Allied air power attacked every element of this network to great effect.*
(US National Archives)

### 11 June 1944

Leigh-Mallory described the events and feelings associated with this day in sombre tones:

> Not a good day. The weather is doing the dirty on us again. The night bombing was again good but the day bombing is bad, and it was a day of great frustration so far as I am concerned. There have been big movements outside the area south of the Seine and the Loire, and we have discovered some big train movements going on which cannot be attacked in this filthy weather. They were found by fighters. The situation is developing, and at the moment I can do little about it.

The need to cut certain critical routes increased as it became obvious that German reinforcements were reaching the battlefield, albeit in small numbers and not as cohesive fighting units. One such bridge was the Blois St Denis rail bridge over the Loire, and on 11 June the 96th Combat Wing (three B-24 groups) was tasked 'to destroy the bridge at all costs'. Crews were instructed to carry out accurate visual attacks, no matter how low they had to go to achieve accurate bombing. Many aircraft bombed from around 5,000ft (1,500m), but in the absence of flak there were no losses and the target was

destroyed. Despite the poor weather the American heavies managed to fly 600 sorties against airfields and railway targets, with just three bombers being lost. The 9th Air Force's bombers had a busy morning on tactical targets, but when the weather clamped down in the afternoon, further missions were impossible. Offensive fighter operations had also been limited.

Harris's bomber crews were after railways again this night, with 329 aircraft hitting Evreux, Massey-Palaiseau, Nantes and Tours.

The Allied air commander might have been a little more at ease had he been privy to this message written on 11 June by Rommel to Field Marshal Keitel:

> Our operations in Normandy are rendered exceptionally difficult by the strong, and in some respects overwhelming, superiority of enemy air forces. As I and officers of my staff have repeatedly convinced ourselves, the enemy has complete command of the air over the battle area up to about 100km behind the front, and by day cuts off, with powerful fighter-bomber and bomber formations, almost all traffic on roads or by-roads or in open country. It is very difficult to bring the necessary fresh supplies of fuel and munitions to the troops. The movement of smaller formations on the battlefield – artillery

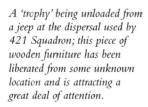

*A 'trophy' being unloaded from a jeep at the dispersal used by 421 Squadron; this piece of wooden furniture has been liberated from some unknown location and is attracting a great deal of attention.*

*Bombers plaster a road bridge on 6 July.*

going into position, placing of armoured cars and the like – is also immediately bombed from the air, with annihilating effect. Troops and staffs have to hide by day in areas with cover to avoid the constant attacks from the air.

Rommel himself later fell victim to such an attack (17 June), being injured and then evacuated back to Germany. His position as head of Army Group B was taken by von Kluge – but the middle of a major battle was not a good time to change the higher command echelon, and in Rommel the Germans lost an officer of flair and ability. General Bayerlein, in his post-war interrogation, commented on this type of attack:

Attacks on Staffs, and the death of COs, often made a deep impression on troops. The travelling of COs in areas threatened by dive-bombers was therefore often postponed altogether.

The fighter-bombers were proving to be the most effective air asset, and as it was now considered that the threat to the shipping lanes had receded sufficiently, the P-38 groups were released from their covering role and sent into the battle over Normandy – much to the delight of the pilots, who were getting bored stooging around over the Channel with no 'trade'.

Leigh-Mallory's diary for 11 June continued:

I am still convinced that the Germans have not got much behind the troops now confronting our armies. More than ever do I want to attack and prevent the build-up, but it is very doubtful because of this weather. However, I am certain that the German build-up is behind-hand, and that he has only got 13 to 14 divisions in the line instead of 16 to 17.

The cautionary note about the weather problems, and the inability to do as much as he would have liked, comes out almost daily, although this was often a reflection of the comments made by land commanders who determined that enemy resistance was stiffening. It is true that German units were making their way to the battlefield, but at the same time the Allied build-up was continuing without interference from enemy air or naval forces: in fact the build-up race was being won, but there was still no place for complacency. The German *Sitrep* for 11 June summarized the position:

Owing to the obstinate resistance of troops in the coastal defence sectors, and the counter-attacks immediately undertaken by the major reserves available, the course of enemy operations has, in spite of the employment of most powerful means of warfare, taken appreciably longer than our adversary had hoped.

ABOVE: *The night hours were one of the few times when the* Luftwaffe *could operate, and the Allies built up a night-defence structure; the P-61s of the 9th Air Force deployed to France as part of the first air movement.* (US National Archives)

*Maj Gen Quesada, commander of IXth TAC, flew the first P-38 into the bridgehead.* (US National Archives)

Having made that reasonably positive statement, the report, which was signed by Rommel, adopted a more gloomy tone:

> Owing to the enemy's overwhelming air superiority, it was not possible to bring up the 1st SS Panzer Corps, the 7th Mortar Brigade, III Flak Corps and II Paratroop Corps quickly into the area between the Orne and the Vire, or to make a counter-attack on the enemy forces which had landed. The Army Group must content itself for the present with forming a cohesive front between the Orne and the Vire with the forces that are gradually coming up, and allowing the enemy to advance. In these circumstances it is unfortunately not possible to relieve troops still resisting in many coastal positions.

The comment was also made that ground operations in this area 'can no longer be supported by our fighter formations, as there are no longer any airfields near the front at our disposal.'

## 12 June 1944

By 12 June all the beach-heads had been linked into a continuous bridgehead with a 50-mile (80km) front, some 8–12 miles (13–19km) deep. Nevertheless, weather problems had not only reduced the scale and effectiveness of the air effort, but had also caused some problems with the logistical build-up; and heavy seas had reduced the scale of sea supply. On the eastern flank the British and Canadian forces were facing increased resistance and were, to all intents and purposes, held up around Caen. However, so far the overall strategy was working, as German reinforcements moved to counter the Allied advance on this flank; it now remained for the sector to hold as the weight of opposition increased, and in this task air power was to play an important role, including the tactical use of strategic bomber forces. Leigh-Mallory's diary:

> Today the situation is changing and enemy movements are spasmodic. The Hun is detraining as far

back as Paris. In the Loire area he is very nearly at a standstill as far as railways are concerned. To prevent shifting of troops down from the north I am going to bomb Amiens, Cambrai and Arras junctions. This will seal off Belgium.

That night Bomber Command laid on one of its heaviest anti-rail efforts to date when 671 bombers attacked Amiens/St Roch, Amiens/Longeau, Arras, Caen, Cambrai and Poitiers. Most of the attacks were reasonably successful, but twenty-three aircraft were lost, mainly to night fighters. A Victoria Cross (posthumous) was awarded to Plt Off Andrew Mynarski of 419 Squadron for his attempt at saving the rear gunner of his aircraft when they were attacked by a night fighter.

Bomber Command mounted a second major raid this night when 303 aircraft attacked oil installations at Gelsenkirchen. Attacks on the German synthetic oil plants had been part of the overall strategy for some time, but were to become increasingly important during 1944.

The shipping lane across the Channel was still busy, and continued efforts were made to keep it safe from surface and air attack. As with much of the air planning, the Allies had to plan for a worse-case scenario and this often meant allocating significant air forces to tasks that, in

the event, were of little effect as the German threat failed to materialize. On 12 June, having lost six U-boats and with another six badly damaged in the period 6–10 June, the commander Naval Forces West ordered a withdrawal of all non-Schnorkel submarines. The losses included the record success of Flying Officer Moore and his 224 Squadron crew who, on the night of the 7th/8th, destroyed two – U-629 and U-373 – in the space of twenty minutes). The U-boat war was by no means over, but it played no further part in the Normandy campaign.

The Allies had been ashore for one week, and despite weather conditions that had reduced the effectiveness of their massive air armada, the general situation was reasonably favourable. A lodgement had been secured at far lower cost than predicted, and the German plan to throw the Allies back into the sea had been comprehensively disrupted. The campaign was by no means won – but it would be increasingly difficult for it to be lost. There was much hard fighting yet to do, and despite the overwhelming Allied air power, the Germans were to proved incredibly resilient and adaptive; indeed, it is unlikely that any other army could have continued to function as well as they did, given the adverse air situation.

*Poitiers under attack on the night of 12/13 June as part of a concerted Bomber Command effort that night (671 bombers) against lines of communication targets. The Poitiers attack was recorded as the most accurate of the night; this target photo was taken by Flt Lt Baker's 97 Squadron aircraft.*

*Night reconnaissance was a vital asset, as it was during the night hours that the Germans made most of their major movements; although this shot by 69 Squadron is dated 1945, it was engaged in this type of work from D-Day.*

## Phase Two: Development of the Bridgehead (13–18 June)

'I sometimes think that the Powers above may have Fascist tendencies, so bad has been the weather.' Leigh-Mallory's diary for 13 June was once more dominated by thoughts of the weather, but he still expressed an overall satisfaction with progress and with the level of losses: 'So far my losses have been light. In the category of fighter-bombers they have been exactly what was estimated; they have been far less in the case of fighters; and extremely light in the case of heavy bombers.'

German resistance had continued to stiffen to such an extent that they were able to launch a series of minor counter-attacks. On 13 June, the 2nd SS Panzer arrived at Villers-Bocage and pushed towards Cherbourg and Caen. This was a tough and well-equipped division, but

fortunately for the Allies its progress towards Normandy was severely delayed and disrupted through a mixture of air attack and Resistance activity.

Other German units suffered similar problems, and as Montgomery commented: 'The strategic bombing policy of the pre-D-Day period was now yielding good dividends, and the growing paralysis over enemy communications was beginning to give us a tremendous advantage. The remorseless air offensive against enemy HQ, communications and detraining stations had caused great disorganization.' On 14 June, Leigh-Mallory had flown to Normandy, his first visit, for a conference with Montgomery, and despite the General's 'post-war' comment quoted above, the air commander's diary records:

I saw Monty this afternoon, and he was not in a good temper, for I had sent him a signal shooting down an airborne operation that he wanted mounted. However, he brisked up a bit when I offered him, in exchange for the operation I was not prepared to carry out, a much more attractive proposal. I have never waited to be told by the army what to do in the air, and my view is not bounded, as seems to be the case with the army, by the nearest hedge or stream. I tried to describe the wider aspects of this battle as I see them, particularly stressing the number of divisions that he might have had to fight, had they not been prevented from appearing on the scene by air action. He was profoundly uninterested.

Over the next few days the air commander's diary continued to be critical of the way that Montgomery was running his part of the campaign.

The British army is static, but the Americans are pushing on. We have got the air battle well in hand … as for the army, I am being more and more driven to the conclusion that Monty won't move unless he has everything on a plate. He has got

*Groundcrew had to keep the aircraft serviceable despite the poor facilities and lack of equipment; servicing a P-47 on an airstrip in France.*
(US National Archives)

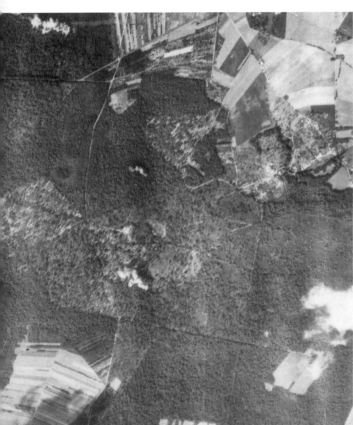 

*Heavy bombers attack a V-weapon supply depot as part of the Crossbow campaign. Fg Off Heath's Lancaster drops eleven 1,000lb (450kg) and four 500lb (225kg) bombs on the target in the Bois-de-Cassan. The second photo is from Flt Sgt Lawrie's aircraft (514 Squadron, Waterbeach).*

much of his army tied up in Villers-Bocage. To sum up the general situation, I would say that the Air Forces have set the arena for the army. They have dislocated the enemy's supplies and thrown him out of his stride, but I don't think the army has taken advantage of this situation or made enough use of it.

15 June: the following day it was more of the same:

> The army is still very sticky, and I am beginning to be afraid that we may miss the boat. The German divisions seem to me to be filtering in, getting together their little bits and pieces, and trying to sort themselves out after a rough journey. [The weather, which was still bad, also came in for comment, but with lack of reconnaissance being the main complaint:]
> The trouble is, I can't get proper reconnaissance, and without it I am beginning to lose continuity. A day or a day-and-a-half's break in reconnaissance means that I lose the thread. It is reconnaissance deeper into France over the back areas that I must have.

This same tone is found in Leigh-Mallory's diary for the next few days, and the main thrusts of his comments concerned what he still perceived as Montgomery's failure to 'get on with it' and with the increased pressure on him to allocate more resources against the V-weapon sites.

> I have no doubt that the Germans would like me to put big bomber formations on the sites launching pilotless aircraft, and they may even have begun to bomb London by this means in order to get me to do so; but I refuse to be diverted from my purpose. I shall wait for a day of fine weather, and then I shall plaster them. In the interests of the battle, if London gets forty or fifty pilotless aircraft shot at it, it must take it, as I am sure it will. [A few days later he wrote:]
> *Crossbow* [pilotless aircraft] are becoming more and more tiresome, and the Government are beginning to get jumpy about them. The Cabinet is nervous and repeatedly calling for action. *Crossbow* has

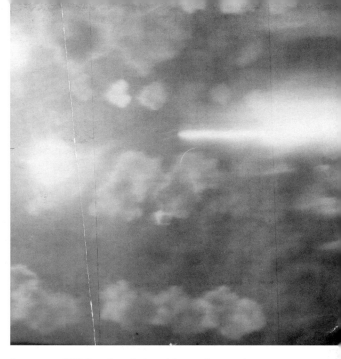

*Lancasters of 50 Squadron during night attack on roads at Limoges, 23/24 June.*

always had a high priority, and I have now detailed 200 aircraft of the American 8th Air Force to be kept at immediate readiness to attack *Crossbow* targets whenever they possibly can.

The Mustangs of 19 Squadron moved to France (B7 Martragny) from Ford on 25 June, the ground party having left some time before, for what had proved a difficult journey. Eric Hughes was one of the pilots that had escorted an attack by medium bombers on the route out from England, but with orders to land at the new strip after the mission:

> Our first responsibility was to supervise the refuelling and re-arming of the aircraft, making use of whatever camouflage cover was available. Then there was debriefing and a visit to the army liaison caravan, to be brought up to date on the current bomb line. With those essential tasks out of the way, we could get something to eat and decide where to sleep. I settled down in a slit trench, as close to my aircraft as possible, and tried to get some sleep. We were less than 2,000yd [1,800m] from the German lines, and once darkness fell they started

# The Second Blitz

At 04:18 in the morning on 13 June 1944, the peace at Swanscombe, near Gravesend, Kent, was shattered by a fierce explosion: the first of Hitler's new 'terror' weapons had landed on English soil. Within an hour, three more of these V-1 flying bombs had come to earth, one crashing into a railway bridge at Grove Road, Bethnal Green, in London, and causing six deaths and a substantial amount of damage.

Intelligence reports had been building since 1943, and it was evident that the weapon would eventually reach operational status and that London would be on the receiving end. Thus in December 1943 a series of studies was undertaken to determine the most effective air defence structure to protect the capital. It was very much a return to the early days of air defence, with a plan for three zones: fighter aircraft, anti-aircraft guns and balloons. The contribution of the bombers to countering this German weapon has already been mentioned, and in this short overview it is the UK-based defences that will be covered.

The revised *Diver* plan of February 1944 called for eight day-fighter squadrons, plus a number of night-fighter units, but for a lower total of anti-aircraft guns. In the twenty-four hour period from 22:30 on 15 June to 16 June 1944, British records show 151 reported launches, with 144 V-1s crossing the English coast. Of those, seventy-three reached the London area. The defences notched up only a modest score, seven falling to the fighters, fourteen to the guns and one shared, whilst a further eleven were shot down by the guns of the Inner Artillery Zone. The Hawker Tempests of No. 150 Wing at Newchurch had been at readiness for defensive patrol since dawn on 15 June.

Early the following day the wing leader, Wing Commander Roland Beamont and his No. 2, were airborne on such a patrol when they sighted a V-1. Giving chase, the fighters were eventually able to carry out an attack, and Beamont scored his first flying bomb 'kill', the missile crashing near Faversham.

Overall, however, it was an inauspicious start. Too many bombs had reached the London area, but there was no simple solution to the problem. The V-1, spanning a little over 17ft 6in (5m), made a very small target, and it flew fast (300–400mph/500–600kmph) and low. Pilots had first to find this small target, and then came the challenge of actually shooting it down. The official RAF account of the campaign summarized the speed problem: 'As for the fighters, the short time in which interception had to be made, demanded that they should be quickly and accurately directed on to the course of the bomb.'

Although 501 Squadron was the last of the Tempest units to enter the campaign, it became one of the most successful. By 29 July, the squadron had received its full complement of Tempest Vs, and was taken off operations to carry out intensive training in *Diver* techniques, but was tasked to specialize in the night role. The squadron, under the command of V-1 ace Squadron Leader Joe Berry, moved to Manston on 2 August to cover the area from the Kent coast to the North Downs.

The first kill went to Flying Officer Bill Polley in Tempest EJ585 on 5 August. He later recalled some of the problems of attacking these weapons:

> Very often we were too close to our targets before we got the opportunity to fire, and the big danger was getting an airburst. On one occasion I was chasing a V-1 too quickly, and I knew that I was overhauling the bomb too quickly and that I was very close to the armoured balloons. I fired a long burst and pulled up steeply to starboard, almost above the V-1, just as it exploded. The blast caught my left wing and tumbled the aircraft in a series of snap rolls. After what seemed an eternity, it regained its stability ... As my gyros had tumbled it was many ageing moments before I realized that I was upside down.

There was a significant risk of self-damage when the bomb exploded. Joe Berry made his stance very clear: 'The squadron must consider itself expendable, and thus will take off and try to effect interception in every weather condition ... even though all other squadrons are grounded.' The Tempest pilots flew along set patrol lines, the ends of which were marked by searchlights, and each patrol lasted some two hours. The sector controller provided positions of target and fighter, with the aim of putting the latter in an advantageous position to achieve a kill. Mosquito units were also active during the night hours, using airborne interception (AI) radar to locate their targets.

The first phase of the flying-bomb campaign ended on 1 September 1944, with the Allied capture of those V-1 launching sites within range of London. Although the campaign never resumed with the same intensity, from 4 September 1944 to 14 January 1945, the city was subjected to attack by V-1s launched from Heinkel He 111 mother aircraft over the North Sea. Defensive patrols remained in force, but there was even less warning of attack, so the ideal solution was to destroy the parent aircraft before they launched their weapons.

In the overall campaign the Germans launched some 9,252 flying bombs, of which around 5,900 crossed the English coast, 2,563 of those reaching the London area. The defences claimed 4,262 destroyed, a very respectable 72.3 per cent of those that crossed into England.

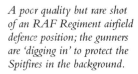
*A poor quality but rare shot of an RAF Regiment airfield defence position; the gunners are 'digging in' to protect the Spitfires in the background.*

shelling us. At daybreak we counted the cost. They had written off twenty-one of our aircraft [of the various units then at B7] and three of our men were killed. They had also hit the field hospital, killing three of the nurses.

This experience was not unusual, and many pilots, more used to the relatively comfortable billets in England, found this nearness to the front line somewhat unnerving! The battle for France was still stalled on the outskirts of Caen, the first of the major objectives for the British and Canadian forces on the eastern flank of the Allied advance. On 26 June, Montgomery launched his offensive, aimed at capturing the high ground south of Caen, a tactic designed to force the Germans to withdraw. 'My mind is very clear on one point:' wrote Leigh-Mallory, 'it is that we must be prepared to use every bit of air we've got, every single aircraft, in order to unstick the army if, as I fear, he gets bogged.' By 'every bit of air' he included the use of heavy bombers in a tactical role.

The advance was slow in the face of heavy German resistance and even limited counter-attacks; on 30 June the land commanders called for the use of heavy bombers, although on this occasion it was to bomb a road junction at Villers-Bocage through which it was thought that two Panzer divisions were planning to move. Bomber Command sent 266 heavies on a daytime attack that was accurately controlled by a Master Bomber. However, of more significance was the attack made by the command on 7 July in direct support of the Caen battle. The daylight attack involved 467 bombers on strongpoints around Caen, during which they dropped 2,276 tons of bombs. The focus of the attack had been subject to a late change of plan, and instead of the fortified villages, the bombers were tasked against stretches of open ground between the villages and Caen. The results were poor as the change of plan had been inappropriate; no progress was made by the ground forces, and on 18 July a larger attack was made against the fortified villages. Under Operation *Goodwood*, over 900 bombers attacked at dawn, dropping over 5,000 tons of bombs. Results were good, and a number of similar attacks were carried out in direct support of the army during August.

With the British and Canadians finally taking Caen in late July, and with the Americans continuing their progress, the Allied campaign, was on the path to final victory. Allied tactical aircraft now occupied numerous airfields in France, including permanent facilities recently 'vacated' by the *Luftwaffe*. With large numbers of aircraft moving base to keep pace with the advancing front line, and with aircraft becoming increasingly expert in the techniques of providing air support, the Allied armies had an incredibly efficient air umbrella. Ground forces came to rely on this

*Refuelling P-47s at a strip in France.* (US National Archives)

support, and at periods when poor weather grounded most air effort, the Allied forces proved vulnerable; indeed the Germans invariably took advantage of periods of poor weather – most dramatically with their last major offensive in the Ardennes (the Battle of the Bulge).

The campaign for the control of France was by no means over, but it was now almost certain that the Allies were here to stay; also the build-up race was now in their favour, as increasing amounts of men and material arrived in Normandy.

## Conclusions

Many of the major points for a considered view of the air campaign have been made above as quotes from Allied and German sources. Before we make the final comments, the following statements reinforce those already made. First from Montgomery:

> An essential preliminary to the assault was the reduction of the GAF to the degree required to ensure mastery of the air over our seaborne forces and over the beaches on the invasion coast. The

*It was important for the Allies to take over permanent airfields; Juvincourt (A68) was located 10 miles (16km) north of Reims.* (US National Archives)

next Army requirement was the interdiction of rail and road communications, with the object of delaying the movement of enemy troops and supplies to the battle area.

Von Runstedt, when asked about the chances of defeating the invasion, said: '... not after the first few days. The Allied air forces paralysed all movement by day and made it very difficult by night. They had smashed the bridges over the Loire as well as the Seine, shutting off the whole area.'

Oberst Hoffner, Chief of German Military Transport Organization, France, had this to say:

Most of the carefully prepared and provisioned airfields assigned to the fighter units had been bombed, and the units had to land at other hastily chosen landing grounds. The poor signals network broke down causing further confusion. Each unit's advance party came by Ju 52, but the main body of the ground staff came by rail, and most arrived days or even weeks later. The attacks on French railways between March and May 1944 reduced the capacity of the network so seriously that in addition to eliminating all French civilian and economic traffic, German economic, armaments and fortifications traffic were progressively abandoned ... had we been able to run our movements on the rates scheduled before the attacks on the railways began in March, the invasion might well not have succeeded.

### Field Marshal von Kluge to Hitler:

[There is] regrettable evidence that in our present position there is no way by which, in the face of the enemy air force complete command, we can find a strategy which will counterbalance its annihilating effect without giving up the field of battle. Whole armoured formations, allotted to the counter-attack, were caught up in bomb carpets of the greatest intensity so that they could be got out of the torn up ground only by prolonged effort. The actual result was that they arrived too late. The psychological effect of such a mass of bombs coming down

*Montgomery was a firm believer in the value of air support, a lesson he had learnt during his campaigns in the Western Desert.*

with all the power of elemental nature on the fighting force, especially the infantry, is a factor which has to be given serious consideration.

### Air Chief Marshal Sir Trafford Leigh-Mallory:

It seems to me that the Press and the wireless are concentrating on the Army and neglecting the air. I don't say this because I want publicity, but because I think the public ought to know the truth, and I am convinced that the truth is that the air has done more to wage this battle, and will have done more to win it, than either of the other two arms. If it had not been for the air attacks by bombers, fighter-bombers and fighters delivered before D-Day and immediately afterwards, it is my view that the Army would have had double, if not three times the amount of resistance which they have in fact

*The RAF was awarded a Battle Honour for the Normandy operation – as shown bottom right on the Standard of No. 100 Squadron.*

BELOW: *Rough and ready but effective; RAF personnel have the 'have squadron, will travel' principle.*

encountered. As it is, the Germans in front of them are short of petrol and ammunition and are in a generally poor state. This is due to air attack.

There is much more in the same vein, all of it from the German side bewailing the extreme difficulties of trying to work in the face of Allied air power. One of the most amazing aspects of the Normandy campaign is that the Germans coped as well as they did, commanders adapted their routines, imposed stringent camouflage regulations and made every effort to avoid the attention of the prowling aircraft. Allied commanders make no secret of the fact that they simply could not have proceeded in the way that they did in anything less than total air superiority; to have attempted to 'run' the causeways off the beach, or build up the logistical stockpiles on the beaches in the face of a viable air threat, would have been impossible.

Liddell-Hart, one of the great military historians, said about 6 June:

> ... at the outset the margin between success and failure was narrow. The ultimate triumph has obscured the fact that the Allies were in great danger at the outset, and had a very narrow shave. If

even the three Panzer divisions, out of ten, that were on the scene by the fourth day had been at hand to intervene on D-Day, the Allied foothold could have been dislodged before they were joined up and consolidated.

As in any military campaign there were mistakes, some things could have been better organized or more smoothly run, casualties might have been avoided, and so on. Nevertheless, as has been shown in this brief account of the air campaign for D-Day, air power was the central element in the success of *Overlord*.

# APPENDIX I
# Allied Order of Battle, June 1944

The Orders of Battle in this appendix are for the major formations directly involved with Operation *Overlord*. It could be argued that every Allied aviation unit in Europe was involved to a greater or lesser extent, even those not directly engaged in the operational areas played a part in diverting German assets, in the air and on the ground.

NOTE: A number of abbreviations are used in this appendix:
Sqn - Squadron; Flt - Flight; det - detachment; FAA - Fleet Air Arm.

**Chain of Air Command**

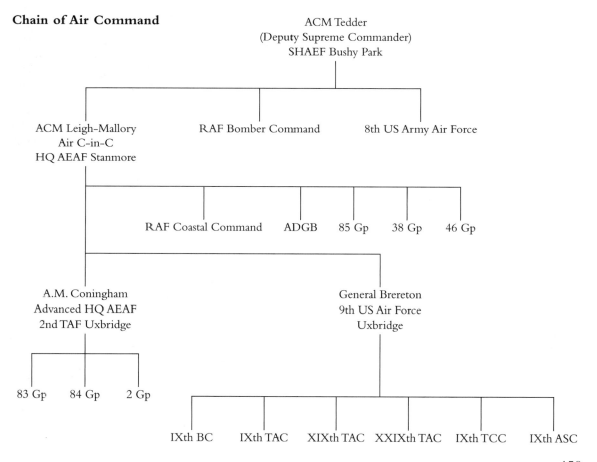

## Supreme HQ Allied Expeditionary Force (AEF)

*Supreme Commander:*
General Dwight D. Eisenhower
*Deputy Supreme Commander:*
Air Chief Marshal Sir Arthur W. Tedder GCB

## HQ Allied Expeditionary Air Forces (AEAF)

*Air Officer Commanding-in-Chief:*
Air Chief Marshal Sir Trafford Leigh-Mallory KCB DSO
*Senior Air Staff Officer:*
Air Vice-Marshal H. E. P. Wiggleworth CBE DSC

## 2nd Tactical Air Force (TAF)

HQ UXBRIDGE
*Air Officer Commanding:*
Air Marshal Sir Arthur Coningham KCB
DSO MC DFC AFC
*Senior Air Staff Officer:*
Air Vice-Marshal V. E. Groom OBE DFC

*No. 34 Wing (Gp Capt C. R. Lousada)*

| | | |
|---|---|---|
| 16 Sqn | Northolt | Spitfire PR.XI |
| 69 Sqn | Northolt | Wellington XIII |
| 140 Sqn | Northolt | Mosquito PR.IX/PR.XVI |

*No. 35 Wing*

| | | |
|---|---|---|
| 2 Sqn | Gatwick | Mustang II |
| 4 Sqn | Gatwick | Spitfire PR.XI |
| 268 Sqn | Gatwick | Mustang IA |

*No. 39 Wing*

| | | |
|---|---|---|
| 168 Sqn | Odiham | Mustang I |
| 400 Sqn | Odiham | Spitfire PR.XI |
| 414 Sqn | Odiham | Mustang I |
| 430 Sqn | Odiham | Mustang I |

*No. 121 Wing (Wg Cdr C. S. Morice)*

| | | |
|---|---|---|
| 174 Sqn | Holmsley South | Typhoon |
| 175 Sqn | Holmsley South | Typhoon |
| 245 Sqn | Holmsley South | Typhoon |

*No. 122 Wing*

| | | |
|---|---|---|
| 19 Sqn | Funtington | Mustang III |
| 65 Sqn | Funtington | Mustang III |
| 122 Sqn | Funtington | Mustang III |

*No. 123 Wing (Wg Cdr D. J. Scott)*

| | | |
|---|---|---|
| 198 Sqn | Thorney Island | Typhoon |
| 609 Sqn | Thorney Island | Typhoon |

*No. 124 Wing (Wg Cdr B. G. Carroll)*

| | | |
|---|---|---|
| 181 Sqn | Hurn | Typhoon |
| 182 Sqn | Hurn | Typhoon |
| 247 Sqn | Hurn | Typhoon |

*Typhoon of 175 Squadron, the unit operated as part of No. 121 Wing out of Holmsley South.*

*Typhoon JR128 (HF-L) of 183 Squadron; the squadron was part of No. 136 Wing at Thorney Island prior to D-Day.*

BELOW: *The Free French units, such as the Boston-equipped 342 Tunisie Squadron, were particularly keen to get back to France. During* Overlord *this unit operated as part of No. 137 Wing from Hartford Bridge.*

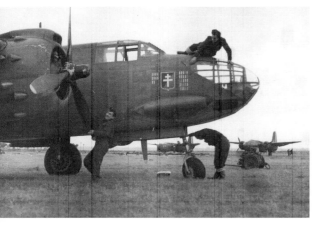

**No. 125 Wing (Wg Cdr J. H. Lapsley)**

| | | |
|---|---|---|
| 132 Sqn | Ford | Spitfire LF.IX |
| 602 Sqn | Ford | Spitfire LF.IX |
| 453 Sqn | Ford | Spitfire LF.IX |

**No. 126 Wing (Wg Cdr K. Hudson)**

| | | |
|---|---|---|
| 401 Sqn | Tangmere | Spitfire LF.IX |
| 411 Sqn | Tangmere | Spitfire LF.IX |
| 412 Sqn | Tangmere | Spitfire LF.IX |

**No. 127 Wing**

| | | |
|---|---|---|
| 403 Sqn | Tangmere | Spitfire LF.IX |
| 416 Sqn | Tangmere | Spitfire LF.IX |
| 421 Sqn | Tangmere | Spitfire LF.IX |

**No. 129 Wing (Wg Cdr D. C. Macdonald)**

| | | |
|---|---|---|
| 184 Sqn | Westhampnett | Typhoon |

**No. 131 Wing**

| | | |
|---|---|---|
| 302 Sqn | Selsey | Spitfire LF.IX |
| 308 Sqn | Selsey | Spitfire LF.IX |
| 317 Sqn | Selsey | Spitfire LF.IX |

**No. 132 Wing**

| | | |
|---|---|---|
| 66 Sqn | Bognor | Spitfire LF.IX |
| 331 Sqn | Bognor | Spitfire LF.IX |
| 332 Sqn | Bognor | Spitfire LF.IX |

**No. 133 Wing**

| | | |
|---|---|---|
| 306 Sqn | Coolham | Mustang III |
| 315 Sqn | Coolham | Mustang III |
| 129 Sqn | Coolham | Mustang III |

**No. 134 Wing (Wg Cdr Vybiral)**

| | | |
|---|---|---|
| 310 Sqn | Appledram | Spitfire LF.IX |
| 312 Sqn | Appledram | Spitfire LF.IX |
| 313 Sqn | Appledram | Spitfire LF.IX |

**No 135 Wing (Wg Cdr Harris)**

| | | |
|---|---|---|
| 222 Sqn | Chailey | Spitfire LF.IX |
| 349 Sqn | Chailey | Spitfire LF.IX |
| 485 Sqn | Chailey | Spitfire LF.IX |

**No. 136 Wing (Wg Cdr J. M. Bryan)**

| | | |
|---|---|---|
| 164 Sqn | Thorney Island | Typhoon |
| 183 Sqn | Thorney Island | Typhoon |

**No. 137 Wing**

| | | |
|---|---|---|
| 88 Sqn | Hartford Bridge | Boston IIIA |
| 226 Sqn | Hartford Bridge | Mitchell II |
| 342 Sqn | Hartford Bridge | Boston IIIA |

*No. 138 Wing*

| | | |
|---|---|---|
| 107 Sqn | Lasham | Mosquito VI |
| 305 Sqn | Lasham | Mosquito VI |
| 613 Sqn | Lasham | Mosquito VI |

*No. 139 Wing*

| | | |
|---|---|---|
| 98 Sqn | Dunsfold | Mitchell II |
| 180 Sqn | Dunsfold | Mitchell II |
| 320 Sqn | Dunsfold | Mitchell II |

*No. 140 Wing*

| | | |
|---|---|---|
| 21 Sqn | Gravesend | Mosquito VI |
| 137 Sqn | Manston | Typhoon |
| 464 Sqn | Gravesend | Mosquito VI |
| 487 Sqn | Gravesend | Mosquito VI |

*No. 143 Wing (Wg Cdr F. W. Hillock)*

| | | |
|---|---|---|
| 438 Sqn | Hurn | Typhoon |
| 439 Sqn | Hurn | Typhoon |
| 440 Sqn | Hurn | Typhoon |

*No. 144 Wing*

| | | |
|---|---|---|
| 441 Sqn | Ford | Spitfire LF.IX |
| 442 Sqn | Ford | Spitfire LF.IX |
| 443 Sqn | Ford | Spitfire LF.IX |

*No. 145 Wing (Wg Cdr Crawford Compton)*

| | | |
|---|---|---|
| 329 Sqn | Merston | Spitfire LF.IX |
| 340 Sqn | Merston | Spitfire LF.IX |
| 341 Sqn | Merston | Spitfire LF.IX |

*No. 146 Wing (Wg Cdr E. R. Baker)*

| | | |
|---|---|---|
| 193 Sqn | Needs Oar Point | Typhoon |
| 197 Sqn | Needs Oar Point | Typhoon |
| 257 Sqn | Needs Oar Point | Typhoon |
| 266 Sqn | Needs Oar Point | Typhoon |

*Great shot of two pilots from 440 Squadron, with an appropriately marked bomb – 'May we drop one for you?'*
(440 Squadron)

*No. 3 Naval (Air Spotting Pool) Wing*

| | | |
|---|---|---|
| 808 Sqn | Lee on Solent | Seafire |
| 885 Sqn | Lee on Solent | Seafire |
| 886 Sqn | Lee on Solent | Seafire |
| 897 Sqn | Lee on Solent | Seafire |

*Air Spotting Pool*

| | | |
|---|---|---|
| 26 Sqn | Lee on Solent | Spitfire V |
| 63 Sqn | Lee on Solent | Spitfire V |

*Spitfire IXs of 443 Squadron deployed to France (to B3 St Croix) on 15 June from their base at Ford.*

## Air Defence of Great Britain (ADGB) Units Under Operational Control of 2nd TAF

| | | |
|---|---|---|
| 33 Sqn | Lympne | Spitfire IX |
| 74 Sqn | Lympne | Spitfire HF.IX |
| 127 Sqn | Lympne | Spitfire HF.IX |
| 80 Sqn | Detling | Spitfire IX |
| 229 Sqn | Detling | Spitfire IX |
| 274 Sqn | Detling | Spitfire IX |
| 350 Sqn | Friston | Spitfire LF.V |
| 501 Sqn | Friston | Spitfire LF.V |
| 130 Sqn | Horne | Spitfire LF.V |
| 303 Sqn | Horne | Spitfire LF.V |
| 402 Sqn | Horne | Spitfire LF.V |
| 64 Sqn | Deanland | Spitfire LF.V |
| 234 Sqn | Deanland | Spitfire LF.V |
| 611 Sqn | Deanland | Spitfire LF.V |
| 345 Sqn | Shoreham | Spitfire LF.V |

## Units of No. 85 Group under Operational Control of 2nd TAF

*No. 141 Wing*

| | | |
|---|---|---|
| 322 Sqn | Hartford Bridge | Spitfire XIV |

*No. 148 Wing*

| | | |
|---|---|---|
| 91 Sqn | West Malling | Spitfire XIV |

*No. 150 Wing*

| | | |
|---|---|---|
| 3 Sqn | Newchurch | Tempest V |
| 56 Sqn | Newchurch | Spitfire LF.IX |
| 486 Sqn | Newchurch | Tempest V |
| 124 Sqn | Bradwell Bay | Spitfire VII |

## Other ADGB/No. 85 Group Units Allocated Tasks within *Overlord*

*ADGB Air Officer Commanding:*
Air Marshal Sir Roderic M. Hill KCB MC AFC
*Senior Air Staff Officer:*
Air Vice-Marshal W. B. Calloway CBE AFC

*No. 10 Group*

| | | |
|---|---|---|
| 616 Sqn | Fairwood Common | Spitfire |
| 68 Sqn | Fairwood Common | Mosquito |
| 1 Sqn | Predannack | Spitfire IX |
| 165 Sqn | Predannack | Spitfire IX |
| 151 Sqn | Predannack | Mosquito |
| 1449 Flt | St Mary's, Scilly Is | Hurricane |
| 610 Sqn | Culmhead | Spitfire XIV |
| 126 Sqn | Culmhead | Spitfire IX |
| 263 Sqn | Harrowbeer | Typhoon |
| 131 Sqn | Harrowbeer | Spitfire |
| 41 Sqn | Bolthead | Spitfire |
| 406 Sqn | Winkleigh | Beaufighter, Mosquito |

*No. 12 Group*

| | | |
|---|---|---|
| 316 Sqn | Coltishall | Mustang |
| 504 Sqn det | Digby | Spitfire |
| 309 Sqn det | Hutton Cranswick | Hurricane |
| 25 Sqn | Coltishall | Mosquito |
| 307 Sqn | Church Fenton | Mosquito |

*No. 11 Group/No. 85 Group Night-Fighter Force*

| | | |
|---|---|---|
| 125 Sqn | Hurn | Mosquito XVII |
| 604 Sqn | Hurn | Mosquito XIII |
| 418 Sqn | Holmsley South | Mosquito VI |
| 456 Sqn | Ford | Mosquito XXX |
| 96 Sqn | West Malling | Mosquito XII/XIII |
| 29 Sqn | West Malling | Mosquito XIII |
| 409 Sqn | West Malling | Mosquito XIII |
| 219 Sqn | Bradwell Bay | Mosquito XXX |
| 605 Sqn | Manston | Mosquito VI |
| 488 Sqn | Zeals | Mosquito XIII |
| 264 Sqn | Hartford Bridge | Mosquito XIII |
| 410 Sqn | Hunsdon | Mosquito XIII |

*Air-Sea Rescue Units*

| | | |
|---|---|---|
| 275 Sqn | Warmwell | Walrus, Anson, Spitfire |
| 276 Sqn | Portreath, Bolthead | Warwick, Walrus, Spitfire |
| 277 Sqn | Shoreham, Hawkinge | Walrus, Sea Otter, Spitfire |
| 278 Sqn | Bradwell Bay, Martlesham | Warwick, Walrus, Spitfire |

## Coastal Command Units for *Overlord*

*Air Officer Commanding:*
Air Chief Marshal Sir Sholto Douglas KCB MC DFC
*Senior Air Staff Officer:*
Air Vice-Marshal A. B. Ellwood CB DSC

*No. 19 Group*

| | | |
|---|---|---|
| 10 Sqn RAAF | Mount Batten | Sunderland |
| 228 Sqn | Pembroke Dock | Sunderland |
| 461 Sqn | Pembroke Dock | Sunderland |
| 201 Sqn | Pembroke Dock | Sunderland |
| 422 Sqn★ | Castle Archdale | Sunderland |
| 423 Sqn★ | Castle Archdale | Sunderland |
| 58 Sqn | St David's | Halifax |
| 502 Sqn | St David's | Halifax |
| 53 Sqn | St Eval | Liberator |
| 224 Sqn | St Eval | Liberator |
| 547 Sqn | St Eval | Liberator |
| 206 Sqn | St Eval | Liberator |
| 103 Sqn | Dunkeswell | Liberator |
| 105 Sqn | Dunkeswell | Liberator |
| 110 Sqn | Dunkeswell | Liberator |
| 311 Sqn | Predannack | Wellington |
| 179 Sqn | Predannack | Wellington |
| 407 Sqn | Chivenor | Wellington |
| 172 Sqn | Chivenor | Wellington |
| 304 Sqn | Chivenor | Wellington |
| 612 Sqn | Chivenor | Wellington |
| 404 Sqn | Davidstow Moor | Beaufighter |
| 144 Sqn | Davidstow Moor | Beaufighter |
| 282 Sqn | Davidstow Moor | Warwick |
| 524 Flt | Davidstow Moor | Wellington |
| 248 Sqn | Portreath | Mosquito |
| 235 Sqn | Portreath | Beaufighter |
| 415 Flt | Winkleigh/Bolthead | Albacore |
| 517 Sqn | Brawdy | Halifax |
| 849 Sqn FAA | Perranporth | Avenger |
| 850 Sqn FAA | Perranporth | Avenger |
| 816 Sqn FAA | Perranporth | Swordfish |
| 838 Sqn FAA | Harrowbeer | Swordfish |

★(No. 15 Group)

*No. 16 Group*

| | | |
|---|---|---|
| 143 Sqn | Manston | Beaufighter |
| 236 Sqn | North Coates | Beaufighter |
| 254 Sqn | North Coates | Beaufighter |
| 455 Sqn | Langham | Beaufighter |
| 498 Sqn | Langham | Beaufighter |
| 279 Sqn | Bircham Newton | Hudson |
| 521 Sqn | Bircham Newton | Ventura/Gladiator |
| 415 det | Docking/Manston | Wellington/Albacore |
| 280 Sqn | Strubby | Warwick |
| 819 Sqn FAA | Manston | Swordfish |
| 848 Sqn FAA | Manston | Avenger |

(Other Coastal Command units in No. 15 Gp, No. 18 Gp, Iceland, Gibraltar, Azores, flew convoy patrols, met. reconnaissance, and anti-submarine ops in the Atlantic)

## Transport Groups

*No. 38 Group*

| | | |
|---|---|---|
| 296 Sqn | Brize Norton | Albemarle |
| 297 Sqn | Brize Norton | Albemarle |
| 295 Sqn | Harwell | Albemarle |
| 570 Sqn | Harwell | Albemarle |
| 190 Sqn | Fairford | Stirling |
| 620 Sqn | Fairford | Stirling |
| 196 Sqn | Keevil | Stirling |
| 299 Sqn | Keevil | Stirling |
| 298 Sqn | Tarrant Rushton | Halifax |
| 644 Sqn | Tarrant Rushton | Halifax |

*No. 46 Group*

| | | |
|---|---|---|
| 233 Sqn | Blakehill Farm | Dakota |
| 512 Sqn | Broadwell | Dakota |
| 575 Sqn | Broadwell | Dakota |
| 48 Sqn | Down Ampney | Dakota |
| 271 Sqn | Down Ampney | Dakota |
| 1696 ADLS | Northolt | various |

## Bomber Command

HQ HIGH WYCOMBE
*Air Officer Commanding:*
Air Chief Marshal Sir Arthur T. Harris
KCB OBE AFC
*Senior Air Staff Officer:*
Air Vice-Marshal H. S. P. Walmsley CBE
MC DFC

*No. 1 Group (Air Vice-Marshal E. A. B. Rice)*

| | | |
|---|---|---|
| 12 Sqn | Wickenby | Lancaster |
| 626 Sqn | Wickenby | Lancaster |
| 100 Sqn | Grimsby | Lancaster |
| 101 Sqn | Ludford Magna | Lancaster |
| 103 Sqn | Elsham Wolds | Lancaster |
| 576 Sqn | Elsham Wolds | Lancaster |
| 166 Sqn | Kirmington | Lancaster |
| 300 Sqn | Faldingworth | Lancaster |
| 460 Sqn | Binbrook | Lancaster |
| 550 Sqn | North Killingholme | Lancaster |
| 625 Sqn | Kelstern | Lancaster |

*No. 3 Group (Air Vice-Marshal R. Harrison)*

| | | |
|---|---|---|
| 90 Sqn | Tuddenham | Lancaster |
| 149 Sqn | Methwold | Stirling |
| 218 Sqn | Woolfox Lodge | Stirling |
| 15 Sqn | Mildenhall | Lancaster |
| 75 Sqn | Mepal | Lancaster |
| 115 Sqn | Witchford | Lancaster |
| 514 Sqn | Waterbeach | Lancaster |
| 622 Sqn | Mildenhall | Lancaster |
| 138 Sqn | Tempsford | Stirling, Halifax |
| 161 Sqn | Tempsford | Lysander, Hudson, Halifax |

*No. 4 Group (Air Vice-Marshal C. R. Carr)*

| | | |
|---|---|---|
| 102 Sqn | Pocklington | Halifax |
| 10 Sqn | Melbourne | Halifax |
| 51 Sqn | Snaith | Halifax |
| 76 Sqn | Holme-on-Spalding Moor | Halifax |
| 78 Sqn | Breighton | Halifax |

*Halifax over the Pas de Calais. With a negligible threat from the Luftwaffe, Bomber Command's heavies were able to operate in daylight in areas where air superiority had been achieved.*

| | | |
|---|---|---|
| 158 Sqn | Lissett | Halifax |
| 466 Sqn | Leconfield | Halifax |
| 640 Sqn | Leconfield | Halifax |
| 578 Sqn | Burn | Halifax |
| 77 Sqn | Full Sutton | Halifax |
| 346 Sqn | Elvington | Halifax |

*No. 5 Group (Air Vice-Marshal A. Cochrane)*

| | | |
|---|---|---|
| 9 Sqn | Bardney | Lancaster |
| 44 Sqn | Dunholme Lodge | Lancaster |
| 49 Sqn | Fiskerton | Lancaster |
| 50 Sqn | Skellingthorpe | Lancaster |
| 61 Sqn | Skellingthorpe | Lancaster |
| 57 Sqn | East Kirkby | Lancaster |
| 630 Sqn | East Kirkby | Lancaster |
| 106 Sqn | Metheringham | Lancaster |
| 207 Sqn | Spilsby | Lancaster |
| 463 Sqn | Waddington | Lancaster |
| 467 Sqn | Waddington | Lancaster |
| 619 Sqn | Dunholme Lodge | Lancaster |
| 617 Sqn | Woodhall Spa | Lancaster |
| 627 Sqn | Woodhall Spa | Mosquito |
| 83 Sqn | Coningsby | Lancaster |
| 97 Sqn | Coningsby | Lancaster |

### No. 6 (RCAF) Group (Air Vice-Marshal C. McEwen)

| | | |
|---|---|---|
| 420 Sqn | Tholthorpe | Halifax |
| 425 Sqn | Tholthorpe | Halifax |
| 424 Sqn | Skipton-on-Swale | Halifax |
| 433 Sqn | Skipton-on-Swale | Halifax |
| 426 Sqn | Linton-on-Ouse | Halifax |
| 408 Sqn | Linton-on-Ouse | Lancaster |
| 427 Sqn | Leeming | Halifax |
| 429 Sqn | Leeming | Halifax |
| 431 Sqn | Croft | Halifax |
| 434 Sqn | Croft | Halifax |
| 432 Sqn | East Moor | Halifax |
| 419 Sqn | Middleton-St-George | Lancaster |
| 428 Sqn | Middleton-St-George | Lancaster, Halifax |

### No. 8 (Pathfinder) Group (Air Vice-Marshal D. C. T. Bennett)

| | | |
|---|---|---|
| 7 Sqn | Oakington | Lancaster |
| 571 Sqn | Oakington | Mosquito |
| 35 Sqn | Graveley | Lancaster |
| 692 Sqn | Graveley | Mosquito |
| 156 Sqn | Upwood | Lancaster |
| 139 Sqn | Upwood | Mosquito |
| 405 Sqn | Gransden Lodge | Lancaster |
| 582 Sqn | Little Staughton | Lancaster |
| 109 Sqn | Little Staughton | Mosquito |
| 635 Sqn | Downham Market | Lancaster |
| 105 Sqn | Bourn | Mosquito |

### No. 100 Group (Air Vice-Marshal E. B. Addison)

| | | |
|---|---|---|
| 141 Sqn | West Raynham | Mosquito |
| 239 Sqn | West Raynham | Mosquito |
| 169 Sqn | Little Snoring | Mosquito |
| 85 Sqn | Swannington | Mosquito |
| 157 Sqn | Swannington | Mosquito |
| 515 Sqn | Little Snoring | Mosquito |
| 23 Sqn | Little Snoring | Mosquito |
| 214 Sqn | Oulton | B-17 |
| 192 Sqn | Foulsham | Halifax, Mosquito |
| 199 Sqn | North Creake | Stirling |

## US 8th Army Air Force

*Commander:*
Lieutenant General James H. Doolittle
*1st Bombardment Division:*
Major General Robert B. Williams
*2nd Bombardment Division:*
Brigadier General James P. Hodges

*3rd Bombardment Division:*
Major General Curtis E. LeMay

## VIIIth Fighter Command

Major General William E. Kepner

### 67th Fighter Wing
### (1st Bombardment Division)

*20th Fighter Group (Lieutenant Colonel Harold J. Rau)*

| | | |
|---|---|---|
| 55th Sqn | Kingscliffe | P-38 |
| 77th Sqn | Kingscliffe | P-38 |
| 79th Sqn | Kingscliffe | P-38 |

*352nd Fighter Group (Colonel Joseph P. Mason)*

| | | |
|---|---|---|
| 328th Sqn | Bodney | P-51 |
| 486th Sqn | Bodney | P-51 |
| 487th Sqn | Bodney | P-51 |

*356th Fighter Group (Lieutenant Colonel Philip E. Tukey)*

| | | |
|---|---|---|
| 359th Sqn | Martlesham | P-47 |
| 360th Sqn | Martlesham | P-47 |
| 361st Sqn | Martlesham | P-47 |

*359th Fighter Group (Colonel Avelin P. Tacon)*

| | | |
|---|---|---|
| 368th Sqn | East Wretham | P-51 |
| 369th Sqn | East Wretham | P-51 |
| 370th Sqn | East Wretham | P-51 |

*364th Fighter Group (Colonel Roy W. Osborn)*

| | | |
|---|---|---|
| 383rd Sqn | Honington | P-38 |
| 384th Sqn | Honington | P-38 |
| 385th Sqn | Honington | P-38 |

### 65th Fighter Wing
### (2nd Bombardment Division)

HQ Saffron Walden Grammar School

*4th Fighter Group (Colonel Donald J. Blakeslee)*

| | | |
|---|---|---|
| 334th Sqn | Debden | P-51 |
| 335th Sqn | Debden | P-51 |
| 336th Sqn | Debden | P-51 |

*56th Fighter Group (Colonel Hubert A. Zemke)*

| | | |
|---|---|---|
| 61st Sqn | Boxted | P-47 |
| 62nd Sqn | Boxted | P-47 |
| 63rd Sqn | Boxted | P-47 |

*Lt Col Jointilla briefs the
353rd FG for a mission
in January 1944.*
(US National Archives)

*355th Fighter Group (Colonel William J. Cummings)*

| | | |
|---|---|---|
| 354th Sqn | Steeple Morden | P-51 |
| 357th Sqn | Steeple Morden | P-51 |
| 358th Sqn | Steeple Morden | P-51 |

*361st Fighter Group (Colonel Thomas J. Christian)*

| | | |
|---|---|---|
| 374th Sqn | Bottisham | P-51 |
| 375th Sqn | Bottisham | P-51 |
| 376th Sqn | Bottisham | P-51 |

*479th Fighter Group (Lieutenant Colonel Kyle L. Riddle)*

| | | |
|---|---|---|
| 434th Sqn | Wattisham | P-38 |
| 435th Sqn | Wattisham | P-38 |
| 436th Sqn | Wattisham | P-38 |

## 66th Fighter Wing (3rd Bombardment Division)

HQ SAWSTON HALL, NR CAMBRIDGE

*55th Fighter Group (Colonel George T. Crowell)*

| | | |
|---|---|---|
| 38th Sqn | Wormingford | P-38 |
| 338th Sqn | Wormingford | P-38 |
| 343rd Sqn | Wormingford | P-38 |

*78th Fighter Group (Colonel Frederic C. Gray)*

| | | |
|---|---|---|
| 82nd Sqn | Duxford | P-47 |
| 83rd Sqn | Duxford | P-47 |
| 84th Sqn | Duxford | P-47 |

*339th Fighter Group (Colonel John B. Henry)*

| | | |
|---|---|---|
| 503rd Sqn | Fowlmere | P-51 |
| 504th Sqn | Fowlmere | P-51 |
| 505th Sqn | Fowlmere | P-51 |

*353rd Fighter Group (Colonel Glenn E. Duncan)*

| | | |
|---|---|---|
| 350th Sqn | Raydon | P-47 |
| 351st Sqn | Raydon | P-47 |
| 352nd Sqn | Raydon | P-47 |

*357th Fighter Group (Colonel Donald W. Graham)*

| | | |
|---|---|---|
| 362nd Sqn | Leiston | P-51 |
| 363rd Sqn | Leiston | P-51 |
| 364th Sqn | Leiston | P-51 |

## USSTAF (Operational Control of 8th and 15th Air Force)

*Commander:*
Lieutenant-General Carl A. Spaatz

## VIIIth Bomber Command

### 1st Combat Wing (1st Bombardment Division)
HQ BASSINGBOURN

*91st Bomb Group (Colonel Henry W. Terry)*

| | | |
|---|---|---|
| 322nd Sqn | Bassingbourn | B-17 |
| 323rd Sqn | Bassingbourn | B-17 |

| | | |
|---|---|---|
| 324th Sqn | Bassingbourn | B-17 |
| 401st Sqn | Bassingbourn | B-17 |

*381st Bomb Group (Colonel Harry P. Leber)*

| | | |
|---|---|---|
| 532nd Sqn | Ridgewell | B-17 |
| 533rd Sqn | Ridgewell | B-17 |
| 534th Sqn | Ridgewell | B-17 |
| 535th Sqn | Ridgewell | B-17 |

*398th Bomb Group (Colonel Frank P. Hunter)*

| | | |
|---|---|---|
| 600th Sqn | Nuthampstead | B-17 |
| 601st Sqn | Nuthampstead | B-17 |
| 602nd Sqn | Nuthampstead | B-17 |
| 603rd Sqn | Nuthampstead | B-17 |

**2nd Combat Wing (2nd Bombardment Division)**
HQ HETHEL

*389th Bomb Group (Colonel Robert B. Miller)*

| | | |
|---|---|---|
| 564th Sqn | Hethel | B-24 |
| 565th Sqn | Hethel | B-24 |
| 566th Sqn | Hethel | B-24 |
| 567th Sqn | Hethel | B-24 |

*445th Bomb Group (Colonel Robert H. Terrill)*

| | | |
|---|---|---|
| 700th Sqn | Tibenham | B-24 |
| 701st Sqn | Tibenham | B-24 |
| 702nd Sqn | Tibenham | B-24 |
| 703rd Sqn | Tibenham | B-24 |

*453rd Bomb Group (Colonel Ramsey D Potts)*

| | | |
|---|---|---|
| 732nd Sqn | Old Buckenham | B-24 |
| 733rd Sqn | Old Buckenham | B-24 |
| 734th Sqn | Old Buckenham | B-24 |
| 735th Sqn | Old Buckenham | B-24 |

**4th Combat Wing (3rd Bombardment Division)**
HQ BURY ST EDMUNDS

*94th Bomb Group (Colonel Charles B. Dougher)*

| | | |
|---|---|---|
| 331st Sqn | Bury St Edmunds | B-17 |
| 332nd Sqn | Bury St Edmunds | B-17 |
| 333rd Sqn | Bury St Edmunds | B-17 |
| 410th Sqn | Bury St Edmunds | B-17 |

*447th Bomb Group (Colonel Hunter Harris)*

| | | |
|---|---|---|
| 708th Sqn | Rattlesden | B-17 |
| 709th Sqn | Rattlesden | B-17 |
| 710th Sqn | Rattlesden | B-17 |
| 711th Sqn | Rattlesden | B-17 |

*486th Bomb Group (Colonel Glendon P. Overing)*

| | | |
|---|---|---|
| 832nd Sqn | Sudbury | B-24 |
| 833rd Sqn | Sudbury | B-24 |
| 834th Sqn | Sudbury | B-24 |
| 835th Sqn | Sudbury | B-24 |

*B-17s of the 381st BG; the four Flying Fortress Squadrons of this Group were led by Col Harry Leber.*

*487th Bomb Group (Colonel Robert Taylor III)*

| | | |
|---|---|---|
| 836th Sqn | Lavenham | B-24 |
| 837th Sqn | Lavenham | B-24 |
| 838th Sqn | Lavenham | B-24 |
| 839th Sqn | Lavenham | B-24 |

## 13th Combat Wing (3rd Bombardment Division)
HQ HORHAM

*95th Bomb Group (Colonel Karl Truesdell)*

| | | |
|---|---|---|
| 334th Sqn | Horham | B-17 |
| 335th Sqn | Horham | B-17 |
| 336th Sqn | Horham | B-17 |
| 412th Sqn | Horham | B-17 |

*100th Bomb Group (Colonel Thomas S. Jeffrey)*

| | | |
|---|---|---|
| 349th Sqn | Thorpe Abbotts | B-17 |
| 350th Sqn | Thorpe Abbotts | B-17 |
| 351st Sqn | Thorpe Abbotts | B-17 |
| 418th Sqn | Thorpe Abbotts | B-17 |

*390th Bomb Group (Colonel Frederick W. Ott)*

| | | |
|---|---|---|
| 568th Sqn | Framlingham | B-17 |
| 569th Sqn | Framlingham | B-17 |
| 570th Sqn | Framlingham | B-17 |
| 571st Sqn | Framlingham | B-17 |

## 14th Combat Wing
HQ SHIPDHAM

*44th Bomb Group (Colonel John H. Bibson)*

| | | |
|---|---|---|
| 66th Sqn | Shipdham | B-24 |
| 67th Sqn | Shipdham | B-24 |
| 68th Sqn | Shipdham | B-24 |
| 506th Sqn | Shipdham | B-24 |

*392nd Bomb Group (Colonel Irvine A. Rendle)*

| | | |
|---|---|---|
| 576th Sqn | Wendling | B-24 |
| 577th Sqn | Wendling | B-24 |
| 578th Sqn | Wendling | B-24 |
| 579th Sqn | Wendling | B-24 |

*492nd Bomb Group (Colonel Eugene H. Snavely)*

| | | |
|---|---|---|
| 856th Sqn | North Pickenham | B-24 |
| 857th Sqn | North Pickenham | B-24 |
| 858th Sqn | North Pickenham | B-24 |
| 859th Sqn | North Pickenham | B-24 |

## 20th Combat Wing (2nd Bombardment Division)
HQ HARDWICK

*93rd Bomb Group (Colonel Leland G. Fiegel)*

| | | |
|---|---|---|
| 328th Sqn | Hardwick | B-24 |
| 329th Sqn | Hardwick | B-24 |
| 330th Sqn | Hardwick | B-24 |
| 409th Sqn | Hardwick | B-24 |

*446th Bomb Group (Colonel Jacob J. Bragger)*

| | | |
|---|---|---|
| 704th Sqn | Bungay | B-24 |
| 705th Sqn | Bungay | B-24 |
| 706th Sqn | Bungay | B-24 |
| 707th Sqn | Bungay | B-24 |

*448th Bomb Group (Colonel Gerry L. Mason)*

| | | |
|---|---|---|
| 712nd Sqn | Seething | B-24 |
| 713rd Sqn | Seething | B-24 |
| 714th Sqn | Seething | B-24 |
| 715th Sqn | Seething | B-24 |

## 40th Combat Wing (1st Bombardment Division)
HQ THURLEIGH

*92nd Bomb Group (Lieutenant Colonel William M. Reid)*

| | | |
|---|---|---|
| 325th Sqn | Podington | B-17 |
| 326th Sqn | Podington | B-17 |
| 327th Sqn | Podington | B-17 |
| 407th Sqn | Podington | B-17 |

*305th Bomb Group (Colonel Ernest Lawson)*

| | | |
|---|---|---|
| 364th Sqn | Chelveston | B-17 |
| 365th Sqn | Chelveston | B-17 |
| 366th Sqn | Chelveston | B-17 |
| 422nd Sqn | Chelveston | B-17 |

*306th Bomb Group (Colonel George L. Robinson)*

| | | |
|---|---|---|
| 367th Sqn | Thurleigh | B-17 |
| 368th Sqn | Thurleigh | B-17 |
| 369th Sqn | Thurleigh | B-17 |
| 423rd Sqn | Thurleigh | B-17 |

## 41st Combat Wing (1st Bombardment Division)
HQ MOLESWORTH

*303rd Bomb Group (Colonel Kent D. Stevens)*

| | | |
|---|---|---|
| 358th Sqn | Molesworth | B-17 |
| 359th Sqn | Molesworth | B-17 |

| | | |
|---|---|---|
| 360th Sqn | Molesworth | B–17 |
| 427th Sqn | Molesworth | B–17 |

*379th Bomb Group (Colonel Maurice A. Preston)*

| | | |
|---|---|---|
| 524th Sqn | Kimbolton | B–17 |
| 525th Sqn | Kimbolton | B–17 |
| 526th Sqn | Kimbolton | B–17 |
| 527th Sqn | Kimbolton | B–17 |

*384th Bomb Group (Colonel Dale R. Smith)*

| | | |
|---|---|---|
| 544th Sqn | Grafton Underwood | B–17 |
| 545th Sqn | Grafton Underwood | B–17 |
| 546th Sqn | Grafton Underwood | B–17 |
| 547th Sqn | Grafton Underwood | B–17 |

## 45th Combat Wing (3rd Bombardment Division)
HQ SNETTERTON HEATH

*96th Bomb Group (Colonel James L. Travis)*

| | | |
|---|---|---|
| 337th Sqn | Snetterton Heath | B–17 |
| 338th Sqn | Snetterton Heath | B–17 |
| 339th Sqn | Snetterton Heath | B–17 |
| 413th Sqn | Snetterton Heath | B–17 |

*388th Bomb Group (Colonel William B. David)*

| | | |
|---|---|---|
| 560th Sqn | Knettishall | B–17 |
| 561st Sqn | Knettishall | B–17 |
| 562nd Sqn | Knettishall | B–17 |
| 563rd Sqn | Knettishall | B–17 |

*452nd Bomb Group (Colonel Thetus C. Odom)*

| | | |
|---|---|---|
| 728th Sqn | Deopham Green | B–17 |
| 729th Sqn | Deopham Green | B–17 |
| 730th Sqn | Deopham Green | B–17 |
| 731st Sqn | Deopham Green | B–17 |

## 93rd Combat Wing (3rd Bombardment Division)
HQ MENDLESHAM

*34th Bomb Group (Colonel Ernest J. Wackwitz)*

| | | |
|---|---|---|
| 4th Sqn | Mendlesham | B–17 |
| 7th Sqn | Mendlesham | B–17 |
| 18th Sqn | Mendlesham | B–17 |
| 391st Sqn | Mendlesham | B–17 |

*385th Bomb Group (Colonel Dale R. Smith)*

| | | |
|---|---|---|
| 548th Sqn | Great Ashfield | B–17 |
| 549th Sqn | Great Ashfield | B–17 |
| 550th Sqn | Great Ashfield | B–17 |
| 551st Sqn | Great Ashfield | B–17 |

*490th Bomb Group (Colonel Lloyd H. Watnee)*

| | | |
|---|---|---|
| 848th Sqn | Eye | B–24 |
| 849th Sqn | Eye | B–24 |
| 850th Sqn | Eye | B–24 |
| 851st Sqn | Eye | B–24 |

*493rd Bomb Group (Colonel Elbert Helton)*

| | | |
|---|---|---|
| 860th Sqn | Debach | B–24 |
| 861st Sqn | Debach | B–24 |
| 862nd Sqn | Debach | B–24 |
| 863rd Sqn | Debach | B–24 |

## 94th Combat Wing (1st Bombardment Division)
HQ POLEBROOK

*351st Bomb Group (Colonel Eugene A. Romig)*

| | | |
|---|---|---|
| 508th Sqn | Polebrook | B–17 |
| 509th Sqn | Polebrook | B–17 |
| 510th Sqn | Polebrook | B–17 |
| 511th Sqn | Polebrook | B–17 |

*401st Bomb Group (Colonel Harold W. Bowman)*

| | | |
|---|---|---|
| 612nd Sqn | Deenethorpe | B–17 |
| 613rd Sqn | Deenethorpe | B–17 |
| 614th Sqn | Deenethorpe | B–17 |
| 615th Sqn | Deenethorpe | B–17 |

*457th Bomb Group (Colonel James R. Luper)*

| | | |
|---|---|---|
| 748th Sqn | Glatton | B–17 |
| 749th Sqn | Glatton | B–17 |
| 750th Sqn | Glatton | B–17 |
| 751st Sqn | Glatton | B–17 |

## 95th Combat Wing (2nd Bombardment Division)
HQ HALESWORTH

*489th Bomb Group (Colonel Ezekiel W. Napier)*

| | | |
|---|---|---|
| 844th Sqn | Halesworth | B–24 |
| 845th Sqn | Halesworth | B–24 |
| 846th Sqn | Halesworth | B–24 |
| 847th Sqn | Halesworth | B–24 |

*491st Bomb Group (Lieutenant Colonel Carl T. Goldenberg)*

| | | |
|---|---|---|
| 852nd Sqn | Metfield | B–24 |
| 853rd Sqn | Metfield | B–24 |
| 854th Sqn | Metfield | B–24 |
| 855th Sqn | Metfield | B–24 |

## 96th Combat Wing (2nd Bombardment Division)
HQ Horsham St Faith

*458th Bomb Group (Colonel James H. Isbell)*

| | | |
|---|---|---|
| 752nd Sqn | Horsham St Faith | B-24 |
| 753rd Sqn | Horsham St Faith | B-24 |
| 754th Sqn | Horsham St Faith | B-24 |
| 755th Sqn | Horsham St Faith | B-24 |

*466th Bomb Group (Colonel Arthur J. Pierce)*

| | | |
|---|---|---|
| 784th Sqn | Attlebridge | B-24 |
| 785th Sqn | Attlebridge | B-24 |
| 786th Sqn | Attlebridge | B-24 |
| 787th Sqn | Attlebridge | B-24 |

*467th Bomb Group (Colonel Albert J. Shower)*

| | | |
|---|---|---|
| 788th Sqn | Rackheath | B-24 |
| 789th Sqn | Rackheath | B-24 |
| 790th Sqn | Rackheath | B-24 |
| 791st Sqn | Rackheath | B-24 |

*7th Photo Group (Lieutenant Colonel Norris E. Hartwell)*

| | | |
|---|---|---|
| 13th Sqn | Mount Farm | F-5 |
| 14th Sqn | Mount Farm | Spitfire XI |
| 22nd Sqn | Mount Farm | P-38 |
| 27th Sqn | Mount Farm | P-38 |

*Other units*

| | | |
|---|---|---|
| 802nd Recce Group | Watton | Mosquito XVI, B-17 |
| 803rd (P) Sqn (RCM) | Oulton | B-17 |
| 422nd Sqn | Chelveston | B-17 |
| Air-Sea Rescue (65th Wing) | Boxted | P-47 |

## US 9th Air Force

*Commander:*
Major General Lewis H. Brereton
*Chief of Staff:*
Brigadier General Victor H. Strahm

*10th Photo Group*

| | | |
|---|---|---|
| 30th Sqn | Chalgrove | F-5B |
| 31st Sqn | Chalgrove | F-5B |
| 33rd Sqn | Chalgrove | F-5B |
| 34th Sqn | Chalgrove | F-5B |
| 423rd Sqn | Chalgrove | P-61, P-70 |

## US IXth Tactical Air Command (TAC)

Tactical HQ Uxbridge
*Commander:*
Major General Elwood R. Quesada

*67th Reconnaissance Group*
HQ Middle Wallop

| | | |
|---|---|---|
| 12th Sqn | Middle Wallop | P-51B |
| 15th Sqn | Middle Wallop | P-51B |
| 107th Sqn | Middle Wallop | P-51B |
| 109th Sqn | Middle Wallop | P-51B |

### 71st Fighter Wing
HQ Andover

*366th Fighter Group*

| | | |
|---|---|---|
| 389th Sqn | Thruxton | P-47 |
| 390th Sqn | Thruxton | P-47 |
| 391st Sqn | Thruxton | P-47 |

*368th Fighter Group*

| | | |
|---|---|---|
| 395th Sqn | Chilbolton | P-47 |
| 396th Sqn | Chilbolton | P-47 |
| 397th Sqn | Chilbolton | P-47 |

*370th Fighter Group*

| | | |
|---|---|---|
| 401st Sqn | Andover | P-38 |
| 402nd Sqn | Andover | P-38 |
| 485th Sqn | Andover | P-38 |

### 84th Fighter Wing
HQ Beaulieu

*404th Fighter Group*

| | | |
|---|---|---|
| 506th Sqn | Winkton | P-47 |
| 507th Sqn | Winkton | P-47 |
| 508th Sqn | Winkton | P-47 |

*50th Fighter Group*

| | | |
|---|---|---|
| 10th Sqn | Lymington | P-47 |
| 31st Sqn | Lymington | P-47 |
| 313th Sqn | Lymington | P-47 |

*365th Fighter Group*

| | | |
|---|---|---|
| 386th Sqn | Beaulieu | P-47 |
| 387th Sqn | Beaulieu | P-47 |
| 388th Sqn | Beaulieu | P-47 |

**405th Fighter Group**
| 509th Sqn | Christchurch | P-47 |
| 510th Sqn | Christchurch | P-47 |
| 511th Sqn | Christchurch | P-47 |

## 70th Fighter Wing
HQ IBSLEY

*48th Fighter Group*
| 492nd Sqn | Ibsley | P-47 |
| 493rd Sqn | Ibsley | P-47 |
| 494th Sqn | Ibsley | P-47 |

*371st Fighter Group*
| 404th Sqn | Bisterne | P-47 |
| 405th Sqn | Bisterne | P-47 |
| 406th Sqn | Bisterne | P-47 |

*367th Fighter Group*
| 392nd Sqn | Stoney Cross | P-38 |
| 393rd Sqn | Stoney Cross | P-38 |
| 394th Sqn | Stoney Cross | P-38 |

*474th Fighter Group*
| 428th Sqn | Warmwell | P-38 |
| 429th Sqn | Warmwell | P-38 |
| 430th Sqn | Warmwell | P-38 |

## US XIXth Tactical Air Command

TACTICAL HQ BIGGIN HILL
*Commander:*
Major General O. P. Weyland

## 100th Fighter Wing
HQ LASHENDEN

*354th Fighter Group*
| 353rd Sqn | Lashenden | P-51 |
| 355th Sqn | Lashenden | P-51 |
| 356th Sqn | Lashenden | P-51 |

*358th Fighter Group*
| 365th Sqn | High Halden | P-47 |
| 366th Sqn | High Halden | P-47 |
| 367th Sqn | High Halden | P-47 |

*362nd Fighter Group*
| 377th Sqn | Headcorn | P-47 |
| 378th Sqn | Headcorn | P-47 |
| 379th Sqn | Headcorn | P-47 |

*Line-up of 378th FS/362nd FG P-47s on an ALG; 'jerry' cans are being used to fill up a fuel bowser.*

*Night-fighter defence included P-61s of the 9th Air Force.*
(US National Archives)

*363rd Fighter Group*

| | | |
|---|---|---|
| 380th Sqn | Staplehurst | P-51 |
| 381st Sqn | Staplehurst | P-51 |
| 382nd Sqn | Staplehurst | P-51 |

**303rd Fighter Wing**
HQ Ashford

*36th Fighter Group*

| | | |
|---|---|---|
| 22nd Sqn | Kingsnorth | P-47 |
| 23rd Sqn | Kingsnorth | P-47 |
| 53rd Sqn | Kingsnorth | P-47 |

*373rd Fighter Group*

| | | |
|---|---|---|
| 410th Sqn | Woodchurch | P-47 |
| 411th Sqn | Woodchurch | P-47 |
| 412th Sqn | Woodchurch | P-47 |

*406th Fighter Group*

| | | |
|---|---|---|
| 512th Sqn | Ashford | P-47 |
| 513th Sqn | Ashford | P-47 |
| 514th Sqn | Ashford | P-47 |

*Night-Fighter Units*

| | | |
|---|---|---|
| 422nd Sqn | Scorton | P-61, P-70 |
| 425th Sqn | Coleby Grange | P-61, P-70 |

**US IXth Bomber Command**

HQ Marks Hall
*Commander:*
Major General Samuel E. Anderson

| | | |
|---|---|---|
| 1st Pathfinder Sqn | Andrewsfield | B-26 |

**98th Bomb Wing (Medium)**

*397th Bomb Group*

| | | |
|---|---|---|
| 596th Sqn | Rivenhall | B-26 |
| 597th Sqn | Rivenhall | B-26 |
| 598th Sqn | Rivenhall | B-26 |
| 599th Sqn | Rivenhall | B-26 |

*387th Bomb Group*

| | | |
|---|---|---|
| 556th Sqn | Chipping Ongar | B-26 |
| 557th Sqn | Chipping Ongar | B-26 |
| 558th Sqn | Chipping Ongar | B-26 |
| 559th Sqn | Chipping Ongar | B-26 |

*323rd Bomb Group*

| | | |
|---|---|---|
| 453rd Sqn | Earl's Colne | B-26 |
| 454th Sqn | Earl's Colne | B-26 |
| 455th Sqn | Earl's Colne | B-26 |
| 456th Sqn | Earl's Colne | B-26 |

*394th Bomb Group*

| | | |
|---|---|---|
| 584th Sqn | Boreham | B-26 |
| 585th Sqn | Boreham | B-26 |

| 586th Sqn | Boreham | B–26 |
|-----------|---------|------|
| 587th Sqn | Boreham | B–26 |

**99th Bomb Wing (Medium)**
HQ GREAT DUNMOW

*322nd Bomb Group*

| 449th Sqn | Andrewsfield | B–26 |
|-----------|--------------|------|
| 450th Sqn | Andrewsfield | B–26 |
| 451st Sqn | Andrewsfield | B–26 |
| 452nd Sqn | Andrewsfield | B–26 |

*344th Bomb Group*

| 494th Sqn | Stansted Mountfitchet | B–26 |
|-----------|-----------------------|------|
| 495th Sqn | Stansted Mountfitchet | B–26 |
| 496th Sqn | Stansted Mountfitchet | B–26 |
| 497th Sqn | Stansted Moutnfitchet | B–26 |

*386th Bomb Group*

| 552nd Sqn | Great Dunmow | B–26 |
|-----------|--------------|------|
| 553rd Sqn | Great Dunmow | B–26 |
| 554th Sqn | Great Dunmow | B–26 |
| 555th Sqn | Great Dunmow | B–26 |

*391st Bomb Group*

| 372nd Sqn | Matching | B–26 |
|-----------|----------|------|
| 373rd Sqn | Matching | B–26 |
| 374th Sqn | Matching | B–26 |
| 375th Sqn | Matching | B–26 |

**97th Bomb Wing (Light)**
HQ LITTLE WALDEN

*416th Bomb Group*

| 668th Sqn | Wethersfield | A–20G |
|-----------|--------------|-------|
| 669th Sqn | Wethersfield | A–20G |
| 670th Sqn | Wethersfield | A–20G |
| 671st Sqn | Wethersfield | A–20G |

*409th Bomb Group*

| 640th Sqn | Little Walden | A–20G |
|-----------|---------------|-------|
| 641st Sqn | Little Walden | A–20G |
| 642nd Sqn | Little Walden | A–20G |
| 643rd Sqn | Little Walden | A–20G |

*The 834th Engineer Aviation Battalion erecting a T-2 hangar at Matching.* (National Archives)

*410th Bomb Group*

| | | |
|---|---|---|
| 644th Sqn | Gosfield | A-20G |
| 645th Sqn | Gosfield | A-20G |
| 646th Sqn | Gosfield | A-20G |
| 647th Sqn | Gosfield | A-20G |

## US IXth Troop Carrier Command

HQ GRANTHAM LODGE
*Commander:*
Brigadier General Paul L. Williams

1st Pathfinder Group   North Witham   C-47, C-53

### 50th Troop Carrier Wing
HQ BOTTESFORD

*439th Troop Carrier*

| | | |
|---|---|---|
| 91st Sqn | Upottery | C-47, C-53 |
| 92nd Sqn | Upottery | C-47, C-53 |
| 93rd Sqn | Upottery | C-47, C-53 |
| 94th Sqn | Upottery | C-47, C-53 |

*440th Troop Carrier*

| | | |
|---|---|---|
| 95th Sqn | Exeter | C-47, C-53 |
| 96th Sqn | Exeter | C-47, C-53 |
| 97th Sqn | Exeter | C-47, C-53 |
| 98th Sqn | Exeter | C-47, C-53 |

*441st Troop Carrier*

| | | |
|---|---|---|
| 99th Sqn | Merryfield | C-47, C-53 |
| 100th Sqn | Merryfield | C-47, C-53 |
| 301st Sqn | Merryfield | C-47, C-53 |
| 302nd Sqn | Merryfield | C-47, C-53 |

### 52nd Troop Carrier Wing
HQ COTTESMORE

*61st Troop Carrier*

| | | |
|---|---|---|
| 14th Sqn | Barkston Heath | C-47, C-53 |
| 15th Sqn | Barkston Heath | C-47, C-53 |
| 53rd Sqn | Barkston Heath | C-47, C-53 |
| 59th Sqn | Barkston Heath | C-47, C-53 |

*313th Troop Carrier*

| | | |
|---|---|---|
| 29th Sqn | Folkingham | C-47, C-53 |
| 47th Sqn | Folkingham | C-47, C-53 |
| 48th Sqn | Folkingham | C-47, C-53 |
| 49th Sqn | Folkingham | C-47, C-53 |

*314th Troop Carrier*

| | | |
|---|---|---|
| 61st Sqn | Saltry | C-47, C-53 |
| 63rd Sqn | Saltry | C-47, C-53 |
| 32nd Sqn | Saltry | C-47, C-53 |
| 50th Sqn | Saltry | C-47, C-53 |

*315th Troop Carrier*

| | | |
|---|---|---|
| 34th Sqn | Spanhoe | C-47, C-53 |
| 43rd Sqn | Spanhoe | C-47, C-53 |

*316th Troop Carrier*

| | | |
|---|---|---|
| 36th Sqn | Cottesmore | C-47, C-53 |
| 37th Sqn | Cottesmore | C-47, C-53 |
| 44th Sqn | Cottesmore | C-47, C-53 |
| 45th Sqn | Cottesmore | C-47, C-53 |

### 53rd Troop Carrier Wing
HQ GREENHAM COMMON

*434th Troop Carrier*

| | | |
|---|---|---|
| 71st Sqn | Aldermaston | C-47, C-53 |
| 72nd Sqn | Aldermaston | C-47, C-53 |
| 73rd Sqn | Aldermaston | C-47, C-53 |
| 74th Sqn | Aldermaston | C-47, C-53 |

*435th Troop Carrier*

| | | |
|---|---|---|
| 75th Sqn | Welford | C-47, C-53 |
| 76th Sqn | Welford | C-47, C-53 |
| 77th Sqn | Welford | C-47, C-53 |
| 78th Sqn | Welford | C-47, C-53 |

*436th Troop Carrier*

| | | |
|---|---|---|
| 79th Sqn | Membury | C-47, C-53 |
| 80th Sqn | Membury | C-47, C-53 |
| 81st Sqn | Membury | C-47, C-53 |
| 82nd Sqn | Membury | C-47, C-53 |

*437th Troop Carrier*

| | | |
|---|---|---|
| 83rd Sqn | Ramsbury | C-47, C-53 |
| 84th Sqn | Ramsbury | C-47, C-53 |
| 85th Sqn | Ramsbury | C-47, C-53 |
| 86th Sqn | Ramsbury | C-47, C-53 |

*438th Troop Carrier*

| | | |
|---|---|---|
| 87th Sqn | Greenham Common | C-47, C-53 |
| 88th Sqn | Greenham Common | C-47, C-53 |
| 89th Sqn | Greenham Common | C-47, C-53 |
| 90th Sqn | Greenham Common | C-47, C-53 |

# APPENDIX II

# Allied Air Forces Available for the Assault on Normandy

| Command/Air Force | No of Sqns | Serviceable aircraft | Command/Air Force | No of Sqns | Serviceable aircraft |
|---|---|---|---|---|---|
| **2nd TAF** | 80 | 1,348 | **No. 38 Gp** | 10 | 313 |
| No. 83 Gp | 34 | | Albemarle | 4 | |
| No. 84 Gp | 31 | | Stirling | 4 | |
| No. 2 Gp | 12 | | Halifax | 2 | |
| No. 34 Wing | 3 | | Gliders (520 ac + 200 reserve) | | |
| *Comprising:* | | | | | |
| Spitfire | 27 | | **No. 46 Gp** | 5 | 165 |
| Typhoon | 18 | | Dakota | 5 | |
| Mustang | 6 | | Gliders (200 ac + 200 reserve) | | |
| Mosquito | 6 | | | | |
| Mitchell | 4 | | **FAA** | 7 | 84 |
| Boston | 2 | | | | |
| Auster | 7 | | **Bomber Command** | 82 | 1,681 |
| Recce types | 10 | | Lancaster | 39.5 | |
| | | | Halifax | 22 | |
| **ADGB** | 45 | 809 | Stirling | 2.5 | |
| No. 10 Gp | 12 | | Mosquito | 6 | |
| No. 11 Gp | 19 | | Special duty types | 12 | |
| No. 12 Gp | 4.5 | | | | |
| No. 13 Gp | 1.5 | | **Coastal Command** | 63 | 678 |
| No. 85 Gp on loan | 6 | | | | |
| ASP | 2 | | **TOTAL RAF** | 304 | 5,252 |
| *Comprising:* | | | | | |
| Spitfire | 26 | | **US 9th AF** | 162 | 2,506 |
| Mustang | 1 | | IXth TAC | 33 | |
| Typhoon | 2 | | XIXth TAC | 25 | |
| Hurricane | 1 | | IXth BC | 44 | |
| Mosquito | 9 | | IXth TCC | 56 | |
| Beaufighter | 2 | | 10th PRG | 4 | |
| ASR types | 4 | | | | |
| | | | **US 8th AF** | 212 | 2,788 |
| **No. 85 Gp** | 12 | 174 | B–17 | 88 | |
| Day fighter | 6 | | B–24 | 76 | |
| Night fighter | 6 | | Fighters | 48 | |
| *Comprising:* | | | | | |
| Mosquito | 6 | | | | |
| Spitfire | 4 | | | | |
| Tempest | 2 | | | | |

# APPENDIX III
# Bomber Command Operations 1–7 June 1944

| Date | Main target | No of aircraft | Date | Main target | No of aircraft |
|------|-------------|----------------|------|-------------|----------------|
| 1st/2nd | Ferme D'Urville | 109 | | Ouistreham | 116 |
| | Saumur | 58 | | Maisy | 116 |
| | Aarhus | 6 | | Houlgate | 116 |
| 2nd/3rd | Trappes | 128 | | Merville-Franceville | 109 |
| | Dieppe | 107 | | Crisbecq | 101 |
| | Neufchatel | 74 | | St Martin de Varreville | 100 |
| | Haringzelles | 67 | | Longues | 99 |
| | Calais | 67 | | Osnabruck | 31 |
| | Wimereux | 65 | 6th/7th | Coutances | 139 |
| | Wissant | 63 | | Caen | 129 |
| | Leverkusen | 23 | | Argentan | 128 |
| 3rd/4th | Ferme D'Urville | 100 | | Conde sur Noireau | 122 |
| | Calais | 70 | | St Lô | 115 |
| | Wimereux | 65 | | Châteaudun | 112 |
| | Argentan | 5 | | Vire | 112 |
| | Ludwigshaven | 20 | | Lisieux | 104 |
| 4th/5th | Calais | 79 | | Achères | 104 |
| | Swingatte | 57 | | Ludwigshaven | 32 |
| | Maisy | 56 | 7th/8th | Foret de Cerisy | 212 |
| | Boulogne | 67 | | Achères | 108 |
| | Argentan | 6 | | Versailles/Matelots | 83 |
| | Cologne | 20 | | Massy | 75 |
| 5th/6th | La Pernelle | 131 | | Juvisy | 71 |
| | Mont Fleury | 124 | | Cologne | 32 |
| | St Pierre du Mont | 124 | | | |

Highest number of sorties despatched in one night: 5/6 June – 1,333.
Highest bomb tonnage dropped in one night: 5/6 June – 5,316 tons.

# APPENDIX IV

# 356th FG Statistical Analysis for June 1944

|                              | 359th FS | 360th FS | 361st FS | Total |
|------------------------------|----------|----------|----------|-------|
| Missions flown               | 505      | 498      | 513      | 1,516 |
| Ac. completing mission       | 470      | 468      | 480      | 1,418 |
| Average no. of aircraft per mission | 11 | 11 | 11 | 33 |
| Av. daily serviceability     | 19       | 21       | 22       | 62    |
| Pilot availability – 69%     |          |          |          |       |

## Missions flown:

| Date | Type | Group leader | Date | Type | Group leader |
|------|------|--------------|------|------|--------------|
| 2 June | Sweep | Lt Col Baccus | 12 June | Strafe-bomb | Lt Col Baccus |
| 3 June | Sweep | Maj White | 13 June | Sweep | Lt Col Tukey |
| 6 June | Sweep | Lt Col Tukey | 14 June | Area patrol | Maj Vogt |
|  | Sweep | Lt Col Baccus | 14 June | Thunderbombing | Lt Col Baccus |
|  | Sweep | Lt Col Baccus | 15 June | Escort | Lt Col Tukey |
|  | Sweep | Lt Col Tukey | 16 June | Thunderbombing | Lt Col Baccus |
|  | Sweep | Maj Vogt | 17 June | Sweep | Maj Thorne |
|  | Sweep | Lt Col Waller | 17 June | Escort | Maj Thorne |
|  | Sweep | Lt Col Baccus |  | Area support | Maj Thorne |
| 7 June | Sweep | Lt Col Tukey | 21 June | Escort | Lt Col Tukey |
|  | Sweep | Capt Bailey |  | Area support | Maj Thorne |
|  | Sweep | Lt Col Waller | 22 June | Area support | Maj Thorne |
|  | Sweep | Lt Col Baccus |  | Area support | Capt Cota |
|  | Dive-bomb | Maj Vogt | 23 June | Area support | Maj Burke |
| 8 June | Sweep | Capt Strait | 24 June | Escort | Lt Col Tukey |
|  | Sweep | Lt Col Tukey | 25 June | Escort | Lt Rubner |
|  | Sweep | Lt Col Baccus |  | Area support | Capt Ogden |
|  | Sweep | Maj Vogt | 27 June | Thunderbombing | Maj Thorne |
|  | Sweep | Maj White | 28 June | Area patrol | Lt Col Baccus |
| 10 June | Area patrol | Lt Col Waller | 29 June | Escort | Capt Meholic |
|  | Area patrol | Lt Col Tukey | 30 June | Fighter-bombing | Maj Vogt |
| 11 June | Area patrol | Lt Col Tukey |  |  |  |

# APPENDIX V

# Air Operations Flown Between 21:00 hours 5 June and 19:00 hours 6 June 1944

The statistics in this table are from the AEAF Operations Summary, and are the raw data from that source. There will be errors and omissions, but it does provide a relatively complete list of the main air operations during the first twenty-four-hour period of the invasion.

**Period 21:00 5 June to sunrise 6 June**

| Type of mission | Aircraft | Unit | Target | TOT bracket |
|---|---|---|---|---|
| **9th Air Force** | | | | |
| Fighter-bomber | 50 P-47 | 358th FG | 1900–2153 | |
| Escort | 48 P-38 | 370th FG | last 0024 | |
| Recce | 31 F-6/P-51 | 67th PRG | 2004–0651 | |
| | 3 Boston | 10th PRU | 2400–0221 | |
| | | | | |
| **2nd TAF** | | | | |
| Fighter/R-P | 8 Typhoon | 198 Sqn | Château Le Vretot | 2145 |
| | 7 Typhoon | 609 Sqn | Château Livetan | 2130 |
| | 7 Typhoon | 198, 609 Sqn | rail/road bridges | 2103–2219 |
| Convoy patrol | 72 Spitfire | 401, 416, 441, 443, 453 Sqns | Channel | 1742–2305 |
| Recce | 2 Typhoon | 164 Sqn | Cherbourg | 2150–2307 |
| | 7 Mosquito | 140 Sqn | night photo | 2300–0215 |
| | 2 Wellington | 69 Sqn | night photo | 2355–0302 |
| Bomber | 12 Mitchell, 2 Mosquito | 320, 613 Sqns | aborted | |
| | 12 Mitchell, 1 Mosquito | 180, 21 Sqns | | 0126–0427 |
| | 12 Mitchell, 2 Mosquito | 98, 21 Sqns | | 0226–0527 |
| Offensive patrol | 4 Mosquito | 107, 21 Sqns | Caen-Barentan road | 2215–0115 |
| | 98 Mosquito | 138, 140 Wings | | 2200–0556 |
| | | | | |
| **ADGB** | | | | |
| Offensive patrol | 2 Mosquito | 25, 307 Sqns | Leeuwarden | 2244–0215 |
| | 2 Beaufighter | 406 Sqn | Morlaix, Lannion | 2256–0240 |
| | 18 Mosquito | 418 Sqn | N. France | 2308–0545 |

*Air Operations Flown Between 21:00 hours 5 June and 19:00 hours 6 June*

| Type of mission | Aircraft | Unit | Target | TOT bracket |
|---|---|---|---|---|
| Offensive patrol | 18 Mosquito | 605 Sqn | N. France, Holland | 2310–0441 |
| | 6 Mosquito | 29 Sqn | N. France, Belgium | 2239–0359 |
| | 2 Mosquito | 151 Sqn | Bastard–Vannes | 0125–0415 |
| Convoy patrol | 40 Spitfire | | No. 10 Gp area | 1935–2316 |
| | 4 Hurricane | | No. 11 Gp area | 1505–2310 |
| | 26 Spitfire | | | |
| Defensive patrol | 19 Mosquito | | No. 10 Gp area | 2243–0551 |
| | 2 Beaufighter | | | |
| | 52 Spitfire, 35 Mosquito | | No. 11 Gp area | 0120–0505 |
| | 35 Mosquito | | | |
| | 12 Mosquito | | No. 12 Gp area | 2325–0522 |
| | 2 Hurricane | | No. 13 Gp area | 2245–0020 |
| | 2 Seafire | | | |
| Recce | 6 Spitfire | 56, 611 Sqns | shipping | 2015–2256 |
| ASR | 6 Spitfire | 277 Sqn | | 2100–2225 |

**IXth TCC**

| Type of mission | Aircraft | Unit | Target | TOT bracket |
|---|---|---|---|---|
| Para/glider ops | 81 C-47 | 438th TCG | | 2232–0245 |
| | 48 C-47 | 315th TCG | | 2306–0440 |
| | 45 C-47 | 435th TCG | | 2355–0330 |
| | 72 C-47 | 316th TCG | | 2300–0510 |
| | 36 C-47 | 436th TCG | | 2300–0330 |
| | 72 C-47 | 61st TCG | | 2352–0505 |
| | 52 C-47 | 437th TCG | | 0157–0610 |
| | 45 C-47 | 442nd TCG | | 2351–0615 |
| | 20 C-47 | PFF | | 2154–0550 |
| | 90 C-47 | 441st TCG | | 2344–0245 |
| | 60 C-47 | 314th TCG | | 2321–0540 |
| | 72 C-47 | 313th TCG | | 2315–0500 |
| | 81 C-47 | 439th TCG | | |
| | 45 C-47 | 440th TCG | | 2350–0315 |
| | 52 C-47 | 434th TCG | | 0119–0550 |

**Nos 38 & 46 Gps**

| Type of mission | Aircraft | Unit | Target | TOT bracket |
|---|---|---|---|---|
| Para ops | 27 Albemarle | 295, 296, 570 Sqns | | 2301–0239 |
| | 46 Stirling | 190, 196 Sqns | | 2323–0235 |
| | 129 Dakota | 48, 233, 271, 512, 575 Sqns | | 2310–0243 |
| Glider ops | 40 Halifax | 298, 644 Sqns | | 2300–0520 |
| | 13 Dakota | 48, 575 Sqns | | 2249–0228 |
| | 45 Albemarle | 295, 297, 570 Sqns | | 0120–0520 |

**RAF Bomber Command**

| Type of mission | Aircraft | Unit | Target | TOT bracket |
|---|---|---|---|---|
| Bomber | 131 | | La Permelle | |
| | 124 | | Mont Fleury | |
| | 125 | | St Pierre du Mont | |
| | 115 | | Maissy | |
| | 116 | | Houlgate | |
| | 101 | | Crisbeq | |
| | 100 | | St Martin de Vareville | |

| Type of mission | Aircraft | Unit | Target | TOT bracket |
|---|---|---|---|---|
| | 116 | | Ouistreham | |
| | 109 | | Merville-Franceville | |
| | 99 | | Longues | |
| | 107 | | special patrol | |
| | 31 | | Osnabruck | |
| | 41 | | bomber support | |
| | 6 | | leaflets | |

## Period sunrise 6 June to 21:00 6 June

| Type of mission | Aircraft | Unit | Target | TOT bracket |
|---|---|---|---|---|
| **2nd TAF** | | | | |
| Smoke screen | 12 Boston | 342 Sqn | Cap Barfleur | 0513–0733 |
| | 19 Boston | 88 Sqn | Le Havre | 0415–0843 |
| Fighter-bomber | 8 Typhoon | 197 Sqn | château | 0725 |
| | 12 Typhoon | 439 Sqn | gun battery | 0729 |
| | 12 Typhoon | 440 Sqn | strongpoint | 0725 |
| | 12 Typhoon | 438 Sqn | strongpoint Le Hamel | 0728 |
| | 8 Typhoon | 266 Sqn | guns | 0755 |
| | 8 Typhoon | 257 Sqn | MT | 1705–1815 |
| | 8 Typhoon | 440 Sqn | MT | 1656–1812 |
| Fighter/R–P | 4 Typhoon | 609 Sqn | radar Le Havre | 1238 |
| | 11 Typhoon | 198 Sqn | château | 0900 |
| | 24 Typhoon | 181, 247 Sqns | guns, Cabourg | 0707–0845 |
| | 8 Typhoon | 174 Sqn | guns | 0800 |
| | 8 Typhoon | 245 Sqn | camp | 0713–0821 |
| | 12 Typhoon | 175 Sqn | Caen/La Falaise | 1527–1651 |
| | 11 Typhoon | 184 Sqn | coastal battery, Cabourg | 1532–1633 |
| | 15 Typhoon | 198, 609 Sqns | Caen area | 1712–1843 |
| | 7 Typhoon | 174 Sqn | Caen area | 1733–1846 |
| Offensive patrol | 36 Spitfire | 403, 416, 421 Sqns | Cherbourg area | 0624–0815 |
| | 12 Typhoon | 183 Sqn | roads, Caen area | 1130–1303 |
| | 12 Typhoon | 164 Sqn | roads, Bayeux area | 1124–1300 |
| | 8 Typhoon | 182 Sqn | Caen area | 1617–1736 |
| | 8 Typhoon | 181 Sqn | Caen area | 1605–1725 |
| | 8 Typhoon | 164 Sqn | Bayeux area | 1734–1900 |
| | 8 Typhoon | 197 Sqn | Caen area | 1750–1920 |
| | 8 Typhoon | 183 Sqn | Caen area | 1838–2003 |
| | 8 Typhoon | 438 Sqn | Caen area | 1725–1846 |
| | 8 Typhoon | 439 Sqn | Bayeux area | 1645–1806 |
| | 12 Typhoon | 247 Sqn | Caen area | 1855–2037 |
| | 8 Typhoon | 193 Sqn | Caen area | 1650–1800 |
| | 8 Typhoon | 245 Sqn | Caen area | 1632–1903 |
| | 8 Typhoon | 266 Sqn | Caen area | 1800–1925 |
| | 10 Typhoon | 182 Sqn | Caen area | 1924–2015 |
| | 2 Typhoon | 247 Sqn | Caen area | 1855–2020 |
| Beach-head patrol | 109 Spitfire | | | 0715–1010 |
| | 216 Spitfire | | | 1020–1533 |

*Air Operations Flown Between 21:00 hours 5 June and 19:00 hours 6 June*

| Type of mission | Aircraft | Unit | Target | TOT bracket |
|---|---|---|---|---|
| | 36 Spitfire | 329, 340, 341 Sqns | eastern area | 0904–1110 |
| | 36 Spitfire | 132, 453, 602 Sqns | western area | 1309–1510 |
| | 36 Spitfire | 302, 308, 317 Sqns | western area | 1545–1727 |
| | 108 Spitfire | | eastern area | 1314–1742 |
| CC escort | 6 Mustang | 122 Sqn | Cap de Le Havre | 0631–0831 |
| Convoy escort | 35 Spitfire | 302, 308, 317 Sqns | western area | 0523–0755 |
| | 36 Spitfire | 441, 442, 443 Sqns | eastern area | 0633–0832 |
| | 36 Spitfire | 132, 453, 602 Sqns | western area | 0809–1010 |
| | 36 Spitfire | 222, 349, 485 Sqns | | 1445–1645 |
| | 12 Mustang | 122 Sqn | | 1229–1700 |
| Recce | 17 Spitfire | 16 Sqn | battle area | 0645–1900 |
| | 6 Mosquito | 140 Sqn | battle area | 0640–1815 |
| | 3 Spitfire | 400 Sqn | | 0830–1922 |
| | 6 Mustang | 400 Sqn | | 1757–2001 |
| | 29 Mustang | 430 Sqn | | 0505–1810 |
| | 8 Mustang | 2 Sqn | | 1940–2119 |
| Air spotting | 344 sorties | ASP | | all day |

**9th Air Force**

| Type of mission | Aircraft | Unit | Target | TOT bracket |
|---|---|---|---|---|
| Bombing | 54 Marauder | 323rd BG | Beau Guillet, Madeleine | 0415–0812 |
| | 17 Marauder | 391st BG | coastal battery, Point du Hoe | 0450–0811 |
| | 16 Marauder | 322nd BG | coastal battery, Ouistreham | 0400–0920 |
| | 16 Marauder | 322nd BG | coastal battery, Montfairville | 0500–0759 |
| | 17 Marauder | 391st BG | coastal battery, Beneville | 0343–0715 |
| | 18 Marauder | 391st BG | coastal battery, Maissy | 0457–0820 |
| | 16 Marauder | 322nd BG | coastal battery, Ouistreham | 0345–0707 |
| | 54 Marauder | 386th BG | coastal defences, Utah beach | 0439–0831 |
| | 53 Marauder | 397th BG | coastal defences, Utah beach | 0407–0836 |
| | 54 Marauder | 387th BG | coastal defences, Utah beach | 0427–0618 |
| | 56 Marauder | 344th BG | coastal defences, Utah beach | 0412–0804 |
| | 36 Marauder | 322nd BG | coastal battery, Gatteville | 1235–1521 |
| | 55 Boston | 409th BG | Valognes | 1201–1535 |
| | 57 Boston | 416th BG | Argentan, Ecouche | 1203–1532 |
| | 36 Marauder | 386th BG | coastal battery, Houlgate | 1808 |
| | 37 Marauder | 391st BG | Caen area | 1657 |
| | 45 Boston | 410th BG | Carentan | 1428 |
| | 37 Marauder | 394th BG | guns, Beneville | 1824 |
| | 36 Marauder | 323rd BG | Caen area | 1619 |
| | 24 Marauder | 387th BG | Falaise area | 1520–1525 |
| | 38 Marauder | 397th BG | Trouville | 1814 |
| Fighter–bomber | 18 P-47 | 366th FG | coastal battery, Maissy | 0638 |
| | 17 P-47 | 366th FG | rail, Carentan | 0550 |
| | 16 P-47 | 368th FG | bridge, St Saveur | 0612 |
| | 15 P-47 | 48th FG | guns, Le Posse | 0620 |
| | 32 P-47 | 48th FG | bridge, Beuzeville | 0620 |
| | 17 P-38 | 474th FG | bridge, la Hayed du Pitts | 0600 |
| | 47 P-47 | 365th FG | Courperville | 0607 |
| | 20 P-47 | 366th FG | coastal battery, Maissy, Beauvais | 0744/1114 |

| Type of mission | Aircraft | Unit | Target | TOT bracket |
|---|---|---|---|---|
| | 18 P-47 | 371st FG | Coutances | 1335–1447 |
| | 20 P-47 | 371st FG | rail, Percy/Hambye | 1255–1254 |
| | 32 P-38 | 474th FG | bridge, Oissel | 1028–1254 |
| | 47 P-47 | 365th FG | bridge, Oissel | 1640–1700 |
| | 48 P-47 | 48th FG | guns | 1828 |
| | 45 P-47 | 366th FG | MT, St Lô | 1523–1753 |
| | 47 P-47 | 368th FG | guns | 1900–2015 |
| | 18 P-47 | 371st FG | guns | |
| | 47 P-47 | 368th FG | MT, Isigny | 1413–1614 |
| | 18 P-47 | 371st FG | | 1516–1714 |
| Beach-head patrol | 48 P-47 | 373rd FG | | 1733–2031 |
| | 49 P-47 | 406th FG | | 1432–1720 |
| | 52 P-47 | 36th FG | | 1532–1909 |
| Bomber escort | 64 P-38 | 367th, 368th FG | | 0352–1103 |
| | 246 P-47 | 36th, 50th, 373rd, 404th, 406th FG | | 0352–1103 |
| Convoy escort | 130 P-47 | 36th, 373rd, 406th FG | | 0933–1530 |
| Recce | 25 F-5 | 10th PRU | | |
| | 23 F-5 | 67th PRG | | |
| | 86 F-6/P-51 | 67th PRG | | |

**ADGB**

| | | | | |
|---|---|---|---|---|
| Offensive patrol | 48 Spitfire | | | 0532–0645 |
| Beach-head patrol | 280 Spitfire | | | |
| CC escort | 2 Tempest | | | |
| Convoy escort | 132 Spitfire, 6 Tempest, 2 Hurricane | | | |
| Defensive patrols | 5 Mosquito, 74 Spitfire, 6 Hurricane | | | |
| Recce | 18 Spitfire, 4 Typhoon, 8 Mustang, 2 Tempest | | | |
| ASR | 58 sorties | | | |

**8th Air Force**

| | |
|---|---|
| Escort and TOO | 287 P-47 |
| | 505 P-51 |
| | 555 P-38 |

Bomber: the bomber missions are recorded under different headings:

| Mission | Aircraft | No. despatched | No. attacking | Tonnage | Target |
|---|---|---|---|---|---|
| 1st | B-17 | 822 | 679 | 2,551 | beaches |
| | B-24 | 543 | 418 | 245 | beaches |
| 2nd | B-24 | 38 | 37 | 109 | Argentan |
| | B-24 | 358 | 0 | 0 | |
| | B-17 | 84 | 0 | 0 | |
| 3rd | B-24 | 73 | 58 | 157 | Caen area |
| 4th | B-24 | 12 | 8 | 22 | Coutances |
| | B-24 | 22 | 19 | 54 | Vire |
| | B-24 | 24 | 23 | 66 | St Lô |
| | B-24 | 29 | 29 | 53 | St Lô |

*Air Operations Flown Between 21:00 hours 5 June and 19:00 hours 6 June*

| Mission | Aircraft | No. despatched | No. attacking | Tonnage | Target |
|---|---|---|---|---|---|
| | B–24 | 26 | 3 | 9 | Coutances |
| | B–24 | 22 | 20 | 57 | Vire |
| | B–24 | 4 | 3 | 7 | St Lô |
| | B–24 | 12 | 12 | 34 | Coutances |
| | B–17 | 36 | 24 | 70 | Th. Harcourt |
| | B–17 | 12 | 2 | 6 | Th. Harcourt |
| | B–17 | 24 | 22 | 76 | Th. Harcourt |
| | B–24 | 10 | 9 | 27 | St Lô |
| | B–17 | 72 | 46 | 144 | Conde sur Noireau |
| | B–17 | ? | 22 | 66 | Vire |
| | B–17 | 74 | 73 | 210 | Falaise |
| | B–17 | 72 | 35 | 99 | Pont L'Evoque |
| | B–17 | ? | 12 | 34 | Flers |
| | B–17 | ? | 21 | 57 | Argentan |
| | B–17 | 73 | 54 | 132 | Argentan |
| | B–24 | 77 | 25 | 74 | Lisieux |
| | B–24 | 24 | 0 | 0 | Vire |
| | B–24 | 38 | 26 | 78 | bridges |
| | B–17 | 46 | 36 | 101 | |

TOO – Targets Of Opportunity on the ground

*British and American gliders recovered from the D-Day landings.* (US National Archives)

# APPENDIX VI
# Planned Reorganization Post Invasion (the *Bigot* Plan)

**2nd TAF** – support 21st Army Group
83 Gp support 1st Canadian Army
84 Gp support 2nd British Army
85 Gp defence of Base Area

**9th Air Force** – support 12th Army Group
IXth TAC support 1st US Army
XIXth TAC support 3rd US Army
XXIXth TAC support 9th US Army
IXth AD Command defence of Base Area

**1st TAF (Provisional)** – support 6th Army Group
XIIth TAC support 7th US Army
1st French Air Corps support 1st French Army

*416th Bomb Group A-20s at Villaroche.* (US National Archives)

# APPENDIX VII
# Allied Airfields in North-West Europe

The Allies adopted an airfield numbering sequence for new-build airfields and for those existing airfields put back into use. In essence the B-numbered airfields were allocated to the RAF and the A-series to the Americans; this did not reflect who was responsible for the construction and it was not always exclusive in terms of who used the airfield. The R series were American-occupied airfields in Austria and France and have been omitted. Likewise, the Y series of airfields were in southern France and have been omitted.

## British Airfields

| | | | | | |
|---|---|---|---|---|---|
| B1 | Asnelles-sur-Mer | B29 | Bernay/Valailles | B60 | Brussels/Grimbergen |
| B2 | Bazenville | B30 | Creton | B61 | Ghent/St Denis Westrem |
| B3 | St Croix-sur-Mer | B31 | Fresnoy Folny | B62 | not known |
| B4 | Beny-sur-Mer | B32 | Camp Neuseville | B63 | Bruges/St Croix |
| B5 | Camilly | B34 | Avrilly | B64 | Diest/Schaffen |
| B6 | Coulombs | B35 | Godelmesnil | B65 | Maldegem |
| B7 | Martragny | B37 | Corroy | B66 | Blankenberg |
| B8 | Sommervieu | B38 | not known | B67 | Ursel |
| B9 | Lantheuil | B39 | Ecouffler | B68 | Le Culot |
| B10 | Plumetot | B40 | Nivillers | B69 | Moerbeke |
| B11 | Longues | B41 | Plouy | B70 | Antwerpen/Deurne |
| B12 | Ellon | B42 | Beauvails/Tille | B71 | Koksijde (Coxyde) |
| B13 | not allocated | B43 | St Omer/Fort Rouge | B72 | not known |
| B14 | Amblie | B44 | Poix | B73 | Moorsele |
| B15 | Ryes | B45 | not known | B74 | not known |
| B16 | Villons-les-Buissons | B46 | Gandvillers | B75 | Nivelles |
| B17 | Caen/Carpiquet | B47 | not known | B76 | Peer |
| B18 | Cristot | B48 | Amiens/Glisy | B77 | Gilze-Rijen |
| B19 | Lingevres | B49 | not known | B78 | Eindhoven/Welschap |
| B20 | not known | B50 | Vitry-en-Artois | B79 | Woensdrecht |
| B21 | St Honorine | B51 | Lille/Vanderville | B80 | Volkel |
| B22 | Auchie | B52 | Douay/Dechy | B81 | Le Madrillet |
| B23 | La Rue Hugenot/ | B53 | Merville | B82 | Grave |
| | Morainville | B54 | Achiet | B83 | Knock le Zoute |
| B24 | St André de l'Eure | B55 | Courtrai/Wevelghem | B84 | Rips |
| B25 | Le Treport | B56 | Evere | B85 | Schijndel |
| B26 | Illiers l'Eveque | B57 | Lille/Wambechies | B86 | Helmond |
| B27 | Boisney | B58 | Brussels/Melsbroek | B87 | Rosieries-en-Santerre |
| B28 | Evreux/Fauville | B59 | Ypres/Vlamertinghe | B88 | Heesch |

| B89 | Mill | B110 | Achmer | B155 | Dedelsdorf |
|-----|------|------|--------|------|------------|
| B90 | Kleine Brogel | B111 | Ahlhorn | B156 | Luneburg |
| B91 | Mijmegan/Kluis | B112 | Hopsten | B157 | Werl |
| B92 | Abville/Drucat | B113 | Varrelbusch | B158 | Lubeck |
| B93 | Valkenburg | B114 | Diepholz | B159 | Mahlen |
| B94 | not known | B115 | Melle | B160 | Kastrup |
| B95 | Teuge | B116 | Wunsdorf | B161 | not known |
| B96 | not known | B117 | Jever | B163 | not known |
| B97 | Amsterdam/Schiphol | B118 | Celle | B162 | Stade |
| B98 | not allocated | B119 | Cologne/Wahn | B164 | Schleswigland |
| B99 | not allocated | B120 | Hannover/ | B165 | not known |
| B100 | Goch | | Langenhagen | B166 | Flensburg |
| B101 | Nordhorn | | | B167 | Kiel/Holtenau |
| B102 | Vorst | B121–B149 *See* note 2 below | | B168 | Fuhlsbuttel |
| B103 | Plantlunee | | | B169 | not known |
| B104 | Damm | B150 | Hustedt/Scheven | B170 | Westerland/Sylt |
| B105 | Drope | B151 | Buckeburg | B171 | not known |
| B106 | Enschede/Twente[1] | B152 | Fassburg | B173 | not known |
| B107 | Lingen | B153 | Bad Oeynhausen | B172 | Husum |
| B108 | Rheine | B154 | Reinsehlen/ | B174 | Utersen |
| B109 | Quackenbruck | | Schneverdingen | | |

NOTES: [1] spelling changed to Twenthe in 1948; [2] Airfield numbers 121–149 were allocated to wings of the 2nd Tactical Air Force whilst at airfields in England, and so have been omitted from this list.

## American Airfields

| A1 | St Pierre du Mont | A24 | Biniville | A47 | Orly |
|-----|-------------------|------|-----------|------|------|
| A2 | Cricqueville | A25 | Biniville | A48 | Bretigny-sur-Orge |
| A3 | Cardonville | A26 | Gorges | A49 | Beille |
| A4 | Deux Jumeaux | A27 | Rennes | A50 | Orleans/Bricy |
| A5 | Chippelle | A28 | Pontorson | A51 | Morlaix |
| A6 | Buzeville | A29 | St James | A52 | Etampes/Mondesir |
| A7 | Azeville | A30 | Courtlis | A53 | Issy-les-Moulineaux |
| A8 | Picauville | A31 | Gael | A54 | Le Bourget |
| A9 | Le Molay | A32 | not used | A55 | Melun/Villaroche |
| A10 | Carentan | A33 | Vannes | A56 | Crecey |
| A11 | St Lambert | A34 | Gorron | A57 | Laval |
| A12 | Lignerolles | A35 | Le Mans | A58 | Coulommiers |
| A13 | Tour-en-Bessin | A36 | St Leonard | A59 | Cormeilles-en-Vexin |
| A14 | Cretteville | A37 | Lombron | A60 | Beaumont-sur-Oise |
| A15 | Maupertus | A38 | Montreuil | A61 | Reims/Champagne |
| A16 | Brucheville | A39 | Châteaudun | A63 | Villeneuve/Vertus |
| A17 | Meautis | A40 | Chartres | A64 | St Dizier/Robinson |
| A18 | St Jean de Daye | A41 | Dreux/Vermouillet | A65 | Perthes |
| A19 | La Vielle | A42 | Villacoublay | A66 | Orconte |
| A20 | Lessay | A43 | St Marceau | A67 | Vitry-en-Artois |
| A21 | St Laurent-sur-Mer | A44 | Peray | A68 | Juvincourt |
| A22 | Colleville-sur-Mer | A45 | Lonray | A69 | Laon/Athies |
| A23 | Querqueville | A46 | Toussus-le-Noble | A70 | Laon/Couvron |

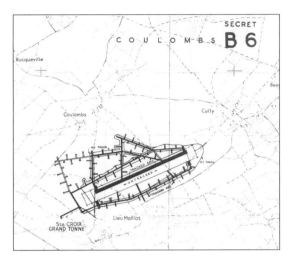

*Airfield B6 Coulombs.*

*14 June, and one of many airfields under construction in the lodgement area.* (US National Archives)

ABOVE: *St Pierre du Mont was built on the edge of the sea and this vertical photo, and the oblique (left) demonstrate how these ALGs were 'carved' out of the French landscape. Construction of St Pierre du Mont was by the 834th EAB.* (US National Archives)

| | | | | | |
|---|---|---|---|---|---|
| A71 | Clastres | A80 | Mourmel On-le-Grand | A89 | Le Culot |
| A72 | Peronne | A81 | Creil/Senlis | A90 | Toul/Croix-de-Metz |
| A73 | Roye/Ami | A82 | Rouvres | A91 | Sedan |
| A74 | Cambrai/Niergnies | A83 | Denain/Prouvy | A92 | St Trond |
| A75 | Cambrai/Epinoy | A84 | Chievres/ Mons | A93 | Liege/Bierset |
| A76 | Athis | A85 | Senzelles | A94 | Conflans |
| A77 | St Livière | A86 | Vitrival | A95 | Azelot |
| A78 | Florennes/Juzaine | A87 | Charleroi | A96 | Nancy/Ochey |
| A79 | Prosnes | A88 | Maubeuge | A97 | Sandweiller |
| | | | | A98 | Rosières-en-Haye |

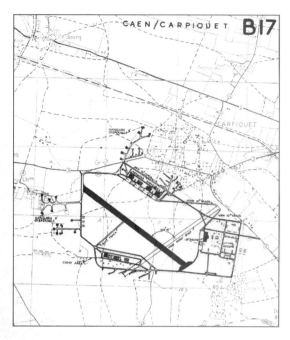

*Airfield B17.*

Airfield A8.

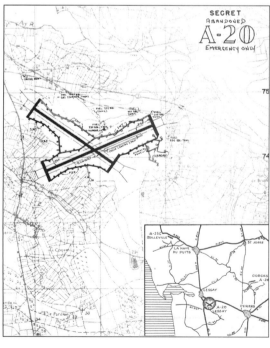

*Airfield A20.*

*Airfield A75.*

# Index

Readers should note that the index does not include full details from the appendices. With major formations such as AEAF, Bomber Command and the USAAF the index references are simply for those formations mentioned by name; however, their involvement in the campaign was so extensive that in reality their activities occur on almost every page.